THE SENATE

# Constitutionalism and Democracy

GREGG IVERS AND KEVIN T. MCGUIRE, EDITORS

# THE SENATE
From White Supremacy to Governmental Gridlock

Daniel Wirls

University of Virginia Press • *Charlottesville and London*

University of Virginia Press
© 2021 by the Rector and Visitors of the University of Virginia
All rights reserved
Printed in the United States of America on acid-free paper

*First published 2021*

9 8 7 6 5 4 3 2 1

Library of Congress Cataloging-in-Publication Data
Names: Wirls, Daniel, author.
Title: The Senate : from white supremacy to governmental gridlock / Daniel Wirls.
Description: Charlottesville : University of Virginia Press, 2021. | Series: Constitutionalism and democracy | Includes bibliographical references and index.
Identifiers: LCCN 2021014324 (print) | LCCN 2021014325 (ebook) | ISBN 9780813946894 (hardcover) | ISBN 9780813946900 (paperback) | ISBN 9780813946917 (ebook)
Subjects: LCSH: United States. Congress. Senate—History. | United States—Race relations—Political aspects—History. | White supremacy movements—Political aspects—United States—History. | Representative government and representation—United States. | Democracy—United States.
Classification: LCC JK1161 .W573 2021 (print) | LCC JK1161 (ebook) | DDC 328.73/071—dc23
LC record available at https://lccn.loc.gov/2021014324
LC ebook record available at https://lccn.loc.gov/2021014325

*Cover art:* Nathaniel Roy/Notch Design

# CONTENTS

| | | |
|---|---|---|
| | Acknowledgments | vii |
| | Introduction: The Senate and American Democracy | 1 |
| 1 | Creating Something Exceptional? Power and Purpose in the Design of the Senate | 13 |
| 2 | Equal Representation: The Perpetual Great Compromise | 38 |
| 3 | Equal Representation's Inexorable Clash with Political and Racial Equality | 58 |
| 4 | The Right of the Living Dead: Staggered Terms, Continuing Bodies, and Constitutional Myths Senators Tell Themselves and America | 84 |
| 5 | The Filibuster: From Southern Citadel to the Sixty-Vote Senate | 110 |
| 6 | "Cooling the Coffee": More Myths Senators Tell Themselves, and the Filibuster's Clash with Effective Government and the Constitution | 141 |
| 7 | The Supermajority Senate Curtailed: Nuclear Options and Mushroom Clouds of Hypocrisy | 167 |
| | Conclusion: Constitutional Repair and Reparations | 193 |
| | Notes | 211 |
| | Index | 255 |

# ACKNOWLEDGMENTS

IN SMALL ways, this book has been in progress since Stephen Wirls and I wrote *The Invention of the United States Senate*, which was published in 2004. That volume's examination of the Senate stopped in the early 1800s. Two books and other projects on unrelated subjects delayed my intended evaluation of the contemporary Senate in light of its creation and development. Over the years, however, research proceeded, along with the publication of a few articles on specific aspects of the book as it evolved. I was finally able to turn most of my attention to this project in the last few years as the Senate itself seemed to become increasingly a subject of news and controversy, culminating in its role during the Trump administration.

Along the way, a host of undergraduate research assistants—all but one of whom came from the ranks of our amazing politics majors at the University of California, Santa Cruz—made vital contributions. I am deeply grateful to Kylie Carpenter, Jannet Ceja, Nick Draper, Lindsey Hutchison (via a Smith College summer program), Ivan Huynh, Sawyer Labbe, Jessica Matlock, Frances Maurer, Marleena Sonico, and Jessica Xu. Two UC Santa Cruz Ph.D. students, Shawn Nichols and Trina Barton, also conducted essential and, in Barton's case, painstaking research.

Many colleagues read and commented on sections of the book as it developed, doing their best to impart their wisdom as I tried to shape the parts into a whole. These friends and colleagues include Gwen Alphonso, Sarah Binder, Gerald Gamm, Matt Green, Tyler Hughes, Frances Lee, and Elizabeth Sanders. My thanks to Greg Koger for sharing his data set on supermajority votes in the Senate. I have to single out David Siemers and Sean Theriault for their extensive comments and sage advice on the penultimate draft of the manuscript; the book is much better for their efforts. Anonymous reviewers gave detailed feedback at other stages. Colleagues in the Politics Department at UC Santa Cruz, including Eva Bertram, Kent Eaton, and Dean Mathiowetz, provided feedback and support. Part of the research involved a series of interviews in 2013 with mostly current and a few former senior Senate staff, focusing on how things worked in the contemporary sixty-vote Senate in an era of partisan polarization. Many thanks to Jeremiah Baumann, Jack Danielson, Bill Dauster, Steven

Duffield, Alan Frumin, Rohit Kumar, Sean Moore, Galen Roehl, Thomas Ross, Shannon Smith, and James Wallner for taking the time to talk to me and share their insights. Ruth Talbot took time out of her busy schedule to transform and refine the book's graphics; I was fortunate to benefit from her considerable talents at a crucial time in the book's preparation.

Thanks to UC Washington Center for providing a home away from home to teach about Congress and conduct research, and to UC Santa Cruz for its generous sabbatical policy, which allowed me to finish a draft of the manuscript during the 2017–18 academic year. My biggest debt of gratitude is owed to Nadine Zimmerli, editor extraordinaire at the University of Virginia Press. More than anyone else, Nadine is responsible for this book's improvement and completion, from her initial interest in the project to her detailed, trenchant, and timely edits of the entire manuscript. My thanks and appreciation to Marjorie Pannell for her expert editorial work and to the rest of the team at the Press.

This book was heading to the finish line as granddaughter Zadie Talbot Schindler came into the world to join the family and brighten our days. And so this book is dedicated to Zadie and her adoring parents, Steven and Zeneva, along with the rest of her loving clan, including Aunt Ruth and Grandma Alice.

THE SENATE

INTRODUCTION

# The Senate and American Democracy

> Living Father, revive the Senate. Infuse it with new life. Dissolve the frustration, the disappointment, the disenchantment. Ignite the fire that burned in the Senators' hearts when first they convinced the people to send them here. Restore the faith, the sense of purpose, the enthusiasm, the dream, the vision. Mighty God, from whom comes all authority, the world waits for the Senate to be the powerful, intelligent, deliberative, legislative leaders so desperately needed today in the Nation and the world. Let it be true, dear Lord. Let it be true. In Jesus' name. Amen.
>
> —The Reverend Richard C. Halverson, Senate chaplain, opening prayer, July 11, 1994

The Reverend Halverson's prayer was never answered. Although it sought a renewed sense of purpose, enthusiasm, and vision from senators as individuals, his supplication asked for an institution that never was and never could be. In the years following this prayer, things only got worse for the Senate, and that was no accident or act of God.

In the wake of everything that has happened since, it is easy to forget that in July 1994—when the chaplain prayed for the Senate as he did—the government was, despite the initial promise of a Clinton presidency bolstered by strong Democratic majorities in both houses of Congress, in the throes of legislative gridlock, and the nation was experiencing the kind of brook-no-compromise, take-no-prisoners partisanship that would become commonplace. The Clinton presidency and the 103rd Congress were collapsing under the Republicans' use of the Senate, despite a solid Democratic majority, to prevent bills from becoming law—something that would become a more or less fixed and bipartisan feature of the political landscape. By the mid-1990s, the Senate had become a citadel from which to thwart or impede what the other party, the House, or the president sought to accomplish.

Since at least 1994, when the Republicans, led by House Minority Whip Newt Gingrich, took control of Congress in the elections that fall, the United States has dealt with and debated its crisis of governance. With divided government, hyperpartisanship, and policy gridlock in especially sharp contrast with a dynamic environment of economic and technological change, Americans have faced increasing doubts about the capacity of their eighteenth-century political institutions to lead the nation into and through a twenty-first-century world. General uncertainties and concerns have found expression in a variety of not particularly harmonious or consistent criticisms, criticisms that too often fluctuate with partisan electoral fortunes. There is too much government or not enough government. Excessive partisan polarization or not enough party control. Dangerous presidential power or perilous congressional gridlock and paralysis. An imperial judiciary. Too much power in Washington; too much power in state capitals. Regardless, the core of the problem is a crisis of governance, an inability of our institutions to address and solve problems. This is a self-perpetuating crisis, moreover, as failure produces frustration and more political polarization.

Americans have devoted most of their attention, however, to changing the people in charge rather than the institutions themselves, their powers, or their relations to each other. If Americans want a better politics and better governance, they must consider whether their ongoing efforts to change politicians, or to grow or shrink the electorate, have done anything to alleviate the crisis. They must carefully consider how the political institutions that govern the country—rather than simply the people who temporarily occupy positions within them—have failed, and why. And in this age of extreme partisan polarization, they must look beyond the results of the last election and which party controls the House, Senate, presidency, or even the Supreme Court to think about the institutional changes and reforms that could benefit us all, regardless of which party wins the next election.

With the crisis of national governance a near constant in American life, this book is an argument about the Senate—the institution itself, rather than the senators who serve in it—but in relation to the other institutions of government, the constitutional system as a whole, and that crisis. Just as the Senate was the crux of the Constitutional Convention's decisions in 1787, so it is at the center of our contemporary constitutional crisis. Should we blame the Senate for the crisis? No, that would be going too far. But if not the main flaw in the American system, the Senate is certainly one of its central defects. It is a principal cause of some problems; it exacerbates others; it solves nothing. Presidential power: has the Senate tamed it? No. Has the Senate reined in a runaway House? No. Instead, it is the Senate that has run away—from democracy—and taken governance with it. It is past time for the people of the United States to look beyond the current politicians and policy problems that must be solved to the governmental structures and relationships that not only are failing to solve those problems but also are alienating the citizens whose support and confidence are essential to successful government. Many things should be on the table. This history and analysis of the Senate's constitutionalism and behavior put that institution front and center—but hardly alone—in a reconsideration of the American system.

Part of the problem with the Senate is something it shares with the nation it represents: its lofty self-image often distorts a clear-eyed analysis and diagnosis of the problems it confronts. Even if by the early years of the twenty-first century the Senate was increasingly subject to criticism and its reputation as "the world's greatest deliberative body" had grown tarnished, the Senate throughout its history has promoted a grandiose self-conception of its special place and purpose. The Senate's constitutional imaginary, widely shared by citizens and commentators, brings to mind a more familiar and encompassing self-conception: the belief that the United States is an "exceptional" nation. If the United States is an exceptional nation, then the US Senate must be an exceptional institution, and in much the same way.[1] American exceptionalism is the belief in the political superiority of the United States, such that the nation stands apart from and above the other nations of the world.[2] In this view, "America" was special even when it existed only as a collection of largely unrelated colonies of settlers seeking freedom and creating forms of self-government. The country's founding, from the Declaration of Independence through the drafting and approval of the Constitution, made the United States the first nation based on collective choice and self-conscious constitutional construction rather than on some combination of conquest and culture. Since then, the United States has been the model for constitutional popular government. And the United States has had, from this perspective, a special duty to lead the family of nations and foster world order.

Alexis de Tocqueville notably was among the earliest to capture this American belief: "For fifty years the inhabitants of the United States have been repeatedly and constantly told that they are the only religious, enlightened, and free people. They see that democratic institutions flourish among them, whereas they come to grief in the rest of the world; consequently they have an immensely high opinion of themselves and are not far from believing that they form a species apart from the rest of the human race."[3] For some, American exceptionalism is part and parcel of a laudable civil religion—those beliefs, rituals, and symbols that unite Americans—but it is also an object of criticism, if not outright ridicule.[4] For our purposes it does not matter whether the exceptionalist doctrine is, like America itself, right or wrong. As many have argued, it has elements of historically undeniable facts, but it can be and has been exaggerated or distorted into a form of unreflective or even mindless nationalism.[5] And, like nearly everything else, it has been sucked into the vortex of partisan polarization.[6]

The Senate's exceptionalism parallels the nation's quite closely. Just as the United States was a unique creation as a political nation defined by its Constitution, Senate exceptionalism sees that body as the special institution created by the founding. The Senate stands apart from and above other legislative bodies both at home and abroad. More than any other invention of the Constitution, the Senate defines what is special about American government and politics. If the United States is the "indispensable" nation, in Madeleine Albright's turn of phrase, the Senate is the indispensable institution of American government.[7] Even though the presidency, the Supreme Court, and the House of Representatives were thoroughly innovative constructs, none of these bodies has garnered the kind of encomiums and tributes inspired by and directed at the Senate. And if, as Tocqueville noted, Americans all but considered themselves another species, senators have tended to see themselves as a special, even exceptional, form of public servant.

As early as 1805, in his farewell speech as vice president, Aaron Burr said that the Senate "is a sanctuary; a citadel of law, of order, and of liberty; and it is here—it is here, in this exalted refuge; here, if anywhere, will resistance be made to the storms of political phrenzy and the silent arts of corruption; and if the Constitution be destined ever to perish by the sacrilegious hands of the demagogue or the usurper, which God avert, its expiring agonies will be witnessed on this floor."[8] A few decades later, Daniel Webster reminded his colleagues that "this is a Senate, a Senate of equals, of men of individual honor and personal character, and of absolute independence. We know no masters, we acknowledge no dictators. This is a hall for mutual consultation and discussion, not an arena for the exhibition of champions."[9] Toward the end of the nineteenth century, Senator David Turpie added this familiar and often repeated characterization: "The universal law and genius of language have given a name to this body derived from its principal attribute. It is a deliberative body—the greatest deliberative body in the world."[10]

Another late nineteenth-century tribute came from the British prime minister William Gladstone, who called the Senate "that remarkable body, the most remarkable of all the inventions of modern politics."[11] Writing in the mid-twentieth century, journalist William White "felt that the one touch of authentic genius in the American political system, apart, of course, from the incomparable majesty and decency and felicity of the Constitution itself, is the Senate of the United States."[12] And to cite just one of many possible examples from more recent senators, Robert Byrd deemed Senate service "the highest political calling in the land," with the Senate itself "the central pillar of our Constitutional system," even "hallowed ground."[13]

These flattering quotations about the Senate, however, can and should invite skepticism in much the same way unrefined American exceptionalism has. Both exceptionalisms are similarly misleading or disingenuous. Behind or beneath the lofty rhetoric and imagery of each is a more complicated and at times sordid reality. The Senate's exceptionalism parallels the denial and duplicity of American exceptionalism, if for no other reason than that the Senate often played a particular role in many of the same events that trouble the typically pollyannaish national self-conception, including slavery, the Civil War, Gilded Age corruption and inequality, Jim Crow, segregation, and Cold War hysteria. Both forms of exceptionalism raise suspicions that the rhetoric is overblown precisely to obscure, overcome, and excuse the rather profound shortcomings and tragedies that are as much a part of the historical record as the triumphs and achievements. Just as American exceptionalism can interfere with a sober assessment of the nation's past and its relationship to present and future decisions about how to employ governmental power at home and abroad, Senate exceptionalism has clouded our assessment of the behavior, purpose, and value of that institution.

I offer a critical analysis and assessment of the Senate's relationship to American democracy. Distinct from the volumes of work that analyze various aspects of the Senate from a purely historical or empirical perspective—that is to say, from an explicitly or implicitly value-neutral perspective—this book is a normative evaluation of the Senate. My central question is not "How does the Senate operate and what are the measurable consequences of its unique characteristics?," even if this book contributes to our empirical understanding of the Senate. Instead, I ask "How do we evaluate and judge the Senate as one of the central institutions in American democracy, both past and present?" What is the relationship of the Senate to the Constitution and the American system of government? Does the Senate's relative power and purpose, along with the ideas that support them, help or hinder democratic government in the twenty-first century? As part of this inquiry, what is the relationship between the Senate and the contemporary crisis in American governance? And if constitutional changes to our institutions are necessary for better governance, then how should the Senate be altered to be part of the solution rather than part of the problem?

These are important questions, but scholars have tended to address them at best indirectly. Most empirical studies of the Senate, which dominate treatments of that institution, have little to offer as far as normative or constitutional evaluation,[14] while normative studies drawing on democratic theory tend not to study or apply their analysis to real institutions.[15] Scholarship in the area of American political development, with its emphasis on changes in institutions and power over time, has certainly concerned itself with questions of constitutionalism, sometimes quite directly. But only a few modern works have touched on Senate constitutionalism.[16] A limited but important segment of legal scholarship comes closest to addressing my set of questions, usually by taking on a particular feature of the Senate, but not in the comprehensive fashion I do here.[17] For the student or citizen seeking an understanding of the Senate's role with an eye toward evaluating its contribution or need for reformation, this book offers a historical argument that explicates and critiques the Senate's role in the American system of government.

In the pages that follow, I advance three interrelated arguments. First, the Senate, with the help of various commentators and the citizenry as a whole, has produced a constitutional mythology about its place and purpose. Across the generations, the Senate has constructed important distinctions for itself—an exceptional role in the American system of government—that have no firm foundation in the Constitution. Second, these ideas about the Senate are part and parcel of its problematic role in the governmental process, a role shaped primarily by the combination of equal representation and the power given to political minorities by Senate rules of procedure. Third, while Senate mythology and the dysfunction are general in their origins and impact, the Senate has been uniquely related to the history of race in America, from the depravity of slavery, through the protracted era of racial subjugation, to the post–civil rights decades of inequality and underrepresentation.[18] I tease apart the

Senate's constitutional self-image, exposing the particular relationship of the "world's greatest deliberative body" to the maintenance of white supremacy, and explain the Senate's broader clash with modern democracy and effective government. In short, the contemporary Senate is neither as the framers intended it to be nor in harmony with the values and needs of a twenty-first-century democracy or republic. No small part of the institution's dysfunction is because it claims to be operating as the founders wanted, when in fact it is not. The Senate's architecture, self-conception, and resulting behavior distort rather than complement or complete, as many senators would like to think, modern republican governance.

The problematic ideas about the Senate's constitutional place and purpose, and the governmental problems they entail, including the relationship to white supremacy, have evolved primarily from four core features of the Senate and the relationships between and among them. They are:

1. Smaller membership: The Senate was designed to be significantly smaller than the House.
2. Equal representation: Each state is represented by two senators, regardless of its population.
3. Staggered six-year terms: Senators are elected for six-year terms, with only about one-third of the entire membership up for election every two years.
4. Minority power: The rules of the Senate allow for filibusters or other forms of obstruction or denial of majority rule.[19]

Smaller membership, equal representation, six-year staggered terms, and the relative power of political minorities in the Senate are independently important components of the Senate, but each is often as misinterpreted as it is significant. I show their relationship to the evolution of the Senate's constitutional and political roles, to each other, and to the problems they have produced. The interpretation of each, separately and in combination, produced a kind of constitutional mythology about the Senate, a misunderstanding and distortion of the Senate's place and purpose. And, to different degrees, the four have evolved to produce profound and irreconcilable conflicts with contemporary notions of democratic equality and practice, and even with the Constitution itself.

In particular, I emphasize how the confluence of equal representation, the filibuster, and the Senate's view of itself as a continuing body fostered the misleading idea that the Senate is the Constitution's explicit safeguard of "minority rights." The irony is that the principal effect of the Senate's combination of representation and rules was to thwart or degrade the human rights of African Americans. It would be easy to portray what follows as a story of myth versus reality, and in part it is just that. But this is a story of constitutional complexity—the social construction of belief, of partial truths that obscure less flattering realities—rather than simply fact versus fiction.

Not surprisingly, our story begins with the 1787 Constitutional Convention. Chapter 1 makes a series of points about the design of the Senate in relation to the other bodies and branches of government. With respect to the Senate's constitutionalism, the smaller membership was for almost every delegate at the Constitutional Convention the essence of a deliberative upper house of older and wiser statesmen elected for long terms. A limited number of such senators would foster and protect the *collective quality* of deliberation. Senatorial deliberation would be the product of its composition, not the rules of procedure senators might write to govern debate. The kind of debate fostered by its small size was complicated, however, by the fraught compromise that resulted in equal representation, or two senators per state. If the Senate was exceptional, it was for the manifest tension and outright contradictions between its role as a body comprising far-sighted and detached national statesmen and a structure based in equal representation of states and consisting of two-person delegations sent by self-interested state legislatures. Moreover, by creating state equality in the Senate, the founders did not intend that body to be the Constitution's shield for minority rights against majority tyranny. The system as a whole would protect against the abuse of power. And that system was composed of institutions—the presidency, the judiciary, and even the House of Representatives—that were as innovative as or more exceptional than the Senate in their form and function.

Chapters 2 and 3 explore and critique equal representation of states in the Senate. Chapter 2 analyzes the politics of equal representation from the founding to the early twentieth century and focuses on the role of the Senate in protecting the slaveholding interests of the southern states prior to the Civil War. After the Civil War, equal representation evolved into a tool for regional and partisan combat as the two parties fought for control of the branches of the national government and new western states were added to the union, to be duly represented in Congress. Ironically, in light of equal representation's prominent role in magnifying the power of both slave states and states of the former Confederacy, a structure put in place in a political compromise to represent states equally regardless of population became the main basis for the social construction of the Senate as the protector of minority rights in general.

In the second half of the twentieth century the original relevance of equal representation all but disappeared as its distortion of other values became increasingly pronounced. Chapter 3 focuses on equal representation's conflict with the fundamental tenet of modern democratic theory, which is also the primary principle of democratic citizenship in modern constitutionalism here and abroad: one person, one vote, or a fundamental equality among citizens in their ability to choose their government. Once the Supreme Court interpreted the Constitution's equal protection clause to create this central standard of modern democracy—one person, one vote—states' equal representation in the Senate lived on as the glaring violation of this principle. And as partisan polarization emerged to dominate American politics in the twenty-first century, two senators per state not only increasingly distorted the voting power of citizens across states but also magnified the power of rural white voters over urban minority voters. The Senate cannot escape its inherent violation of political equality in general and its bias against racial equality in particular.

As the impact of equal representation evolved, the Senate developed a notion of itself as the unique "continuing body" intended by the founders, which is the subject of chapter 4. Much as equal representation of states led to the more general idea that the Senate was designed to protect minority rights in general, senators distorted the rationale for the institution's longer, staggered terms into a constitutional doctrine that the Senate was an immortal continuing body. In turn, this conceit became one of the foundations for the Senate's exaggerated self-image in general and for the immutable, Olympus-like status of its rules of procedure, especially those that empower what we think of as the filibuster. This conception of the continuing body helped to protect the rules of the Senate that empowered filibusters, a weapon employed most prominently and persistently in defense of white supremacy. Equal representation and the continuing body doctrine combined to foster the idea that the Senate has a unique—indeed, constitutionally essential and sanctioned—deliberative function tied, again, to a misleading and ironic conception of minority rights.

Beyond the constitutional mandate of equal representation, the Senate creates minority power through its rules of procedure. Chapter 5 analyzes the evolution and impact of the filibuster as a product of those rules.

As the Senate grew and the nation changed, the emphasis on the collective quality of debate gave way to norms and procedures that emphasized the *individual right* to hold the floor—the potentially unlimited quantity of debate—regardless of quality. Senate rules of procedure create minority power to delay or prevent decisions by majority rule, making it possible for a minority of senators to delay, obstruct, or prevent what the majority of legislators would like to accomplish. The word most often associated with minority obstruction in its various forms is "filibuster." The filibuster is the use of procedural tactics to delay or prevent a majority decision. Supermajority cloture—the main Senate rule, first adopted in 1917, that empowers filibusters—requires, when any number of senators object, three-fifths of all senators (a supermajority rather than a simple majority) to close debate on a pending measure. The power and use of this rule eventually created the "sixty-vote Senate," the near requirement of three-fifths of all senators to do anything of importance. Along the way, from the late nineteenth century through the 1960s, the filibuster and the use and abuse of supermajority cloture were associated with one issue: opposition to the civil rights of African Americans and the defense of southern white supremacy. And even as the triumph of civil rights law eroded that tight relationship, the rise of the sixty-vote Senate made clear the filibuster's sizable contribution to policy gridlock, diminished deliberation, and congressional incapacity.

As potent as any provision in the Constitution, supermajority cloture became a minority veto that cannot be found in the Constitution or justified by it, even though, as we shall see in chapter 6, many senators and commentators claimed just the opposite. In fact, the sixty-vote Senate is an affront to the document as crafted and explicated by the framers. Over the past century, and despite its intimate connection to white supremacy, the filibuster or supermajority cloture became so important, so central and vital to the Senate's constitutionalism, that many of its supporters have come to think of it as the sine qua non of the institution itself. It is the core, essence, or even "soul" of the Senate.[20] For many, the filibuster is what makes the Senate supposedly the greatest deliberative body in the world, rather than, as has been the case, its near antithesis. Chapter 6 shows how supermajority cloture contradicts the Constitution by upsetting, among other things, the delicate balancing act that defines the system of separated powers combined with checks and balances.

The tortured relationship of the contemporary Senate to the filibuster and the power of minorities to thwart Senate decisions, especially as the two parties and congressional representation became increasingly polarized, generated controversy and calls for reform, even as many still defended supermajority cloture. Chapter 7 examines how the filibuster has been restricted in recent decades. First, and relatively uncontroversial and bipartisan, have been legislated exceptions that circumvent potential Senate obstruction in consideration of particular measures, such as approval of trade agreements. Second, and the result of bitter partisan frustrations, the Senate in 2013 and 2017 voted to eliminate the use of the filibuster and supermajority cloture in consideration of all presidential appointments to the executive branch and the federal judiciary, including the Supreme Court. The changes diminished and constricted the sixty-vote Senate, but the impact of the supermajority cloture remained a powerful force in determining what happened in that body and across the government as a whole.

The combination of equal representation and supermajority cloture, supported by the continuing body doctrine, puts the Senate in direct confrontation with contemporary democratic values and practice, and even with fundamental principles of the Constitution itself. Minority power in the form of supermajority cloture, layered as it was on top of the minority power created by equal representation, came to be defended as a form of voice when it was from the start really about victory. It is not about deliberation and compromise; it is a decision rule that allocates an effective veto. And together, these distorted forms of representation and rules have been at the core of the Senate's history as the institution of national government most closely tied to white supremacy. The Senate as it operates today is built on these distortions and contradictions. The book concludes with reforms—including the elimination of equal representation and the filibuster—as ways to construct a Senate able to meet the requirements of twenty-first-century constitutionalism and government.

Charles Lindblom closes his magnum opus, *Politics and Markets,* with a final comment on the power of the modern business corporation "as a peculiar organization in an ostensible democracy." The large private corporation, he writes, "fits oddly into democratic theory and vision. Indeed, it does not fit."[21] The same can be said of the contemporary US Senate, which, unlike Walmart or Google, is a governmental institution. It is past time for the people of the United States to look beyond the immediate problems that must be solved to the governmental structures and relationships that not only are failing to solve those problems but also are alienating the citizens whose support and confidence are essential to successful government. Many things should be on the table. This history and analysis of the Senate's constitutionalism and behavior put that institution front and center—but hardly alone—in a reconsideration of the American system.

# 1
# Creating Something Exceptional?
POWER AND PURPOSE IN THE DESIGN OF THE SENATE

THE SENATE *was* different, if not exceptional, from the start. But so were the presidency, the judiciary, and even the House of Representatives. If the Senate was exceptional it was not because of its elegant design and clarity of purpose. Emerging from the deliberations in Philadelphia, the Senate was rather like the committee's version of a horse, which is to say a camel.[1] The Senate was placed at the crossroads of the national system of separated institutions sharing power and at the intersection of state and national sovereignty. First, the Senate was half of a bicameral Congress endowed with legislative power. Second, it shared in the executive power of appointments and treaties, with a potentially decisive role in the composition of the Supreme Court. Finally, the politics of the Constitutional Convention added another special purpose—the Senate would be the institutional embodiment of federalism and state power in the national government. It was to be the smaller, wiser, and more detached legislative chamber, the institutional home of state power and state equality and the quasi-council to the executive on appointments and treaties. In this way the Senate became the crucible for resolving several of the thorniest problems of American constitutionalism. In particular, the Senate was exceptional for the manifest tension and outright contradictions between its roles as both a Senate of far-sighted and detached national statesmen and a Senate of delegates sent by self-interested state legislatures. That tension was at the heart of the Constitutional Convention, and from the time the Senate first achieved a quorum, on April 6, 1789, to today, it has never been resolved.

Its rich mixture of purposes and powers continues to make the Senate unique among the world's political institutions. As the equal partner in one of the world's most independent and robust legislatures, it is the most powerful upper house in the world. Whereas many countries have unicameral legislatures or upper houses or senates with significantly less power or even only symbolic importance, the US Senate combines a formidable array of institutional characteristics and powers that make it distinctive and autonomous. The higher age and citizenship requirements for members, as well as the longer and staggered terms, contribute, more or less, to differences in the character of the upper house compared to the lower. Similarly, state equality in the Senate contrasts sharply with the proportional representation of the House. The distinctions produced by elections are reinforced by the institutional elements. The House and Senate are granted nearly equal powers; in fact, the Senate has a few exclusive powers, including the approval of treaties and appointments, that give it a singular status among upper houses. And unlike many upper houses, the modern Senate has enjoyed at least equal (un)popularity and (dis)respect among the people.[2]

But it is this hybridity and complexity that have allowed the Senate over the years to conflate the various aspects of its constitutional role into a generalized idea that it has a special and different purpose that transcends the multiple but carefully defined roles given it by the Constitution. In particular, senators have drawn on and distorted the collection of attributes and responsibilities outlined above to justify what became the dominant feature of the Senate: its rules of procedure, which create and protect minority power, and the effect of those rules on Senate behavior. Modern senators have tended to portray minority power, as structured by Senate rules of procedure, as the sine qua non and raison d'être of their institution. This goes directly against what the Constitution actually mandated. The constitutional means to the end of better deliberation—first and foremost its smaller size, but also the age of senators and their length of citizenship, longer terms, and, originally, selection by state legislatures—have, over time, been displaced in favor of rules created by the Senate that empower minority obstruction.

This chapter focuses on key aspects of the Senate's creation at the 1787 Constitutional Convention to show the Senate's complex if not exceptional design: what the convention created, but also what it did not create. Each of the first three sections of the Constitution (Articles I on Congress, II on the executive, and III on the judiciary) divides into an opening section on composition and a second section on powers. That is, each article begins with how the branch is composed, particularly its mode of selection, qualifications for office, and duration of selection or appointment.[3] The second part of each article is about powers, specifying the branch's duties and authority. This chapter concentrates on two sides of the Senate's composition. On one side were the elements of relative consensus, which were nearly everything about the Senate's republican purpose and the characteristics suited to that, including age of senatorial candidates, length of citizenship, duration in office, indirect method of selection, and especially the small size of the Senate. On the other side was the element of nearly insurmountable conflict, which was the basis of representation: Would the Senate be proportioned by state population, like the proposed House of Representatives, or by state equality, like the existing Congress of the Confederation? The result of that blending of consensus and conflict was a hybrid and conflicted Senate.

Instead of providing a comprehensive account of the decisions made that summer in Philadelphia, this chapter highlights that all government institutions—the Senate, the House, the executive, and the judiciary—were equally novel creations; in some respects, the latter three were more innovative than the Senate. Also, it is important to recognize that the framers did not intend to enhance the power of a Senate minority; minority rights were not a central concern of those who drafted the Constitution, and equal representation in the Senate was not about minority rights. The framers' decision to base Senate representation on state equality produced a compromised Senate with a conflicted mandate, however. Overall, the Senate was not the hub of Madison's balancing act to "enable the government to control the governed; and in the next place oblige it to control itself." It was the entire governmental system—composed of Congress, the executive, the court, and sovereign states—not the Senate per se that would prevent majority tyranny and allow for the safe and effective use of governmental power.

## Consensus: A Republican Senate

Though they confronted a daunting task, the delegates who convened in Philadelphia in 1787 were not without some advantages. The formidable talents of many of the participants notwithstanding, many of the sharpest minds opposed to the project of fortifying the national government decided to boycott the meeting, partly in the expectation that it would collapse under its own weight. The convention was, as a result, populated by many of the most nationally minded among the political elite. This not only greatly enhanced the prospects for something more than a mere reformation of the Articles of Confederation, it broadened the level of agreement on several features of a good government. The delegates shared similar conclusions based on their republican beliefs and experiences in their state governments. One such conclusion was a widely shared belief in the desirability of a two-chamber legislature, with an upper house balanced against the more popular lower house.

At several points during the debates, the delegates expressed confidence about the self-evident appeal of bicameralism. Virginia's George Mason argued that "the mind of the people of America, as elsewhere, was unsettled as to some points; but settled as to others." He was sure it was well settled on two points, "1. in an attachment to republican government. 2. in an attachment to more than one branch in the Legislature."[4] Even the democratic soul of the convention from unicameral Pennsylvania, James Wilson, vigorously defended the need for a two-chamber legislature: "Is there no danger of a Legislative despotism? Theory and practice both proclaim it. If the Legislative authority be not restrained, there can be neither liberty nor stability; and it can only be restrained by dividing it within itself, into distinct and independent branches. In a single house there is no check, but the inadequate one, of the virtue and good sense of those who compose it."[5]

The extent of this accord on bicameralism is evident from the opening actions of the convention. Madison and the Virginia delegation came to Philadelphia prepared with a detailed argument about the defects of the Articles of Confederation and, more important, a set of resolutions outlining the structure and powers of a new national government. Edmund Randolph "opened the main business" of the convention on May 29 by presenting both, and the fifteen Virginia resolutions became the basis of debate and deliberation on May 30. The first of these resolutions was a general call to action to correct and enlarge the Articles of Confederation. The second and third resolutions were about the structure of the new legislature. The second stated that representation in the national legislature "ought to be proportioned to the Quotas of contribution, or to the number of free inhabitants." And the third resolved that "the National Legislature ought to consist of two branches."[6] In other words, the core of the entire proposal was a bicameral legislature based on some form of representation proportional to population.

The resolution for a two-house legislature was the opening item on May 31, and it engendered no debate or opposition. As Madison recorded in his notes, "The Third (3d) Resolution 'that the national Legislature ought to consist of two branches' was agreed to without debate or dissent, except that of Pennsylvania, given probably from complaisance to Doc. Franklin who was understood to be partial to a single House of legislation."⁷ But Pennsylvania's dissent on this issue disappeared thereafter. This effectively unanimous vote on bicameralism took place even after it was clear that the Virginia Plan would end the equal representation of states, which had been a foundational feature of the Confederation.

The proposal for proportional representation, discussed the day before, was more controversial and was ultimately postponed. Nevertheless, the delegates came close to agreeing that "the equality of suffrage established by the articles of Confederation ought not to prevail in the national Legislature, and that an equitable ratio of representation ought to be substituted." However, when a delegate from Delaware reminded the convention of his state's explicit instructions to protect state equality, even if it meant abandoning the proceedings, the convention agreed to a postponement.⁸ Yet Delaware did not object on the first vote on bicameralism the next day. Small states, it would seem, at first saw the need for bicameralism as more important than the potential threat to state representation.

The accord on bicameralism was based in no small part on the delegates' widely shared assumptions about the distinct and special purposes of the upper house. As part of earlier work on the creation of the Senate, I found and categorized every remark or speech that made reference to a desired or ideal trait or purpose of a properly designed Senate.⁹ From the beginning of the proceedings to July 16 and the vote on the so-called Great Compromise, the decision to have the upper house composed of two senators from each state, nineteen delegates, most of the active participants during the period, offered at least some opinion about what they felt were the important characteristics of a Senate. Some only hinted at their preferences; others expounded repeatedly and at some length. A total of forty remarks or speeches contain one or more preferred traits or purposes of a Senate, producing a total of sixty-five individual invocations of one or another characteristic.¹⁰

Though the delegates voiced a number of opinions, the list is a harmoniously interrelated one and the level of agreement is evident. Aside from seven mentions of the importance of a second chamber as a check on legislative power, five characteristics dominate: small size (fourteen mentions), select appointment (eight), independence (eight), wisdom (eight), and stability (eight). These five account for 71 percent of the references to an ideal upper house. Moreover, they elicited no dissent beyond John Dickinson's one claim that small size was not important. At fourteen references, small size is the most frequently invoked trait, and its central importance became apparent as the debate over legislative apportionment unfolded and dominated the convention. The remarks about size manifested concern for producing the quality of debate in which only a small group can engage. Madison would later provide this trenchant summary of the logic of numbers: "In all very numerous assemblies, of whatever characters composed, passion never fails to wrest the scepter from reason. Had every Athenian citizen been a Socrates, every Athenian assembly would still have been a mob."[11] Almost every delegate agreed with this judgment; they deemed small size the principal characteristic that would foster quality deliberation.

Small size would be complemented by a select appointment. As noted, these remarks were made prior to the final decisions about the composition of the Senate, but even so, it was clear that the upper chamber would not be directly elected. The Virginia Plan had the upper house selected by the lower chamber from nominations made by states. Complicated as it was by the later compromise in favor of having two senators per state, the eventual decision to have the Senate selected by state legislatures reflected the delegates' consensus preference for an indirect and refined selection process. And regardless of the final form it took, the goal was to produce wiser, more experienced, and independent senators. It should be noted that the refined process of selection was as close as the delegates got to a proxy for wealth and property. A few delegates linked the Senate to representation and protection of property, but their views constituted a minority, even amid the secret deliberations. Even so, such remarks were usually not simply about representing the interests of property; instead, possession of considerable property would imbue officeholders with the wisdom and independence to form an effective Senate. Property, independence, education, and breadth of experience, in the belief of most of the delegates, came together as a package in society.

In turn, independence and stability would be enhanced by additional factors beyond the mode of selection, in particular the length of term. The Virginia Plan did not specify a length of term for either branch of the legislature. There was a blank to be filled in for the number of years for the first branch. The members of the other branch were "to hold their offices for a term sufficient to ensure their independency."[12] This implied only that the term of the second branch should be longer. In fact, this distinction between the two legislative chambers was confirmed and reinforced with every discussion and vote on the issue of terms. The initial votes gave the House a term of three years and the Senate a term of seven years. At other points, two delegates, Hamilton and Read, even proposed life terms for senators. While there was almost no support for life terms, there was no doubt that a significant difference between the two chambers would prevail. A few expressed concerns about the longest terms proposed, including nine, seven, and six years. Some resistance to much longer terms relative to the House came from small-state delegates who were holding on to the idea—which thus far had not been winning the day—that the upper house would represent states primarily. And some stemmed from anti-aristocratic if not democratic beliefs from delegates whose states had annual elections or who feared that senators, especially those from distant states, might get too independent and forget those who sent them. Nevertheless, the final decision on two years for the House and six-year staggered terms for the Senate evinced the delegates' commitment to the kind of independence and stability that a longer term would produce.

An important note on staggered terms: they were designed and included to balance the dangers of the longer term by allowing partial renewal and change in the Senate every two years. Staggered terms, as we shall see in chapter 4, were not part of the Senate's conservative design. They were not intended to make the Senate into a continuing body to prevent change. The convention never discussed such a concept.

Finally, the convention considered two other electoral qualifications relevant to such things as independence, wisdom, and stability. These were age and length of citizenship. Should there be a minimum age and period of citizenship to be eligible to serve in one or the other chamber of the national legislature? As with many such details, the Virginia Plan left these matters unspecified, leaving a blank space for the minimum age and not even mentioning citizenship. The age blank was filled in early on, well before the apportionment compromise was reached, when the consensus on the characteristics of an ideal Senate still drove the process. The convention decided initially to not have any age qualification for the first branch but specified thirty years for the Senate. The unspoken logic was clear: let the voters decide for the first branch, but a minimum age is prudent for the Senate. The convention amended this ten days later with a decision in favor of twenty-five years as a minimum age for members of the House.[13]

Decided much later, length of citizenship was more controversial than age, but not so much as a distinction between the legislative chambers. Citizenship qualifications did not appear until early August, with the draft presented by the Committee on Detail. Length of citizenship for both chambers then went through a bidding war between those delegates who sought the highest possible number of years and those who thought minimal requirements would do. Aside from general support for more stringent Senate requirements, the greater role of the Senate in foreign affairs via the power of treaties suggested the need for longer citizenship. In the end, with the decisions in favor of seven years for the House and nine for the Senate, rather stringent citizenship requirements adhered to both chambers.[14]

The small size, length of term, process of selection, and even age and citizenship would mitigate the passions and precipitation to which more numerous and popular assemblies are prone. A small number of senators, who would be, by and large, better men because they had achieved their positions through some refining mode of selection, and who were independent of any other branch of government, could best achieve the purposes or goals of a Senate. All these characteristics promoted superior deliberation, characterized by dispassion, wisdom, and a value for stability. This stability and wisdom would be primarily a check on the democratic excesses of the lower chamber (the comments on stability often implied a check on democracy). A properly constructed Senate would provide some institutional memory, a knowledge of and experience with various proposals and policies, and, as a result, would reduce the likelihood of constantly fluctuating laws and policies. The evidence from the Constitutional Convention and other founding documents such as *The Federalist*, particularly numbers 62 and 63, affirm that, rather than rules of procedure the Senate might later develop, it was the constitutionally mandated attributes of the Senate—the mode of selection, the smaller size, the length of term, and so forth—that were to structure and foster its quality as a deliberative body.

## Conflict: Equal Representation and the Compromised Senate

Despite the delegates' agreement on bicameralism and the best ways to ensure a high quality of deliberation in the proposed upper house of the new national legislature, the structure of legislative representation emerged as the most vexing issue of the Constitutional Convention. This became the main point of contention because the basic nature of the republic would be determined by the form or forms of representation in the national legislature. Discussions came close to collapsing in the face of this obstruction; once it was overcome, though other difficulties remained, the convention appeared certain to produce a final document.

As James Madison lamented during the debates, "The great difficulty lies in the affair of Representation; and if this could be adjusted, all others would be surmountable."[15] At the center of this struggle was the composition of the Senate. Though this is common knowledge, the richness and complexity of how the Senate affected and was affected by the struggle over representation are lost or obscured in many accounts of the process.

While it would be stretching the truth to argue the representational compromise came into existence because of the Senate or, more precisely, because of the near consensus on the need for an upper house, the widespread agreement on the need for a Senate in a stronger national system helped to shape and produce the compromise, rather than the other way around. A republican Senate was crucial to the new system, regardless of any political compromises. The problem, however, was that the Senate would become essential as well to the resolution of the question of federalism, that is, the extent to which the new constitution would embrace or eliminate the role of states as sovereign actors. As a result, despite the agreement on a Senate in principle, and for republican purposes, the actual Senate that would emerge from the convention was the complicated and compromised product of the most important and bitter struggle that summer.

To portray the fight over representation as simply between large-state delegations for proportional representation and small-state delegations demanding state equality would be to strip the proceedings of the most interesting complexities in the mixture of interests and principles at work. In addition to these conflicting interests, two main relationships that became increasingly apparent over the course of the summer structured the conflict. The consensus on bicameralism and the general agreement that the government needed to be more national in character all but guaranteed that one of the legislative chambers would be proportional to population and directly elected. Yet nearly any form of proportional representation for the Senate would make it too large, and thereby vitiate its most important characteristics as a deliberative institution. This pushed many large-state delegates in the direction of equal representation in the proposed Senate, not just to placate small states but to keep that body small enough to fulfill its primary function.

As to the first relationship, it would take days of debate before the intractable relationship between the number of legislative chambers and the ratio of representation became apparent to the delegates as the crux of the proceedings. After the connection was made, bicameralism faced its only threat in the form of the so-called New Jersey Plan. Two weeks of debate that kept circling inevitably back to the question of representation culminated on June 15 in a 6–5 vote in favor of proportional representation in the Senate. Only a few days before this the delegates had agreed to proportional representation in the House by a 9–2 vote, demonstrating the broad support for both bicameralism and a different basis for representation in the lower house. But the 6–5 vote for the same in the Senate prompted the small states to rally and offer an alternative. William Patterson presented the New Jersey Plan on June 15. Up to this point, the opposition had no clear alternative. In part this was because there was broad agreement on the overall thrust of the Virginia Plan—the only point of significant dispute had been the issue of equal representation of states. The need for a more effective response to this bone of contention necessitated a more complete alternative. And until this point there had been no significant opposition to bicameralism. The New Jersey Plan, which called for a moderately strengthened Congress of the Confederation, retained the unicameral, equally apportioned legislature of the articles. This aspect of the design did not imply a philosophical preference for a single-house legislature. Patterson offered the plan in reaction to the convention's initial and narrow support of proportional representation in both legislative chambers. The small states had voted, it should be remembered, for bicameralism at the beginning. After some debate this dramatically different alternative was rejected fairly easily on June 19 by a 7-3-1 vote.[16] But it indicated that the small-state coalition, which had accepted and even embraced proportional representation in the House, was likely to hold out for equal representation in the Senate.[17]

As the deadlock over Senate representation developed, many delegates began to grow concerned about the size of the Senate. Simple mathematics made it clear that even a modified form of proportional representation in the Senate would produce a large body, and one that would grow rapidly with the addition of new states. This had not been a problem in the Virginia resolutions, which proposed that the membership of the second branch of the national legislature "ought to be elected by those of the first, out of a proper number of persons nominated by the individual Legislatures." State legislatures would nominate candidates for the Senate and the House would select among them. Consequently, the second branch or Senate could be as small as desired because there was no geographic distribution. The House would select the best candidates regardless of residence. But many delegates rejected this idea for a refined selection of the Senate because this would make the Senate a creature of the House. Refined selection was still important, but not if it came at the expense of institutional independence.

After rejecting selection by the House, the convention agreed, in a 10–0 vote, to have state legislatures choose senators.[18] This constituted a refined selection, but it also required some form of apportionment of senators among the states. Hence the second intractable problem: the adverse impact on the size of the Senate that would be produced by any form of proportionality. This surfaced several times during the debate, confirming delegates' strong preference for a small Senate, significantly smaller than strict proportional representation would produce. Even very early on, Massachusetts delegate Rufus King drew the logical conclusion: the proposal to have the state legislatures select the second branch would make the Senate, from the outset, too numerous, unless "the idea of proportion among the States was to be disregarded."[19] Much later, as the convention edged toward the Great Compromise, North Carolina's William Davie lamented the impact any form of proportional representation would have on Senate size: "It was impossible that so numerous a body could possess the activity and other qualities required in it."[20] King and Davie were not alone in such sentiments. Thrown back to the states for the primary role in selection and constricted by the nearly universal desire for a small Senate, the delegates were on the road toward the Great Compromise whether they realized it or not. As the problem of size and the role of state selection eroded support for proportional representation in the Senate, equal representation emerged as the only viable alternative. The politics of the Great Compromise were a complicated mixture of interest and principle. While perhaps not decisive, the widely shared sentiments of an ideal Senate—independent to be an effective check, small to promote deliberation, and selected (rather than elected) to enhance both deliberation and the check—pushed the convention toward the compromise. Efforts to elaborate purely interest-based explanations mistakenly overlook this evidence from the record. Among the factors that shaped the compromise and swayed the votes of a few individual delegates, these shared principles manifested their importance throughout the deliberations, even on the brink of compromise, and after.[21]

Following the Great Compromise, two other compositional issues with potentially profound consequences were solved rather easily, but with the effects of the apportionment compromise woven once again into the debate and decisions. First, states would be represented equally, but how many senators per state? Second, state equality implied that state representation in the Senate would be corporate, as in the Confederation Congress. If there were more than one senator per state, would they vote by state or per capita as individual senators?

These two profoundly important details were settled simultaneously on July 23 with relatively little debate and near consensus on the final votes. After considerable attention to unrelated articles in the Virginia resolutions, including the mode of ratification, Gouverneur Morris and Rufus King moved "that the representation in the second branch consist of ____ members from each state who shall vote per capita." This was part of an overall counterattack to limit the damage done to the Senate by the equal representation compromise. By specifying that senators would vote as individuals, these large-state delegates were trying to ensure that the Senate would not be a replication of the Confederation Congress and to minimize the chances that senators would act simply as mouthpieces for state legislatures. This approach to voting also was closer to the ideal of a Senate composed of fewer and wiser men for better deliberation. Clearly, no one considered one per state a safe number, not only for purposes of deliberation but also for the purely pragmatic reasons of absences, illnesses, and deaths. Nathaniel Gorham, a supporter of per capita voting, called for two per state because a small number was best for "deciding on peace & war &c, which he expected would be vested in the 2d. Branch. The number of states will also increase." Reflecting the delegates' consistent preference for a small upper house, Mason agreed that more than two, with the addition of new states, would produce too large a Senate. Two per state was then agreed to unanimously. This was followed immediately by Luther Martin's objection to per capita voting "as departing from the idea of the *States* being represented in the 2d. branch." But the delegates quickly voted on the whole motion, including two per state voting per capita, and gave their approval by a 9–1 vote, with only Maryland in opposition.[22] Even most small-state delegates, though committed to state equality, wanted to retain some of the Senate's original purpose. Equality of votes might have been a political necessity, but not at the complete sacrifice of senatorial independence. Perhaps for some small-state delegates, this was their own compromise of interests and principles in the making of the Senate.[23]

From start to finish, the issue of Senate representation pervaded the deliberations of the delegates and affected some of their most important decisions. The nature and purpose of that body were vital issues to the end of the deliberations.²⁴ For our purposes, the point is to understand how the ideal republican Senate and the compromised Senate of state equality came to be combined, whether harmoniously or not, in the same institution.

## Minority Power or Rights

Senators, especially those serving after the nineteenth century, have with great frequency and conviction associated their institution with a special role: the protection of minority rights, or "the rights of the minority," as senators often put it. To cite just two examples, former senator and Republican Majority Leader Howard Baker stated in 1993 that "the Senate is the only body in the federal government where . . . minority rights are fully and specifically protected. It was designed for that purpose by America's Founders."²⁵ A couple of decades later, Democratic Majority Leader Harry Reid echoed Baker's words: "There's a reason for the filibuster. I understand it. It's to protect the rights of the minority. The Senate was set up to protect the rights of the minority."²⁶ Such sweeping claims are devoid of historical evidence and made without pausing to define the key terms. What minorities and what rights? Minority interests are sometimes linked to states and federalism, but far more frequently minority rights are expressed in broad and unspecified terms. That is, the "minority" could be any individual or collective, whether defined by party or region or by some other interest. Likewise, "right" or "rights" are typically left hanging, as though self-evident. A review of thousands of pages of Senate debates from the nineteenth and twentieth centuries shows that the specific thing most commonly associated with minority rights is the right to be heard. This right to "voice" has often been characterized as "freedom of debate." The actual history of the filibuster and supermajority cloture suggests that there is a bit more to it than that. As we shall see in later chapters, the rules of the Senate could encourage debate. They don't. Despite what senators say, the rules have never been about allowing for more debate. They have been about power. The minority does not want to make its case; it wants to win. The hue and cry in the Senate about minority rights over the years has not been so much about *voice* as it has been about *victory*, that is, the power to obstruct, extract concessions, or veto outright what the majority would like to accomplish.

So what role did conceptions of "minority rights" play in the creation of the Constitution? Depending on which minorities and which rights were considered, what protections, if any, were afforded them? And was the Senate tasked with defending such rights in general? At the Constitutional Convention, minority rights as such were not a central concern. Convention delegates, in fact, worried more about forms of minority power or control. Even as the Senate was many different things to the authors of the Constitution, one thing it was not was a citadel for minority rights. In fact, strictly speaking, the framers never connected the Senate to any notion of minority power, let alone rights. In its primary and at times contradictory roles as both the federal institution constituted by state equality and comprising an older and wiser group of statesmen, the Senate represents a potential different *majority* (of states or simply senators). Or it represents a different quality of deliberation, owing to chamber size, the longer term, indirect election, and age-related experience. The records of the Constitutional Convention contain no discussion of the rights of the minority in general or any connection to the Senate specifically. In fact, they evince far more care for majority rule than they do concerns about minority rights. Insofar as equal representation in the Senate entailed an advantage for smaller-population states (and some delegates argued that population would not prove to be the enduring division among the states), then the Senate protected this very specific form of minority rights. But the debates made no mention of a more general notion of minority rights or the Senate's role as their safeguard.

To begin, it bears repeating that the Senate of the Virginia Plan—Madison's deliberative Senate, intended to balance the larger democratic House—would have been apportioned by population. That is, it would have reflected the majority of the population, not some minority, however construed. Madison and a majority of the delegates, for most of the convention, did not even want the Senate to represent states as states, let alone valorize the Senate as the guardian of states' rights. When proportional representation for the Senate proved both unacceptable to smaller states and incompatible with a small Senate, equal representation of states became the barely acceptable alternative. Notice, however, that equal representation was really about representing or balancing *two potentially different majorities:* the majority of sovereign states in the Senate versus the majority of the national population in the House. The Great Compromise was so fraught that it is a fraud to extract a principle of minority rights from the highly contentious votes that nearly ended the proceedings. The basis of Senate representation that emerged from the convention was state equality: states, not any other potential minorities.

A search for the terms "minority" and "majority" in the entirety of the records of the convention reveals the following.[27] The comments surrounding any use of the term "minority" are overwhelmingly against the ability of minorities to decide or prevent a decision by the majority. The only specific endorsements of minority decision-making power, not rights as such, concern states and their role in the national government. And even these are surprisingly few. As the political scientist Patrick Coby points out, "At the Convention there are three minority interests that receive the delegates' sustained attention and solicitude. They are small states, all states, and southern states."[28] The fourth minority interest is property, but it draws less attention at the convention and does not end up with any direct protection in the Constitution.[29]

States, in this case, were not portrayed as exemplars of some universal notion that minorities of any variety should be protected. They were not stand-ins for some broader category. They were considered as specific political entities: discrete and preexisting political units that were given corporate and equal representation in the Senate only because a determined minority of the state delegations at the Convention were prepared to end the entire proceedings if this demand was not met.

Of the forty-three substantive comments surrounding any invocation of the term "minority," only six refer exclusively to the Senate, as opposed to the government or the political process more generally. And five of those six are decidedly against the exercise of minority power by or within the Senate. The one exception came from Madison, who, while defending a long Senate term, noted that the Senate would or should represent the interests of larger property holders, who would be in the minority. It should be noted that this speech was more about the Senate as a source of wisdom and stability and it preceded the Great Compromise, after which Madison sought to take some power from the upper house structured by state equality. Property was, for the delegates who spoke on the subject, a proxy for independence and wisdom rather than the possession of a minority that needed protection.

Even the more general references to majority tyranny do not imply anything about the Senate. During the debates, Madison recorded himself as twice making versions of what would become his famous argument in *Federalist* no. 10. In familiar language, he warned that "In all cases where a majority are united by a common interest or passion, the rights of the minority are in danger."[30] But, as in no. 10, Madison found the cure for this danger in the size and diversity of the republic and the overall form of its institutions. His fellow Virginian, George Mason, also twice expressed concern about the tendency of the majority to oppress the minority, but for Mason this was about states and the power of the northern states, not some general principle. And he clearly ascribed the ability to defeat this defect of republics to the design of the whole system, not the virtues of the Senate. In fact, the Senate came in for some scorn from Mason because he felt it should not be given too much power and be able to entrench itself.[31] Moreover, he also contradicted himself by worrying about a minority controlling the majority when, as he mistakenly forecast, the national population would shift in favor of the South and West.[32]

Instead, concerns about *minority power*, in general or in the Senate specifically, dominated. Delegates such as Wilson, Madison, King, Mason, Franklin, Morris, and General Pinckney argued against various forms of minority power or minority vetoes in areas such as trade, treaties, appointments, the creation of new states, and so forth.[33] A particular example was the debate over the threshold for quorum for both chambers of Congress, with delegates expressing concerns about the delays and mischief that could attend supermajority quorum requirements.[34] They rejected motions that would have required a higher quorum in the Senate for treaties and general business.[35] They also rejected a motion to allow a single member of the Senate "to enter his dissent" on any vote (that is, enter the reasons for his vote in the journal).[36] Moreover, the records are replete with concerns about a potential Senate aristocracy, from small- and large-state delegates alike. This also contradicts any idea that the Senate should be a forum for minority rights. Even Roger Sherman, one of the most important advocates for state equality, expressed opposition to excessive minority power, at least when it came to overriding presidential vetoes. He favored two-thirds rather than three-fourths—which was still in the draft Constitution on September 12—for overriding presidential vetoes, because "the States would not like to see so small a minority and the President, prevailing over the general voice. In making laws regard should be had to the sense of the people."[37]

This might seem surprising given that "majority tyranny" and the fear of it are often portrayed as all but paramount among the concerns of at least some of the founders, particularly Madison. There is, however, a substantial difference between a fear of majority tyranny and a concern for minority rights writ large. Majority tyranny is about the durable or consistent domination of a minority by a cohesive majority. And, as implied by Madison in *Federalist* no. 10, for example, a majority faction is tyrannical only if it is united by a "common impulse of passion, or of interest, adverse to the rights of other citizens, or to the permanent and aggregate interests of the community."[38] That is, a majority decision by a government is not inherently tyrannical because it did not somehow listen to or compromise with the minority. The minority, just like the majority, can be a faction adverse to others' rights or to the aggregate interests of the community. The difference is that the danger of minority factions is mitigated by majority rule, "which enables the majority to defeat its sinister views by regular vote."[39] In short, the majority has the right to decide on any particular issue, but the system is designed to mitigate or prevent domination over time. That is what the extended republic of sovereign states and the multiple decision-making institutions in the national government are meant to do.

When it comes to their institution, however, senators tend to equate minority rights with the following: that on any issue the minority must have some degree of influence over the process or outcome. That logic is in none of the decisions made at the convention.[40] The default position of the Constitution is majority rule. To highlight that default position, the framers made specific exceptions to require supermajorities for five extraordinary actions: the override of a presidential veto, expulsion from Congress, the approval of treaties, conviction on impeachment, and the proposal of amendments to the Constitution.

At the Constitutional Convention, delegates used the term "tyranny" in reference to a number of things, including an executive that was too powerful or one that was not powerful enough. Concerns about majority tyranny specifically were few and far between and were expressed most directly by Madison previewing his *Federalist* no. 10 argument. As numerous were direct references to *minority* tyranny. North Carolinian Hugh Williamson was sure "it must be tyranny, if the smaller states can tax the greater, in order to ease themselves."[41] Or James Wilson of Pennsylvania, who thought "It is a part of the definition . . . of tyranny, that the smaller number governs the greater."[42] And finally, Roger Sherman, the leader of the small-state coalition, thought that "to require more than a majority to decide a question was always embarrassing as had been experienced in cases requiring the votes of nine States in Congress."[43]

## The Exceptional President, Supreme Court, and House of Representatives

As we have seen, the story of the Great Compromise, stripped of its essential details, can leave the impression that a second legislative chamber was introduced to save the day and the convention. This makes the Senate look like the bold innovation. Christopher Dodd, in his 2010 farewell speech to the Senate, made this mistake when he attributed the Senate to the actions of two Connecticut delegates, Roger Sherman and Oliver Ellsworth, "who proposed the idea of a bicameral national legislature."[44] This is simply false, as we have seen. The Connecticut delegates can be credited with advocating for taking what was already agreed to, a bicameral legislature, and using it as the basis for giving each side, so to speak, what it wanted, with proportional representation in one chamber and equal representation in the other. The representational compromise and what followed was something borrowed, something blue, mostly old, and a bit new, but with the necessity of a second chamber as all but a given. And however complicated the Senate became, it was a bit less innovative and a lot less elegant than the exceptionalism argument implies. What about the other branches? In short, the executive, judiciary, and the House of Representatives were in many respects as or more innovative than the Senate, and certainly more elegant in the clarity of their design and purpose.

We can begin with the fact that the United States under the Articles of Confederation had no executive or president. The closest the articles came to such a thing was a "Committee of the States," composed of one member from each state, which convened only when Congress was in recess. A "president" was selected by Congress to "preside" over the Committee of the States, nothing more. States had governors, but the postrevolutionary constitutions created mostly weak executives, who were often picked by the state legislature or very much circumscribed by legislative power. Pennsylvania's constitution, for example, had a twelve-member "executive council" instead of a governor. Georgia's one-house legislature selected the governor, who served a one-year term and was all but under the control of a twelve-member executive council picked from the legislature. Indeed, whether powerful or not, such executive councils were included in most state constitutions. Two states, New York and Massachusetts, had created more autonomous executives. New York had an independently elected governor, and the governor was part of a "council to revise," which included supreme court judges, that reviewed the constitutionality of legislation. Only Massachusetts had an independently elected governor with exclusive veto power subject to a two-thirds override. Overall, the first state constitutions remained some distance from an embrace of a strong executive.[45]

Despite fears of monarchical power, the presidency created by the Constitution was both an independent and a potentially powerful executive. Hamilton's *Federalist* no. 70 laid out the "ingredients which constitute energy in the Executive": unity, duration, an adequate provision for its support, and competent powers. To this end, the president was selected independently from the legislature for a longer term than the House and endowed with a veto that could be overcome only by mustering two-thirds in both the Senate and House. The convention rejected a plural executive and did not create anything like an executive council. This was a strong and unitary executive, designed for effective administration of the national government. Its autonomy from control by the legislature created a true separation of powers, something that had heretofore been an object of theorizing more than actual practice.

An independent judiciary was necessary to complete the distinctly republican separation of powers. This was a major leap forward. The colonies had had courts, but primarily those that handled ordinary legal disputes. As the historian Peter Charles Hoffer and colleagues write, "In some of the colonies, notably Connecticut, the legislatures performed the role of high courts."[46] The revolutionary state constitutions had then made strides toward a formal separation of powers and the recognition of judicial authority and independence. Nevertheless, as with the executive, many of these initial state constitutions did not have a fully independent or powerful high court. Pennsylvania's constitution created a supreme court, but it was essentially just the peak of the pyramid of ordinary law courts. Constitutional questions were handled by a "Council of Censors" that met every seven years. South Carolina's constitution mentioned various types of ordinary lower courts but specified that the lieutenant governor and privy council would serve as the court of chancery or equity. And during these years only a handful of cases suggested or asserted the authority of state courts to rule on the constitutionality of state acts or laws. At the national level, the Articles of Confederation said nothing about courts of any kind.

In sharp contrast, Article III of the Constitution announces that "the judicial Power of the United States, shall be vested in one supreme Court" and other inferior courts Congress is empowered to create. By dividing the appointment power between the president and the Senate and by giving federal judges and justices indefinite tenure "during good Behavior," the Constitution goes nearly as far as possible in creating an independent court. Judicial power, moreover, "shall extend to all Cases, in Law and Equity, arising under this Constitution, the Laws of the United States," and more. And while the concept and practice of judicial review—the court's implicit authority to rule on constitutional questions—would take some time to evolve, this institutional architecture and broad constitutional mandate was a new and substantial addition to the practice of republican government, especially at the level of the nation-state.

The arguments about the innovative if not revolutionary nature of the presidency and judiciary are straightforward and perhaps unsurprising. Neither had existed in anything like the forms proposed in the Constitution. Nevertheless, reminding ourselves of the striking nature of these institutions, which were anything but givens or obvious, casts grave doubt on claims such as those cited in the introduction about the compromised and conflicted Senate as the "one touch of authentic genius" or "the most remarkable of all the inventions of modern politics." And remarkable as each institution was, the true genius lay in the whole rather than in its parts.

But what about the House of Representatives? Surely, it is the least innovative among the four entities composing the branches of government. The House would seem to be the prosaic given of any parliament: a more or less popularly elected body with some or all of the authority to write laws. From a contemporary perspective, the House can seem like an unremarkable necessity rather than an extraordinary invention. I think that this is a significant distortion. In the most crucial constitutional respect, the House of Representatives was the true institutional innovation. Its relative simplicity and the relative lack of discussion about its creation are deceptive because they obscure the sea change the House represented. Madison and his allies lost a great deal in the battle for the ideal republican, and specifically more national, Senate. But that was in large measure because they won the central victory with the House. This victory centered on the creation of a bicameral legislature with at least one chamber selected directly by the people, not by or through their state governments. The House represents the creation of the crucial constituent connection, and thus power, for the national government.

While there were colonial and state assemblies that resembled the House in many respects, a popular legislature had not been part of the national government under the Articles of Confederation. They had created a unicameral Congress based on equal representation of states as states. States could send no fewer than two and as many as seven delegates. The number did not matter because states voted as states: one vote per state regardless of size. As we have seen, the New Jersey Plan with a unicameral legislature based on state equality was put before the convention only as a challenge to the insistence by many large-state delegations on proportional representation in both chambers of the legislature. This small-state alternative basically replicated the Confederation Congress. And it failed. The convention struggled with how representation would be structured in the Senate, but from the beginning, a strong majority of delegates favored a bicameral system with direct representation of citizens in at least one chamber.

This innovation, the direct representation of citizens in the national legislature, was the linchpin of "inventing the people," in the words of historian Edmund Morgan. To create a genuinely national government, Morgan explains, "Madison was inventing a sovereign American people to overcome the sovereign states," and in this creation the "composition of the lower house would thus be decisive" because everything else would be built from that foundation.[47] George Mason made this clear early in the proceedings in Philadelphia. "Under the existing Confederacy," he noted, "Congs. represent the States not the people of the States: their acts operate on the States not on the individuals. The case will be changed in the new plan of Govt. The people will be represented; they ought therefore to choose the Representatives."[48] The people would directly select their representatives, who would then make laws that acted directly on and for them, rather than on or through the states.

The resulting House of Representatives was radically democratic in design and potential, especially for the national legislature of a large country. Its British counterpart, the House of Commons, was based on a medieval form of geographic representation—places, towns, estates. American colonial and state legislatures were typically similar, with most distributing state assembly seats to towns and counties.[49] Breaking from representation based on place per se, the House was apportioned by the population of each state based on an "actual Enumeration," what we now know as the census. One can argue that states were preexisting "places," and that point is well taken. But the key fact is that the Constitutional Convention did its best to divorce representation of citizens in the House from state control. States were all but unavoidable as the intermediary geographic unit for the distribution of House seats. Only states would be capable of administering the elections over the length and breadth of what was already a vast nation, with huge territories such as those just slated for formation into new states by the Northwest Ordinance, a law passed by the Congress of the Confederation in July 1787. The convention saved itself a world of trouble by giving the task of election management over to states. The jealousy of the states might not have tolerated a more nationalized system, but that was hardly an issue because the practical problems of a central government administering nationwide elections made such a system unimaginable. Nevertheless, the "people" within each state would directly pick their representatives to the national government. Moreover, the franchise would be as democratic as what each state allowed for in its "most numerous" branch of its legislature.

The new government was premised on a democratic assembly endowed with the primary powers of government. On this kind of geographic scale, this was a historic innovation. In 1787, the British House of Commons was marginally democratic and represented mostly the 50,000 square miles of England, with handfuls of seats in Scotland and Wales. Pennsylvania and New Jersey, two of the states still defined by their eighteenth-century boundaries, by themselves comprised about 55,000 square miles. And no other branch of the government was intended to be democratically selected. Even in the Virginia Plan, as we have seen, the upper chamber was to be proportioned by population, but selected by the lower house from nominations by the states. Almost none of the delegates imagined an unmediated democratic form of selection for the president, to say nothing of the judiciary.[50] In fact, the antidemocratic mechanisms for selection of the other branches reinforce the point that the direct election of the House is certainly a more innovative feature of the new Constitution than the indirect selection of the Senate and the state equality attached to it.

## It's the System, Not the Senate

The Constitutional Convention created a multifaceted but also compromised and conflicted Senate. But no matter what the founders' exact intentions were for the upper house of Congress, it was always part of a system. That system was composed of two layers. First, there was the extended republic of many states, which retained important aspects of sovereignty or self-government and which were characterized by a diversity of interests resulting from differences in geography, economy, and culture. Second, there was the national government itself, composed of multiple decision-making institutions of separated and shared powers. As we have seen, the Constitution created several exceptional institutions—the House, the executive, and the judiciary, along with the multifaceted Senate. Nevertheless, however important and innovative each part of the system was individually, they were designed, whether with complete success or not, to work together in a republican architecture of independent institutions. Each was to play a vital role in the project of "contriving the interior structure of the government, as that its several constituent parts may, by their mutual relations, be the means of keeping each other in their proper places."[51]

Thus it was the Constitution as a whole that protected against majority tyranny, not any one part, such as the Senate. The Senate was part of this, but it was not the designated guardian of minority rights. Madison put it this way:

> In all Govts. there is a power which is capable of oppressive exercise. In Monarchies and Aristocracies oppression proceeds from a want of sympathy & responsibility in the Govt. towards the people. In popular Governments the danger lies in an undue sympathy among individuals composing a majority, and a want of responsibility in the majority to the minority. The characteristic excellence of the political System of the U. S. arises from a distribution and organization of its powers, which at the same time that they secure the dependence of the Govt. on the will of the nation, provides better guards than are found in any other popular Govt. against interested combinations of a Majority against the rights of a Minority.[52]

The Senate was, and is, part of a system that in its totality was the true ingenuity. This system was innovative in the Constitution's balancing act of the powers attached to each institution, in how each was organized, and in the relationship of each institution to a constituency that would support or resist its power.[53]

As we have seen, the most common characteristics ascribed to an ideal Senate by the framers were a limited number of members, a select form of appointment, and independence. A small number of carefully selected senators appointed for long terms would foster wisdom, stability, and effective deliberation. The quality of deliberation was likely to be better in wisdom and temperament than that of the House because of the elements of the Senate's composition, namely, the much smaller membership, appointment by state legislatures, the longer term, and even the higher age and citizenship requirements of members. In all this, there was no discussion of the quantity of debate or even the right to debate. And there certainly was no discussion about rules of procedure at all, let alone as part of any bicameral differences with regard to deliberation.

In short, the exceptionalist mythology that senators and others regularly attach to that institution misses the truth on two fronts. First, it all but ignores the Constitution's original *intra-institutional* components of the Senate's deliberative difference and substitutes instead the Senate's rules of procedure, which have been written and altered by senators from the Senate's first meeting onward. Second, it reifies the Senate as the constitutional barrier against majority tyranny, when it is *the inter-institutional system,* the system as a whole, and not the Senate in particular, that protects against the abuse or unchecked aggregation of power.

The Senate was a product of multiple forces and motivations, and the product reflects this mixture. In the end, I would argue that knowing the exact balance of motivations of the framers is less important than understanding the consequences of the sometimes confused deliberations, sharp disagreements, and grudging compromises. Whatever the exact motivations behind all the decisions that produced the Senate, it was, as a result, a compromised institution, intended to embody two potentially incompatible purposes. Rufus King reminded the delegates of this dilemma on the last day of debate before the compromise vote: "According to the idea of securing the State Govts. there ought to be three distinct legislative branches. The 2d. was admitted to be necessary, and was actually meant to check the 1st. branch, to give more wisdom, system, & stability to the Govt. and ought clearly as it was to operate on the people to be proportioned to them. For the third purpose of securing the States, there ought then to be a 3d. branch, representing the States as such and guarding by equal votes their rights and dignities."[54] Did the compromised Senate represent the states, or was it still the national institution and steward of governmental policy? Could the two functions be combined? Confusion and disagreement on the former question reigned throughout the rest of the convention. The latter question was never addressed and would have to be answered if and when the new constitution was put into practice.

On September 15, the busy final day of substantive debate on the proposed constitution, the last successful motion was about equality in the Senate.[55] A few days before, the convention had added without debate one restriction on the procedure to amend the Constitution: "no amendment which may be made prior to the year 1808 shall in any manner affect" the provisions protecting the importation of slaves and the three-fifths formula on taxation. Roger Sherman noted the addition of this restriction and thought it "should be extended" such that "no State shall without its consent be affected in its internal police, or deprived of its equal suffrage in the Senate." After dropping the internal police provision, the convention approved the second half of Sherman's restriction without debate or dissent, "being dictated by the circulating murmurs of the small States."[56] The implication of this wording was that instead of undergoing the general and already arduous process for amending the Constitution, any proposed change to equal representation in the Senate would require the approval of every state. Thus was entered into Article V the only indefinite and seemingly insurmountable limitation on the power to amend the Constitution. The Great Compromise, the creation and effects of which had pervaded the deliberations of the Constitutional Convention from start to finish, was not only great, it was apparently permanent as well. And it is to this fundamental feature of the Senate and the Constitution that we now turn.

# 2

# Equal Representation

THE PERPETUAL GREAT COMPROMISE

> The inequality of representation in the Senate [is] always a subject more or less disturbing to logical minds.
>
> —S. E. MOFFETT, 1895

## Why Washington, D.C., Is Not a State: It's the Senate, Stupid!

The Twenty-Third Amendment to the Constitution, giving Washington, D.C., electoral votes in the election of the president and vice president, was passed by the Eighty-Sixth Congress on June 16, 1960, and ratified by March 29, 1961. Even though only one state from the former Confederacy voted to endorse the proposed amendment, ratification by the required three quarters of states took just nine months and twelve days, making it the third fastest addition to the Constitution.[1] Even the repeal of Prohibition took longer.

Washington was still a relatively sleepy and southern town during the same months that John F. Kennedy was campaigning for and then starting his presidency. Nevertheless, with 752,000 residents, the District in 1961 was more populous than eleven states. Moreover, with civil rights becoming a central issue in American politics, the 1960 census revealed that the majority of the District's population was African American.[2] So, while southern states were no doubt concerned about how the amendment might affect the national balance of power for the presidency, D.C. got its three electoral votes. Most of the nation embraced the principle of democratic representation for the population of this major city because the impact was likely to be rather insignificant.

A decade later, with the District thoroughly Democratic and still greater in population than ten states, Republican president Richard Nixon would sign legislation granting the District one nonvoting delegate to the House of Representatives. But representation in the Senate had been and would remain an entirely different matter. In 1978, Congress—at an apex of Democratic power in both chambers of Congress—submitted the District of Columbia Voting Rights Amendment to the states for ratification.[3] The proposed amendment specified that the District "shall be treated as though it were a State" as far as representation in Congress and the election of the president and vice president were concerned. The amendment received only a handful of Republican votes, and only sixteen states ratified it in six years; the record shows that the main opposition was due to the impact on the Senate. Republicans offered unsuccessful alternatives: first, to allow D.C. residents to vote in Maryland's elections for US senators instead of the District getting its own senators, and, second, to have the amendment apply only to representation in the House. This failure notwithstanding, there has been an ongoing statehood movement ever since, even as D.C. slipped in relative population.[4] In the census of 1980, the District was bigger than only four states, then three in 1990, and then only Wyoming in 2000.[5] In 2020, the Democratic House of Representatives passed a bill to grant D.C. statehood, but it went nowhere in the Republican Senate.[6]

The odd status of Washington, D.C., reveals both the political importance and representational irrationality of the Senate. Who could imagine giving a metropolitan area of 68 square miles and fewer than 600,000 residents two senators? Wyoming, by contrast, with fewer residents than D.C., but 98,000 square miles and far more cattle than people, must have its two senators.

A common view is that D.C. would never be admitted as a state because of the "four toos": it is "too liberal, too urban, too black, or too Democratic."[7] Race and its relationship to liberal policies and the Democratic Party matter, of course. But that is looking at the problem the wrong way. Adding one more liberal Black representative to the House—with full voting rights—is not such a significant concern that it would stop a concerted effort to achieve the equivalent of D.C. statehood, just as it would not stop the equivalent for a hypothetical district that was largely white and conservative. But two liberal and possibly Black senators is another matter entirely. It could tip the balance of power in the Senate indefinitely, especially a Senate with the filibuster; that is, supermajority requirements to end debate.

The strained arguments against D.C. statehood reveal what they awkwardly seek to obscure: the absurdity of Senate representation. The very thing—equal representation—that is otherwise a bedrock of the Constitution and, for many, a measure of the founders' genius is the unspoken reason that D.C. or Puerto Rico cannot be granted the status that supposedly makes the American system special. The disenfranchisement of D.C.—which would be the state with the highest percentage of African Americans—highlights as well a central theme of this chapter and the next: the strong historical bond between equal representation in the Senate and efforts to maintain white supremacy. Two senators from the District of Columbia would be small recompense for the over two hundred years of the Senate's generally ignominious role in the oppression of Black Americans.

In this chapter, I explore the role and evolution of equal representation in American constitutionalism and democracy and make four arguments about its development and impact. First, the Senate as it developed via new state admissions was just what the Great Compromise portended: a battleground over regional interests. This was the case before and after the Civil War. And state admissions were the weapon in that battle. Second, prior to the Civil War, the main beneficiary of equal representation and state admissions were the slave-holding states of the South. Equal representation's outstanding role in early American history was to serve as the institutional core of the so-called "slave power." Third, emerging from and as part of this use of equal representation before the war, southern senators—who saw themselves as a minority oppressed by the northern majority—helped forge the idea that the Senate was the Constitution's citadel to protect minority interests, even though no such thing was intended, as I showed in the last chapter. Finally, despite the manifest use of equal representation and state admissions in party and regional competition for the entire nineteenth century, equal representation did not become the focus of efforts to reform the Senate. Instead, forces of democratic change would converge on another defining feature of the Senate: selection by state legislature. An ultimately successful movement rallied behind direct election of senators, resulting in the Seventeenth Amendment in 1913. As the Senate was democratized in this way, growing inequities of equal representation were left intact for logical minds to ponder as the Senate forged its way into the new century.

## The Great and Permanent Compromise

It is called the Great Compromise for a reason. The decision at the 1787 Constitutional Convention to give each state equal representation in the Senate was the most controversial and difficult of that summer. Led by

Virginia, a coalition of "large" states sought forms of proportional representation in both chambers of the proposed national legislature, while the so-called "small" states held out for equal representation in at least one chamber. However much that summary oversimplifies a more complex situation, it captures what became the linchpin of the entire convention. Midway through the summer the proceedings nearly collapsed when the question arose of how the Senate would be constituted, and, as Madison predicted in the midst of the crisis, if this problem were solved, "all others would be surmountable."[8] That proved to be the case.

A few months later, when the time came to justify the Senate's architecture in the *Federalist Papers,* Madison thinly disguised his distaste for this feature of the proposed government and portrayed it as an invention of political necessity:

> The equality of representation in the Senate is another point, which, being evidently the result of compromise between the opposite pretensions of the large and the small states, does not call for much discussion. . . . It is superfluous to try by the standards of theory, a part of the Constitution which is allowed on all hands to be the result not of theory, but "of a spirit of amity, and that mutual deference and concession which the peculiarity of our political situation rendered indispensable." . . . A government founded on principles more consonant to the wishes of the larger states, is not likely to be obtained from the smaller states. The only option then for the former lies between the proposed government and a government still more objectionable. Under this alternative the advice of prudence must be, to embrace the lesser evil; and instead of indulging a fruitless anticipation of the possible mischiefs which may ensue, to contemplate rather the advantageous consequences which may qualify the sacrifice.[9]

Madison's argument—like the rest of the *Federalist* essays—was first published in a New York newspaper. At the time, New York's population was slightly above the average of the states' populations, but its delegation to the Constitutional Convention repeatedly supported state equality, including the unicameral New Jersey Plan, and voted against proportional representation in the House.[10] In fact, Alexander Hamilton was left to fend for himself and his state when his New York colleagues, John Lansing and Robert Yates, abandoned the proceedings after July 10 and returned home because the work of the convention portended, in their view, a centralized system.[11] New York was seen as the key swing state in the battle for ratification, and that is why Hamilton organized the effort there to produce and publish the arguments that would become the *Federalist Papers*. From this perspective, Madison's less than subtle criticism is somewhat startling. Instead of extolling equal representation for the benefit of antifederalist New Yorkers, Madison seemed to be writing for large-state citizens suspicious of, or actively opposed to, equal representation.

Though it was the pivotal controversy at the convention, equal representation proved to be less of an issue during ratification than one might have expected. Nevertheless, if it was going to be challenged, the challenge had to happen as states considered the new plan. Unlike anything else in the Constitution, once equal representation was ratified, the door would be shut and double-bolted. With ratification, it was left to be seen whether Madison's hope would be fulfilled. Would equal representation's "advantageous consequences" he urged us to contemplate ensue? Or would the mischiefs be many, the advantages negligible, and the sacrifice increasingly glaring?

## The Antebellum Irony of Equal Representation

However farsighted the founders seem to have been in many areas of politics, some of their notions of demographics seem naïve from our perspective. No small part of the anxiety the founders had about state size and regional representation was based on projections of population growth. In turn, those projections were based largely on the physical size of the states and the presence or absence of slavery. A quick glance at a map of the states at the time of the Constitutional Convention shows how physically large the southern states were compared to most of the northern states. Some southern states did not have western borders and instead extended all the way to the Mississippi. The intuitive eighteenth-century assumption was that the larger the territory, the greater the potential population.[12] And slavery was, of course, part of the potential for southern growth. This was an agrarian perspective that did not give much weight to the potential for urban concentration around trade and industrial production.

At the Constitutional Convention, the conflicting interests between slave and free states surfaced on a few occasions over questions of representation. And the conflicts between slave-holding and free states intersected with issues around small versus large states in interesting ways. The Great Compromise was preceded by what some have called the "greatest compromise," more commonly known as the three-fifths compromise: the decision to include three-fifths of any state's total enslaved population in its apportionment population for the House of Representatives. This ratio, familiar to the delegates as the rule of revenue or "quota of contribution" created by the Congress of the Confederation, was adopted with little debate by a vote of 9–2.[13] The greatest compromise might have softened the way for the Great Compromise, even if that is difficult to discern in the voting by states and individual delegates.

The extra representation in the House might have made it easier for some large-state southern convention delegates to accept equality in the Senate; in turn, the potential domination of the House by the South might have given some northerners a reason to accede to senate equality.[14] The potential power of the South in the House—and Virginia was by some margin the largest state—was another argument for making the Senate into a northern institution. At the convention, there were six "northern" or border states that were free or with insignificant enslaved populations and six southern or border states with significant enslaved populations.[15] And if the convention succeeded and Rhode Island, which did not send delegates to Philadelphia, joined the union, then the balance would be seven to six. That small initial northern advantage in the Senate seemed likely to grow sooner rather than later with the transformation of the Northwest Territories into states, states that were preordained to be free by the Northwest Ordinance. But that is not how the nation evolved in its initial decades.

The irony is that it did not take long for the tables to turn as northern states gained population much faster than southern states. This was not due to the admission of new states. The original six "slave" states had at the start a slim population advantage over the seven northern states, now including Rhode Island (by about 65,000 residents, according to the 1790 census). Only twenty years later those same seven northern states, with New York and Pennsylvania leading the way, had over half a million more residents than the original group of slave states. This was the census head count including all slaves, not the apportionment population with enslaved populations counted by three-fifths. And in the 1810 census, enslaved individuals accounted for 37 percent of total population of the original six slave states, not counting Kentucky and Tennessee, which had been added to their ranks.[16] Many in the North considered the three-fifths clause an unjustifiable addition to southern representation. Nevertheless, the northern states were destined to dominate the apportionment for the House of Representatives in spite of slavery. By 1820 the North had a greater than 800,000-person advantage in total population over the South, including all the states that had entered the union to that point. The resulting apportionment for the House of Representatives gave the North a 123–90 seat advantage. Twenty years later the gap had increased to 135–88. What about the Senate? Could the South use the Senate to offset the northern state advantage in the House?

## The "Slave Power" and Equal Representation

Politicians in Washington could not control population growth, which determines the number and distribution of representatives in the House, but they could control state admissions, which is the only thing that matters for the Senate. The fairness of equal representation—as a principle of government—does not seem to have been a notable subject of discussion or concern during the first half of the nineteenth century. Sectional power certainly was, however, and as it became the dominant controversy in national politics, the Senate was the central battleground. And one factor loomed above all others: the determination of slave states to maintain parity with northern states in the Senate because there was nothing they could do about the House, even as many northerners lamented the boost given to southern representation in the House by the Constitution's three-fifths clause. As a result, the consequences of state equality in the Senate constantly influenced the politics of antebellum state admissions. This was a contest of sectional clout, not political principle, and the Senate would be the institutional bastion of what critics labeled the "slave power."[17]

As the South lost ground in the House, it maintained a balance of power in the Senate through a process of state admissions that kept the number of free and slave states, and thereby the number of senators from each region, equal or nearly so. The balancing act in the Senate began with the admission of Vermont and Kentucky, one free, one slave, in 1791 and 1792.[18] Coming well before the conflicts between North and South emerged, this first pair maintained a one-state advantage for the North. The admission of Tennessee produced a 50–50 Senate in 1796, which was upset by Ohio's entry in 1803 as the first state from the Northwest Territories. This was balanced by Louisiana's entry as a slave state in 1812, followed by three pairs in close succession: Indiana and Mississippi, Illinois and Alabama, and, most famously, Maine and Missouri in the Missouri Compromise of 1820.[19] By 1821 eleven states had been added, five free (Vermont, Ohio, Indiana, Illinois, Maine) and six slave-holding states (Kentucky, Tennessee, Louisiana, Mississippi, Alabama, Missouri). This produced a balance of twelve free and twelve slave states, and thus an evenly divided Senate.

The final pairing in state admissions was Arkansas and Michigan in 1836 and 1837. The South had its last hurrah with Florida and Texas in 1845, achieving a short-lived two-state advantage of 15–13 in the Senate while making up just under 40 percent of the House. This process and strategy fell apart, however, in the late 1840s and early 1850s at the same time as the South ran out of territory to convert to slave states. After Florida and Texas came the trio of Iowa, Wisconsin, and California, producing a 16–15 northern or non-slave-state majority. Minnesota and Oregon would be added as the sectional rupture headed toward civil war. Figure 1 shows the steady loss of southern power in the House relative to the Senate. In this way, the Great Compromise of 1787 lived on in the series of compromises over state admissions. Equal representation, the linchpin of this sectional balancing act, perhaps delayed but could not stave off secession and the conflagration that soon followed.

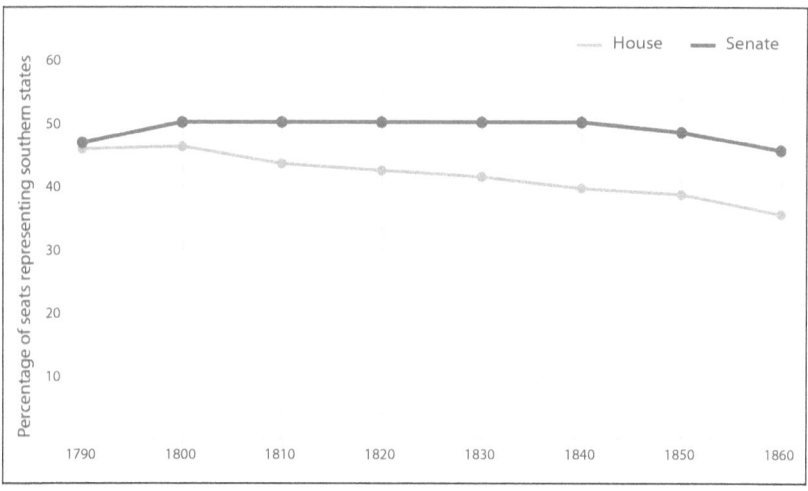

FIG. 1. Southern representation in the House and Senate, 1790–1860

Historians have explored the various forces that limited but did not entirely suppress sectional conflict from the early 1800s to at least the Compromise of 1850.[20] The equilibrium in the Senate meant that the South typically had enough votes to stop any legislation it deemed contrary to its vital interests. The House, by contrast, could and sometimes did pass antislavery measures. This goes back as far as 1804 and an amendment to prohibit slavery in the territory of the Louisiana Purchase.[21] That failed in the Senate, as did an amendment passed by the House in 1819 to abolish slavery in Missouri as part of its admission as a state. After years of delaying the admission of Texas, the House voted to add an amendment to the Texas statehood bill that would have divided it into one slave and one free state. As well, starting in 1846 the House more than once passed the Wilmot Proviso to prohibit slavery in territory gained from war with Mexico. Finally, while the Kansas-Nebraska Act of 1854 was a foregone, if rather contentious, conclusion in the Senate, passing 37–14, the House fight culminated in a much closer 113–100 vote that signaled the fragmentation of the Democratic Party over slavery.

Despite a general and strategic preference by party leaders to avoid sectional conflict, the House repeatedly expressed majority opposition to the expansion of slavery, but these legislative initiatives could not get past the South's institutional veto in the Senate. The Senate also had rules of debate (the subject of chapter 5) that allowed for minority obstruction in the form of dilatory motions and filibusters in the form of extended debate, and the South took advantage of those obstructive possibilities. As Gregory Wawro shows, slave state senators utilized their chamber's rules to obstruct particularly as their minority status increased later in this era.[22] But during these decades the House also had freewheeling debates, and minority obstruction was possible and took place there as well.[23] The core of the slave power was equal representation in the Senate.

## Antebellum Equal Representation and Minority Interests

The central importance of equal representation is also evident in the most influential and infamous strand of American political theory of the antebellum period. John C. Calhoun—representative, secretary of war, vice president, secretary of state, senator, and above all passionate defender of slavery as a positive and permanent good—developed his theory of the "concurrent majority" in response to the emerging minority status of the South. Calhoun believed the Constitution afforded inadequate protection to minority interests. The separation of power, the system of checks and balances, and federalism, in his view, could not prevent the formation around a major issue of a majority faction that could and most likely would use the instruments of government to injure or oppress the minority "interest or portion."[24] So much for Madison's celebrated theory, expounded in *Federalist* no. 10 and no. 51, that a large and diverse federal republic would foil majority tyranny. Instead, the prevention of majority tyranny required that any proposed governmental action be subject to the approval of minority factions or interests.[25]

Calhoun presented the theory of the concurrent majority in his *A Disquisition on Government,* published posthumously in 1851. The work is utterly abstract and does not mention the South or slavery. But there is no mistaking its motivation and purpose. To be fair, Calhoun's and southern concerns about domination by northern states and interests go back as far as 1828 and a sectional divide over tariffs rather than over slavery as such.[26] This culminated in the bitter nullification crisis in 1832 and 1833, which included passage of what southerners labeled the "Force Bill," the legislative instrument Congress provided President Jackson to enforce compliance with the tariff. Calhoun, who was Jackson's vice president, resigned as part of this struggle so that he could take a seat in the Senate and fight more effectively from that vantage.

Important as the tariff fight might have been, it was quickly eclipsed by the contests of power involving slavery. "Southern political thought was a creature of circumstance," argues Jesse T. Carpenter in his book on the subject, "devised solely to meet the exigencies of practical situations and pressing conditions."[27] The exigency or pressing condition was the protection of slavery. To this end, Calhoun proposed that his unspecified interests or portions have a veto power on governmental initiatives. "It is this negative power—the power of preventing or arresting the action of the government, be it called by what term it may, veto, interposition, nullification, check, or balance of power, which in fact forms the constitution" that Calhoun was proposing.[28] How many minority interests or portions might warrant such a constitutional veto Calhoun does not say. He reasoned that such a power would deter proposals from factions that would advance particular interests at the expense of others and thereby "force them to unite in such measures only as would promote the prosperity of all."[29] Without further specification, his theory comes off as a recipe for political deadlock. Back in the real world, it had only one application, to the portion that was the South and its singular interest in enslavement. In concrete terms, the maintenance of an equal or nearly equal number of slave versus free states was the closest Calhoun and his allies were going to get to a such a veto.

Thus the first concrete manifestation and theoretical justification for the Senate as the bastion of what might be considered minority rights—more precisely, minority power—was the bond forged between equal representation and the interests of the states that sought, first and foremost, to protect and preserve the institution of slavery. Supporting the argument I am making here, Sarah Binder and Steven Smith argue that it was "Calhoun, along with other southern senators, who placed the protection of minority interests at the heart of Senate tradition."[30] The first step in this process was the transubstantiation of the raw politics of the Great Compromise and equal representation into a general notion that the Senate was designed to protect minority interests or rights. As Binder and Smith note, this spilled over into a justification for the Senate's emerging tradition of extended debate and the ability to filibuster, another tool prewar southern senators were using to protect their interests, and a connection we take up in later chapters.[31] In this way, the straightforward provision for two senators per state regardless of population intersected with the political interests of slave states to become the foundation for the Senate's mythology about its special and supposedly constitutional role as guardian of the minority voice in the national government.

## Party Politics: Equal Representation from Reconstruction through Redemption

That Senate mythology would endure and eventually grow despite the onset of the Civil War and the destruction of both the southern interest that led to the conflagration and any notions of concurrent majorities in theory or practice. Meanwhile, equal representation would serve largely as a partisan tool in the ongoing struggle for control of the branches of government in the decades after the war. In fact, that process started as part of the war itself with the admissions of West Virginia and Nevada. By splitting off from Virginia after its secession from the Union, the self-proclaimed leaders of West Virginia presented Lincoln and the Congress with a constitutional conundrum. Would the admission of such an entity comply with the restrictions in Article IV of the Constitution on new states being "formed or erected within the Jurisdiction of any other state"? The details are not important for our purposes, but Lincoln and many members of Congress saw admission, proclaimed in April 1863, as an expedient war measure that was probably not fully in compliance with the Constitution. West Virginia had a fairly large population, so there were no concerns about its size. It produced two Republican senators through the end of Reconstruction; after that the state elected two Democrats for most of the rest of the century.

By contrast, the recently formed Nevada Territory contained very few people and was far removed geographically from the war. Nevertheless, as with West Virginia, the politics of war greased the wheels of admission, resulting in the rapid formation of a state with the smallest population ever to be admitted. In 1860, the Nevada Territory contained a mere 6,857 people. At the time, the recently created Oregon was the smallest state, with a rapidly increasing population of over 52,000. Despite some disagreement among Nevada's residents about the wisdom of statehood, Congress passed an enabling act early in 1864 inviting the territory to seek admission. Which it did, becoming the thirty-sixth state on October 31, just in time to take part in the 1864 national elections. Nevada's electoral votes, along with other political considerations, motivated swift congressional action.[32]

Nevada had a silver-induced population boom over the next decade, reaching a paltry 42,941 in the 1870 census. However, by 1900 Nevada's population was less than it had been thirty years earlier. More than any other state admission to date, Nevada's raised the issue of so-called "rotten boroughs" (also called "pocket boroughs"), which is a reference to parliamentary electoral districts, especially rural ones, in England that had very few voters. In these rotten boroughs, a handful of voters were under the thumb of an aristocratic patron who controlled the land and constituency. But British pocket boroughs produced only a single member of Parliament. Likewise, the admission of a state as small in population as Nevada, with one representative, had a small impact on the House. But the effect on the Senate was substantial in percentage and partisan terms. Nevada, with the exception of one senator for a single term, would elect two Republican senators through the end of the nineteenth century.

Nebraska was admitted in 1867, just after the war, while the Republicans were still firmly in control of the national machinery. Nine years later Colorado would enter the union in the summer before the election of 1876, which would mark the end of Reconstruction. Nebraska had two Republican senators for all thirty-two years except a single term by Populist William V. Allen. Colorado had two Republican Senators from admission through the end of the century except for one senator who switched parties for the last four years.

Following Reconstruction and the return of a nationally competitive Democratic Party, the two parties resumed an often bitter fight for control of the institutions of national government. Although the presidency would remain in Republican hands for twenty-four of the thirty-two years from the election of Ulysses S. Grant to the end of the nineteenth century, the Democrats had the majority of the House as early as 1875 and controlled that chamber for sixteen of the same thirty-two years. In the Senate, however, Democrats mustered a majority for only four years in the same period. No small part of this relative difference in Republican control was due to state admissions from the Civil War to 1890. Much as the South, the regional core of the Democratic Party, used the equal representation provision prior to the Civil War to retain some control over the national government, the Republican Party, which dominated politics in most states in the North and West, used the Senate's peculiar form of representation for the same purpose.

This era culminated in the admission of six physically large but sparsely populated states—North Dakota, South Dakota, Montana, Washington, Idaho, Wyoming—in a nine-month period from November 1889 to July 1890.[33] This led to more charges of rotten boroughs. Invoking the contemporaneous free silver movement, Democrats and other critics argued that the Republicans were engaging in the "free coinage" of senators, and Republican senators at that. The Democratic Party at this time stood behind the use of silver, along with gold, as currency. Democrats believed this more expansive monetary policy was beneficial to some of their core constituents, including farmers. Republicans accused Democrats of an inflationary policy that hurt the interests of many of their supporters. Democrats mocked the rapid creation of senators as the Republicans' version of political free coinage. This charge was hard to deny, even though two of these new creations were as populous as or more populous than some of the smallest already existing states.[34] These states were small and, for the most part, reliably Republican. While Montana and Wyoming were more competitive, the other four states had Republican senators over 85 percent of time from their admission in 1889 or 1890 to 1920. The admission of these six, which included four of the five smallest states in the country, came at the same time that the two largest, New York and Pennsylvania, for example, grew by almost a million residents each from 1880 to 1890 (an 18.1 percent increase for New York and an almost

23 percent increase for Pennsylvania) as the great wave of immigration was having its enormous impact. This produced the largest disparity in the nation's history between the average populations of the largest and smallest states.

The late-century contest for power between the Republican and Democratic parties was fraught and bitter, with strong levels of party discipline in Congress and among voters, with fights over many issues, especially those related to the relative economic interests of an industrial North and an agrarian South. It was not, however, an ideological or moral contest over the rights of African Americans. After Reconstruction, the parties split geographically, with one-party Democratic rule in the South working toward the rigid and often violent enforcement of what would be by the 1890s the twin pillars of white supremacy: Jim Crow segregation and electoral disenfranchisement of Blacks.[35] Unable to compete effectively in southern states and districts, the Republican Party dominated many northern and western states that contained very few African American voters. The Grand Old Party was willing to wave the "bloody shirt"—that is, invoke the memory of the Civil War—but that was far more about the martyred (and white) Union dead and hundreds of thousands of loyal Union veterans than about the rights of Blacks that had been sacrificed after Reconstruction.[36] The unsuccessful effort in 1890 to pass a federal elections bill that, in theory at least, could have enforced suffrage rights in the South marked the end of any congressional efforts to enforce the Fifteenth Amendment.[37] The elections bill was killed by a senate filibuster. As well, a Supreme Court appointed largely by Republican presidents and confirmed mostly by Republican Senates would six years later make "separate but equal" the law of the land in the infamous *Plessy v. Ferguson* decision. Hence the irony. While southern power in the Senate served the cause of white supremacy before the Civil War, northern dominance of the Senate in the late nineteenth century did nothing for the plight of African Americans as the nation descended into decades of American apartheid.

Notice that it was the majority party, the Republicans, that used state admissions to ensure institutional control, to bolster the chances that they would remain the majority party or at least retain control of the Senate by stacking it through the admission of new states. As this was happening, no politician invoked abstract notions of minority rights to justify the admission of these states. Rather, the majority party pursued a project of institutional engineering to shore up its congressional power.

In this context, equal representation could become an issue, but more as a question of power than of principle. Only a few scholars and other commentators of the day, such as S. E. Moffett, quoted at the start of this chapter, complained about the manifest oddity and general inequities of equal representation, which western state admissions demonstrated quite clearly. Consequently, a symptom—the effect on partisan control—was the focus in this contest for power, not the disease itself. Instead, a different feature of the Senate's original architecture became the focus of reform.

## Not Equal Representation but Direct Election

If few Americans voiced displeasure with the growing disparities caused by equal representation, another founding feature of the Senate, indirect election by state legislatures, was attracting more and more attention and opposition. Over the same decades of the nineteenth century, as new states were admitted and new senators minted, the politics of democratization—the general if uneven trend toward an expanding franchise directly selecting its representatives—put Senate selection by state legislatures rather than equal representation on a collision course with the political evolution of the country. This ultimately culminated in the Seventeenth Amendment, ratified in 1913, and the direct and popular election of senators by voters instead of state legislatures. One irony is that the same western states, the ones that benefited mightily from equal representation, were leaders in the popular movement for direct and democratic election of the Senate.

The original combination of equal representation and selection by state legislatures implied a form of corporate representation. A senator represented the collective will of the state that chose him. This was a sensible assumption, but one, as noted earlier, that combined what Madison and some of the other founders saw as oil and water. Equal representation was the great compromise to recognize state sovereignty. But election by state legislatures was primarily a form of elevated selection. At the Constitutional Convention, the Virginia Plan, the proposals that set the agenda for the convention's deliberations, included a provision to have the lower house select the members of the upper house "out of a proper number of persons nominated by the individual [state] Legislatures." This had nothing to do with states as states—far from it. This method would have further distanced senators from any connection to a particular geographic constituency. Various considerations led to a final decision in favor of state selection, particularly the concern that election by the members of the House of Representatives would make the Senate too dependent on that body. Although the Madisonian vision of a detached and nationalist Senate did not perish immediately, it lived on mostly in rhetoric about the Senate's lofty constitutional purpose. By contrast, the reality was that many state legislatures saw senators as delegates sent by them to represent state interests.[38]

At the same time, however, the country was democratizing, and voters were being integrated into party politics and party voting, with the presidential election increasingly seen as a plebiscite to determine national control. The people did not vote directly for the president, but that did not stop them from making it into the near equivalent of a direct election by the 1830s with the help of Andrew Jackson and the Democratic Party.[39] Just as the operation and purpose of the Electoral College were effectively overturned by the power and requirements of parties and democratization, the founding purpose and operation of selection of the Senate by state legislatures would be overtaken by party politics. Could senators in such a system maintain Madisonian insulation and independence? Not exactly. The same forces of democratization and party politics swept senatorial selection into their vortex. As party politics became the central organizing force in American government, senators were selected not so much by state legislatures, on behalf of the state, but by political parties within the states, on behalf of the control of national politics.

Parties and voters in a good number of states, without changing the Constitution, or at first even any state election laws, converted indirect election of senators into a popularity contest for control of the state. The mechanism was the so-called "canvass" or straw poll primary. This was, as William Riker describes it, "a canvass, that is, of voters rather than of state legislators, a canvass in which candidates for the Senate helped elect those state legislators who were more or less formally pledged to vote for them."[40] If that sounds obscure, we can use a rather famous moment from American political history to illustrate how selection of senators evolved: the Lincoln-Douglas debates of 1858, when the two were opponents in the contest for the US Senate. If senators were selected by state legislatures, what were the candidates doing holding public debates before large crowds around the state? They were leaders of their parties. The nationalization of politics and policy—especially with the nation on the brink of a civil war—elevated the Senate candidates above the state legislators who supposedly picked them. With a large and increasing number of Senate contests becoming the focal point for popular politics, state legislators were at times beholden to the successful Senate canvasser for their office. Lincoln and Douglas had been nominated by their respective state party conventions, which in practical terms meant that the potential state legislators were pledged—well before they were even elected—to vote for that candidate for Senate. This combination, the nomination of senatorial candidates by state convention and the subsequent public canvass, did not become typical until the 1880s. To quote Riker again, "These devices, the public canvass and pledged legislators, were at their height soon after 1900. How well they worked is shown by the idiom: people spoke of the 'election' of senators in November, when in fact only state legislators were then elected."[41] The principal point I wish to make here is the degree to which partisan politics rather than state interests determined who would become a senator in the era before direct election.[42]

Even though any democratic pressure on the Senate took the form of popular election rather than equal representation, from time to time, equal representation did become a political issue. In 1895 when S. E. Moffett argued that equal representation is "always a subject more or less disturbing to logical minds," he noted that it had been "pushed into peculiar prominence" by, among other things, the admission of low-population western states and the relation of that to contentious political issues such as the tariff and silver question.[43] Coming only five years after the six-state "free coinage" of western Republican senators, Moffett was writing as the nation was debating the potential—and controversial for other reasons, as well—admission of Utah, which would come in January 1896. Oklahoma, Arizona, and New Mexico were also under consideration, though those would not be admitted until the early twentieth century. Moffett was also writing at a time when the Senate had become "intensely unpopular" owing to its connection to antidemocratic corruption related to powerful party machines dominating some states.

Despite his unflattering comments about the Senate, the answer to the question that Moffett posed as the title of his article, "Is the Senate Unfairly Constituted?," was no, at least as far as equal representation was concerned. Moffett's was an early, perhaps the first, scholarly claim that equal representation did not matter because voting in the Senate—based on his analysis of over twenty votes on major legislation from 1798 to 1893—had not been divided on the basis of state population. He concluded, "What is needed . . . is to make senators continuously and effectively responsible to their constituents, by depriving the legislatures of the power of election and giving the people power to recall unfaithful senators."[44] In other words, forget about equal representation because it does not matter and it cannot be eliminated regardless, and concentrate on getting direct election to change the Senate. This is what happened, and the movement, with support blossoming from the early 1890s onward, eventually triumphed after years of Senate resistance with the ratification of the Seventeenth Amendment in 1913.

In the Seventeenth Amendment's progress from movement to ratification, however, is yet another connection between the Senate and white supremacy. Much of the opposition to direct election over the years was the result of constitutional conservatism, party politics, and the resistance of incumbent senators fearful of facing popular election. But southern senators had a unique concern: the potential threat posed by any constitutional amendment that expanded voting rights. As members of the Democratic Party, the party more committed to direct election, most southern senators and representatives backed such an amendment. But they sought to modify it with what became known as the "race rider" provision ("rider" being typically a pejorative term for an unrelated or divisive amendment to a bill). Directly negating Congress's constitutional authority to regulate the time, place, and manner of national elections, this southern amendment specified that states would control those things when it came to Senate elections. This would have been another assurance that the Jim Crow South could maintain the disenfranchisement of African Americans with this addition to the offices filled by popular vote. A factor throughout the debates and votes on what would become the Seventeenth Amendment, the race rider was part of the successful House vote on the direct election amendment during the Sixty-First Congress, but its removal from the Senate version caused enough defections by southern senators that the vote in that chamber fell short of the necessary two-thirds. Only after the elections of 1910 added to the ranks of progressive senators in the next Congress was the amendment finally—and without the race rider—passed and sent to the states for ratification, which was achieved less than a year later without the support of eight of the eleven states of the former Confederacy.[45]

It is not difficult to argue that the Seventeenth Amendment's impact was more symbolic than substantive. The ineluctable norm of popular vote for legislators had triumphed, but what difference it made in the substance of representation was not obvious at the time. Nor has its effect been clarified in retrospect, using the tools of modern political analysis.[46] But the search for clear effects misses the point. In many ways, democracy was the means and the end. The search by social scientists for changes in senatorial behavior after the implementation of direct election might be interesting, but it says almost nothing about what the amendment accomplished because it was self-executing. Direct election was the accomplishment and effect.

The Senate had evolved with the Seventeenth Amendment and had been democratized in that way. In bringing this about, however, Congress and the ratifying states had done something perhaps quite unintentional. As Riker argues, the impact direct election might have on federalism was hardly debated before its passage, but it was another centralizing or nationalizing change in the Senate; subsequently, state legislatures paid attention to state policy, and senators were free to concentrate on national and even international affairs.[47] In this way, the attempt to reform the Senate for the twentieth century had undermined one of the original foundations of equal representation. The selection of senators by state legislators had put a distinct emphasis on the corporate or collective nature of the Senate—that is, that senators represented states as corporate entities—and in this way reinforced the logic of the Great Compromise. After the Seventeenth Amendment was implemented, however, senators represented voters—their voters. Of course, a senator was still the junior or senior senator from the great state of New York or Wyoming, but only in the same way as a member of the House was the representative from the great Third District of Ohio or Florida.

Direct election revitalized the Senate by renewing its legitimacy, but it did not eliminate the logical and democratic problem of equal representation. In 1926, just over a decade following the implementation of the Seventeenth Amendment, the political scientist Carroll Wooddy posed the same stubborn question that S. E. Moffett had years before passage of the amendment: "Is the Senate Unrepresentative?"[48] If nothing else, the popular election of senators ineluctably highlighted the number of voters in each state, the number of individual citizens, capable of electing two senators from any given state. By eliminating the idea of corporate representation and establishing the democratic basis of Senate representation, the Seventeenth Amendment unintentionally highlighted, at least in theory, the increasingly glaring contrast between Senate representation and evolving ideas of democratic fairness and equality. Democratized in one way, by direct election, the Senate's other fundamental feature—equal representation—was heading toward a mid-century collision with what would become the bedrock tenet of modern democracy: one person, one vote.

# 3

# Equal Representation's Inexorable Clash with Political and Racial Equality

THE CAMPAIGN for direct election of the Senate progressed toward its final triumph at the same time as the last territories in the continental United States were converted into states. After the 1896 admission of Utah brought that touchy subject to a close, the early twentieth century saw the admission of Oklahoma in 1907, and then New Mexico and Arizona, both in 1912, just a few months before Congress sent the proposed Seventeenth Amendment to the states for their consideration. With the completion of the contiguous forty-eight states, the sometimes contentious politics of equal representation that attended state admissions was seemingly relegated to the pages of history just as the Senate was about to receive its democratic credentials for the new century in the form of popular election. And for the first half of the twentieth century, direct election of the Senate and women getting the vote through the Nineteenth Amendment in 1919 were the only significant developments in the advancement of electoral democracy in America.

Despite the revolutionary developments produced by the New Deal and World War II as concerned the power and policies of the US government, the institutions of democracy remained remarkably stable as the nation moved through the 1950s. But trouble—trouble that was always there but suppressed—was brewing. The early years of the Cold War era were accompanied by increasing confrontations over civil rights, culminating first in the *Brown v. Board* decision of 1954. Much like slavery and the build-up to the Civil War, a century later civil rights seemed to be increasingly at the center of almost everything. And in these struggles over civil rights the Senate would once again be a citadel for white supremacy as it, eventually alone among the institutions of national government, resisted political and social equality for African Americans.

Meanwhile, the issue of equal representation had not quite died with the completion of the lower forty-eight states. As the civil rights era was emerging, it intersected briefly with the final frontiers of American imperialism. The campaigns for and fights against the admission of Alaska and Hawaii long predated their admissions in 1959, and many of the usual arguments were employed for and against admission. Alaska in particular raised concerns because of its small population and lack of economic development. With a population of 228,000 in the 1960 census, Alaska would become the smallest state by a margin of some 60,000, displacing Nevada for that honor. Hawaii, with 642,000 residents, would come in a respectable forty-third. The fact that both were far removed from the contiguous forty-eight states was a novel concern, as were the indigenous populations of both territories, particularly Hawaii.

Efforts for statehood began in earnest after World War II, and President Truman called for admission of both territories in his 1946 State of the Union address.[1] But resistance came particularly from the Senate, and sectional and partisan politics freely mixed. With civil rights controversies piling up together, from the *Brown* decision in 1954 to the events in Little Rock in 1957, and with Congress embroiled in struggles over modest civil rights measures in 1957 and 1959, the proposed admission of new states meant, much as it had a century earlier, a potentially new balance of power in the Senate. Of course, the states of the former Confederacy were badly outnumbered in the mid-twentieth-century Senate, but senators opposed to civil rights, whether from those states or others, had a powerful tool unavailable to like-minded members of the House of Representatives: the filibuster, backed by the Senate rule of procedure that required, at that time, two-thirds of senators to end debate on a measure under consideration. The addition of four senators who might support civil rights measures by helping to end filibusters endangered that vital source of minority power.[2]

Southern Democrats feared the admission of both these Pacific territories but seemed to be more alarmed by Hawaii because it would be the first majority-minority state and one likely dominated by Republican voters. And the party of Lincoln was still more committed, in words at least, to civil rights than were the Democrats. Alaska would certainly be a very northern state even if Democratic in its partisanship. Southern Democrats had a litmus test for any issue: How might the matter under discussion affect the balance of power on civil rights and the federal government's ability to intervene in the politics of southern states? Both territories were a threat on that score. But the pairing of Republican Hawaii with Democratic Alaska—with a major historical irony in store for both parties—was part of the partisan politics that allowed both statehood measures to move through Congress.[3] The nation's Civil War past was not dead; it was not even past.

## One Person, One Vote: The Inescapable Requirement of Modern Democracy Except for the Senate

The admission of Alaska and Hawaii came as the Supreme Court under Chief Justice Earl Warren was about to confront a major issue that would put its decisions on a collision course with the logic of the Senate, even though the Senate and the apportionment of its seats based on state equality rather than state population were not the subject of controversy or any of the rulings. Logical minds no doubt continued to be disturbed by the odd nature of Senate representation, especially when highlighted by the admission of small-population states, but in the second half of the twentieth century it was representation in the House of Representatives that began to attract political and constitutional attention. The House had its own, and similar, representational problem, which became more acute as the country grew and urbanized. As the twentieth century proceeded, House districts in many areas of the country were becoming radically unequal in population.

Whereas the representational oddity of the Senate was an *interstate* phenomenon, the problem attached to the House was *intrastate*. That is, one could recognize the democratic flaw in the Senate's equal representation by comparing New York and Delaware; to see the parallel problem in the House required a comparison of districts within one state, such as those within Tennessee or within California. It is worth a reminder that the seats for the House of Representatives are distributed or "apportioned" on the basis of population following the census and according to the Constitution's stipulation that "Representatives and direct Taxes shall be apportioned among the several States which may be included within this Union, according to their respective numbers." After each state is awarded one seat, the rest are awarded by population following a formula legislated by Congress.[4] But the Constitution says nothing about how the elections to fill those seats would be handled by the states.

From the founding forward, the basic structures of elections, the right to vote, and the power of a citizen's vote had been under the control of state governments. The one national voting right was found in Article I's provision that, when it comes to voting for the House, "Electors in each State shall have the Qualifications requisite for Electors of the most numerous Branch of the State Legislature." Otherwise, voting rights were defined by state constitutions and state laws, which were given the power to prescribe "the Times, Places, and Manner" for national elections. Congress made little use of its ability to "make or alter such Regulations" created by the states.

The major congressional intervention came in the form of an insistence that all states that were apportioned more than one representative create single-member districts of contiguous territory. This stipulation began with the 1842 Apportionment Act. Prior to the single-member district mandate, a few states had used statewide at-large elections or multimember districts. But the single-member district requirement was not enforced, and the House agreed to seat more than one delegation elected by at-large systems. In 1872 they added that districts contain "as nearly as practicable an equal number of inhabitants."[5] This too was not enforced. Incorporated into apportionment acts up to and including the one from 1911, these specifications regarding single-member, contiguity, and equality were dropped in 1929, following a decade in which Congress could not agree to enact an apportionment.

In the absence of any national control, many states produced increasingly unequal districts for the House and for their state legislatures, the latter of which were not under federal control anyway. This practice is often characterized as "malapportionment." A relative term, malapportionment can refer to any inequitable method of distributing representation in a legislative body. In the context of early twentieth-century America, it was applied to districting that deviated substantially from population. Even if there was not at this time any constitutional standard, the distribution of House seats on the basis of the census and population was a pretty strong implication of equality. As well, some state constitutions stipulated districting based on population. But many were not putting that into practice. After World War II this was increasingly seen as a problem. Tennessee, for example, had not reapportioned its state legislature since 1901. Much of this resulted from the efforts of rural politicians and voters to preserve their power against the inexorable shift of population—documented by the census that was to determine reapportionment—to urban centers. That is what caused the deadlock in Congress in the early 1920s over reapportionment. The 1920 census showed, for the first time, that a majority (just over 51 percent) of the nation lived in urban areas. As late as 1890, it had been only 35 percent (figure 2). States north and south were guilty of apportioning legislative districts in favor of rural areas—and the California State Senate was by some measures the worst—but many of the most egregious cases were in the South.[6]

And southern redistricting practices were not just about the rural-urban divide but also about the suppression of Black voting. Some of the only locations where Blacks were able to vote in significant numbers were in the southern cities to which they moved as part of the Great Migration from the late 1910s into the 1950s. During this period, millions of southern Blacks moved north from predominantly rural areas, mostly to large cities in the Northeast and Midwest, such as New York, Philadelphia, Chicago, and Detroit. But they also concentrated in southern cities such as Memphis and Birmingham.[7] The two trends converged: as the United States was changing from a rural to an urban nation, many

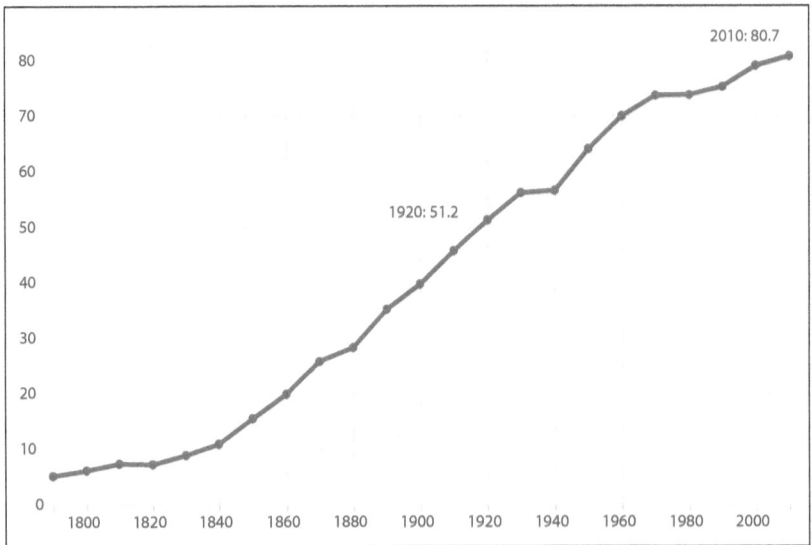

FIG. 2. Percentage urban population in U.S. Census, 1790–2010
*Source:* US Census Bureau.

of its cities were becoming home to more African Americans. Any form of electoral districting that disadvantaged city dwellers in general was going to disadvantage Blacks in particular.

States were, in effect, replicating within their borders the kind of democratic distortion created by equal representation in the Senate at the national level. The Senate distortion was between small and large states, while districting within states often pitted small counties against more populous counties and, more generally, urban voters against rural ones. State assemblies often had large-population urban districts and lower-density rural districts. Many state senates were based on county boundaries. States sometimes drew on a logic that echoed that of the Great Compromise. Rural voters and the counties in which they resided (as natural political communities), in this view, required protection from the overwhelming influence urban voters and interests would have if state legislators adhered to numerical equality across districts.[8]

Significantly unequal districts appeared at all levels—in the US House of Representatives, state assemblies, and state senates—but the analogy to the US Senate and the Great Compromise was applied particularly to state senates. The implicit parallel was between the relationship of states to the Senate in the national Constitution and the role of state senators as representatives of counties in many states and state constitutions. In fact, in the 1920s, California, via a direct popular vote on a constitutional amendment, mandated that the state senate be apportioned equally by county: one county, one senator.[9] This resulted in the effective disenfranchisement of most of Los Angeles, whose six million residents chose one state senator, the same as rural counties with populations as low as 14,000. While usually less egregiously malapportioned than many state legislatures, districts for the US House of Representatives also often varied significantly in population. And these house districts were drawn by the same state legislators who had been elected from often radically unequal state districts. The Supreme Court would later describe all this as "a crazy quilt without rational basis."[10]

No matter how crazy or lacking in rational basis, the federal courts initially shied away from involving themselves with the cases brought by citizens in various states who felt such districting violated their state constitutions or national rights under the equal protection clause of the Constitution. As early as 1946, the Supreme Court decided that it should not wade into the "political thicket" of districting.[11] Under prevailing constitutional doctrine at the time, apportionment and districting were political questions that were better left to resolution by the democratic processes at the national or state level. That is, certain disputes between the institutions of government or stemming from the electoral process were best resolved by the democratically accountable branches as questions of political judgment rather than constitutionality. Judicial intervention was possible but not prudent.

In the case of apportionment, aggrieved voters had to take their complaints to the politicians in their states, the ones who drew the electoral maps that were so biased. And for another sixteen years, the political question doctrine frustrated the movement to address this inequity. The initial constitutional breakthrough came with *Baker v. Carr* in 1962 when the Warren Court ruled that legislative apportionment was a constitutional issue that could be adjudicated in federal courts. The court's decision was limited to this jurisdictional question and did not reach the substance of the case, which was about Tennessee's apparent violation of its own constitutional provisions regarding apportionment of the state legislature.[12] But the Supreme Court would soon be ruling on the substance of apportionment cases that were coming from dozens of states.

The first step forward in post-*Baker* jurisprudence came a year later, in March 1963, when Justice Douglas announced in *Gray v. Sanders* that "the conception of political equality from the Declaration of Independence, to Lincoln's Gettysburg Address, to the Fifteenth, Seventeenth, and Nineteenth Amendments can mean only one thing—one person, one vote."[13] *Gray* was about Georgia's system of primary elections for statewide and federal offices, a system based on county units rather than population. As such the ruling against Georgia's primaries did not directly affect apportionment for state legislatures or the House of Representatives. Nevertheless, the direction in which the court was heading seemed rather clear. Whether or not Douglas's lineage of great texts really all pointed to this one inescapable conclusion is beside the point. Representative democracy had evolved in such a way that it was difficult to imagine and justify a different standard.

The following year the Warren Court applied the one person, one vote standard to the apportionment of districts for the US House of Representatives and state legislatures. In *Wesberry v. Sanders,* the court relied on the Constitution's specification in section 2 of Article I that the "House of Representatives shall be composed of Members chosen . . . by the People of the several States" to apply this standard to the House. Those words meant, according to Justice Black's majority opinion, "that, as nearly as is practicable, one man's vote in a congressional election is to be worth as much as another's."[14]

The same degree of equality applied to state legislatures as well, this time via the Fourteenth Amendment's equal protection clause. The prohibition "No State shall make or enforce any law which shall . . . deny to any person within its jurisdiction the equal protection of the laws" had lain effectively dormant from that amendment's ratification in 1868 until 1954's *Brown v. Board* decision on segregation in public schools. The Warren Court used it again to cement its constitutional revolution in political equality. In using equal protection to end malapportionment in state legislative districts, the court confronted a final major question: Could states have a second legislative chamber, analogous to the US Senate, that was apportioned on a basis other than population, such as by county, in a way that inevitably gave disproportionate influence to rural areas and voters? One of the six apportionment cases from 1964, *Reynolds v. Sims,* confronted this final question in a case from the state of Alabama.

No, was the court's answer in an 8–1 decision. The Alabama state assembly might have more and smaller districts than its senate, but all assembly districts had to be equal to each other in population, and all senate districts had to be equal to each other as well. "We hold," wrote Warren for the court, "that, as a basic constitutional standard, the Equal Protection Clause requires that the seats in both houses of a bicameral state legislature must be apportioned on a population basis. Simply stated, an individual's right to vote for state legislators is unconstitutionally impaired when its weight is in a substantial fashion diluted when compared with votes of citizens living in other parts of the State."[15] More succinctly, and memorably, "Legislators represent people, not trees or acres. Legislators are elected by voters, not farms or cities or economic interests."[16] And, drawing on the words from a unanimous decision in 1960, the court argued: "The fact that an individual lives here or there is not a legitimate reason for overweighting or diluting the efficacy of his vote. The complexions of societies and civilizations change, often with amazing rapidity. A nation once primarily rural in character becomes predominantly urban. Representation schemes once fair and equitable become archaic and outdated. But the basic principle of representative government remains, and must remain, unchanged—the weight of a citizen's vote cannot be made to depend on where he lives" because to "the extent that a citizen's right to vote is debased, he is that much less a citizen."[17] Regardless of the security of its constitutional footing, the court's grasp of the logic of modern democracy and its premise of political equality was unshakable and persuasive.[18]

More than once near the end of his career Warren deemed *Baker v. Carr* and the subsequent apportionment decisions down through *Reynolds* to be the most consequential of his tenure as chief justice, more important in his view than *Brown v. Board of Education*. While acknowledging the widely held opinion that Brown was "the most important case of my tenure on the Court," Warren "never thought so." Instead, "that accolade should go to the case of *Baker v. Carr*," which led to one person, one vote.[19] Taken as a whole, the apportionment decisions directly affected nearly every state and compelled all but immediate action to remedy disparities in representation for the House Representatives, state senates, and most state assemblies. The decisions elicited an uproar from many states, and from some members of Congress, but one that dissipated very quickly. While unpopular among many elected officials, and with huge ramifications for their political power and security, the decisions were generally popular with the public.[20] Unlike some other Warren Court decisions that received hostile or more mixed public receptions, the application of one person, one vote—the idea that one's vote should be equal to those of other citizens—made sense, and the injustices of malapportionment were too manifest. As one scholar put it, "Reynolds went from debatable in 1964 to unquestionable in 1968."[21]

Measured in terms of immediacy and national impact, the apportionment cases were bigger than the school desegregation decisions, which, while morally profound, had limited effect on the problem at hand. But the two issues—Black civil rights and apportionment—were also closely connected logically, and in the mind at least of the great chief justice. Indeed, the connection was perhaps the main reason Warren accorded the apportionment decisions that lofty status. As the chief justice reasoned, "If *Baker v. Carr* had been in existence fifty years ago, we would have saved ourselves acute racial troubles. Many of our problems would have been solved a long time ago if everyone had the right to vote and his vote counted the same as everybody else's. Most of these problems could have been solved through the political process rather than through the courts."[22]

Warren was suggesting that apportionment, which was presented as a problem of overrepresentation of rural versus urban populations, was also an issue of race and civil rights. For example, during the court's conference meeting on *Baker*, Justice Black noted that court intervention in malapportionment was a threat to white control in the South.[23] The demographic forces that were increasing urban populations included the migration of Blacks to cities north and south. Malapportionment was another way to diminish the influence of African Americans. Even if relatively few southern Blacks had been able to vote prior to the mid-1960s, many of those who could, lived in cities.

If white supremacy was a mostly unspoken subtext of the apportionment cases, the US Senate was the elephant in the courtroom, especially in *Reynolds*. Having ruled unconstitutional the majority of upper houses in the country, and having articulated a compelling logic of democratic representation, Warren had to make the senatorial elephant vanish, or at least shrink it down to an ignorable size. In particular, the court was compelled to address the "so-called federal analogy" posed by state senates—that states should be required to have one chamber composed of equal population districts, like the House, and allowed one chamber, like the Senate, that is apportioned on the basis of, essentially, geography. "We . . . find the federal analogy inapposite and irrelevant to state legislative districting schemes," concluded Warren for the court. "Attempted reliance on the federal analogy appears often to be little more than an after-the-fact rationalization offered in defense of maladjusted state apportionment arrangements."[24] States created counties, or other special lines that might be drawn to create unequal state senate districts, and these districts had no prior or independent status as political entities. This is unlike the original states that made up the United States and formed the country by their agreement as prior, separate, and sovereign governments and territories.

The court did not have to justify the US Senate's apportionment. It is in the Constitution; by definition, it is constitutional. But Warren did discuss this, and in so doing perhaps weakened his own argument insofar as he had trouble coming up with a rational basis for the ongoing inequities of Senate representation:

> The system of representation in the two Houses of the Federal Congress is one ingrained in our Constitution, as part of the law of the land. It is one conceived out of compromise and concession indispensable to the establishment of our federal republic. Arising from unique historical circumstances, it is based on the consideration that, in establishing our type of federalism a group of formerly independent States bound themselves together under one national government. Admittedly, the original

13 States surrendered some of their sovereignty in agreeing to join together 'to form a more perfect Union.' But at the heart of our constitutional system remains the concept of separate and distinct governmental entities which have delegated some, but not all, of their formerly held powers to the single national government. The fact that almost three-fourths of our present States were never, in fact, independently sovereign does not detract from our view that the so-called federal analogy is inapplicable as a sustaining precedent for state legislative apportionments. The developing history and growth of our republic cannot cloud the fact that, at the time of the inception of the system of representation in the Federal Congress, a compromise between the larger and smaller States on this matter averted a deadlock in the Constitutional Convention which had threatened to abort the birth of our Nation.[25]

Just as the court's democratic theory of one person, one vote is difficult to dispute, its historical understanding of the founding compromises is sound. "But," as one pair of scholars put it, "historical explanation is not contemporary justification."[26] *Reynolds* shows that equal representation in the Senate skates on the increasingly thin ice of the founding and tradition, something to be tolerated primarily because it was part of the original bargain, not so much for its current contribution or purpose, and despite the fact that it is increasingly at odds with modern democracy. In short, I agree with Supreme Court historian Lucas Powe that "the way *Reynolds* rejected the federal analogy was a direct slap at the United States Senate. . . . There is no other reading of *Reynolds* except one that concludes the United States Senate's overrepresentation of the smaller states violates the nation's principles of political fairness."[27]

If the *Reynolds* decision did a solid job of explaining why state localities did not deserve representation divorced from population, it did not have much to say in support of Senate equality. In fact, insofar as the court implicitly criticized the consequences of unequal representation in state legislatures, it is not clear why its critique did not apply in equal measure to the US Senate:

The right of a citizen to equal representation and to have his vote weighted equally with those of all other citizens in the election of members of one house of a bicameral state legislature would amount to little if States could effectively submerge the equal population principle in the apportionment of seats in the other house. If such a scheme were permissible, an individual citizen's ability to exercise an effective voice in the only instrument of state government directly representative of the people might be almost as effectively thwarted as if neither house were apportioned on a population basis. Deadlock between the two bodies might result in compromise and concession on some issues. But, in all too many cases, the more probable result would be frustration of the majority will through minority veto in the house not apportioned on a population basis, stemming directly from the failure to accord adequate overall legislative representation to all of the State's citizens on a nondiscriminatory basis.[28]

The court's logic notwithstanding, one person, one vote was mandated for every American legislative body except the US Senate, and that new constitutional standard was implemented only a few years after Alaska and Hawaii entered the union with their collective three representatives and four senators.[29] As we have seen, in *Reynolds* Chief Justice Warren addressed the argument that almost three quarters of the fifty states were not party to the original bargain of 1787. Instead of predating the union, the subsequent states were creations of the national government. The consequences of the Great Compromise were replicated beyond the framers' imagination as dozens of mostly small-population territories were admitted as states, ending with Alaska and Hawaii. And when judged against the new democratic standard of one person, one vote, equal representation in the Senate had become more egregious over time. It was a greater affront to political equality in the second half of the twentieth century, and into the twenty-first, than at its creation or in the 150 years between.

## Who Is Underrepresented by Equal Representation in the Senate?

Because two senators per state is dictated by the Constitution, the "Senate is malapportioned by design."[30] Consequently, it is a bit odd to refer to the Senate as precisely that, even though by the standard of one person, one vote, it is arguably the most malapportioned legislative body in the world. There is more than one way to gauge malapportionment, whether in the United States or elsewhere. One of the most used is the minimum percentage of the population able to elect a majority of the legislative body.[31] The lower the percentage that can elect a majority, the more malapportioned the legislature. And from the start, a small percentage of the population has been necessary to elect a majority of senators (figure 3). In the case of the Senate, one starts from the smallest state and counts up to the state that would produce a majority of the Senate (since 1960, the twenty-sixth from the bottom). The sum of the populations of those states can then be calculated as a percentage of the total national population. The percentage peaked in the 1830s at 24.8 percent. That was the highest percentage of the total population electing a majority of the Senate. Since then it has averaged just under 19 percent, and was 17.8 percent after the 2010 census. From 1790 through the 1940s, the average was 20.7 percent. From 1950 through 2020, the average was 17.6 percent.

As part of this evolution, the gap between the largest and smallest states has grown. The first census in 1790 revealed that Virginia, the largest state, had a population of 747,550, while the smallest, Delaware, contained 59,096, a ratio of 12.6 to 1. Based on the 2010 census, the same ratio between largest (California) and smallest (Wyoming) is about 66 to 1. The two, Virginia and California, were or are also by far the most populated states; that is, Virginia was significantly larger than the next state in population (a ratio of 1.72 to 1 compared to Pennsylvania) as is California (a ratio of 1.48 to 1 compared to Texas) today. If we take a group of states at the top and bottom to negate the effect of outliers like Virginia in its

FIG. 3. Senate malapportionment, 1790–2010

day and California in recent decades, we see the same increasing gap. For example, the ratio between the top five and bottom five in the 1790s was 7.5 to 1, whereas in 2010 the ratio of population between the largest five and smallest five was 33.5 to 1.[32]

As noted, one voter in Wyoming is worth a bit more than sixty-six Californians when it comes to electing senators in their respective states. Wyoming, the Equality State, with the nation's smallest population and an ironically accurate nickname, had 563,626 residents in the 2010 census, about the same as Fresno, California, that state's fifth largest city. California, by far the largest state, had 37,253,956 residents. Starting from Wyoming and working up from the bottom, combining the less populous states until a California-equivalent population of over 37 million is reached, you have to go all the way to Connecticut, a total of twenty-two states, with forty-four senators. The voters of California get two senators while their equivalent, spread across twenty-two states, get nearly half the Senate. Add three more states and exactly half the Senate is represented by states accounting for only 16 percent of the nation's population.[33]

If we start from the other direction, from the largest down, it takes only nine states to reach over one-half of the national population, represented by eighteen senators, less than one-fifth of that body. Sixteen percent of the country gets fifty senators while 50 percent gets eighteen. There are so many ways to parse this massive inequity. As another example, owing to the allocation system that assures each state at least one seat in the House of Representatives, seven states have one representative each, constituting a total of 1.6 percent of the House, but those same seven states constitute 14 percent of the Senate.[34]

Figures like the ones just offered are frequently cited to remind Americans of the scale of this distortion and representational injustice. And that distortion and the injustice it embodies are enough to condemn equal representation without further qualification. But comparisons of overall state populations obscure other distortions that add to the problems posed by Senate equality. As we have seen, the decisions from *Baker* through *Reynolds* were centered on the overrepresentation of rural interests and the underrepresentation of urban and minority populations, particularly African American. And just as the cases and the jurisprudence that led to one person, one vote concentrated on the manifest impact on urban voters of legislative malapportionment in the House and state legislatures, equal representation in the Senate is not so much about small versus large states as such as it is about rural versus urban voters and everything else that rough division has come to entail, particularly the power granted to mostly white voters in many smaller states relative to minority voters in larger states. As a result, political scientists and economists have left behind the traditional and familiar concerns about small versus large states and have focused on other effects. In an era of a more diverse, urban, welfare state, what are the distributive and representative consequences of Senate equality for the residents of more urbanized and diverse states? In short, Senate representation has become an ever more egregious and multilayered embodiment of the distortions of democracy that led to one person, one vote and the strict equality that applies to the districting of other legislative bodies in the United States.

A number of studies have tracked the bias of equal representation when it comes to such demographic characteristics as population density, race and ethnicity, and political ideology.[35] As one scholar summed up, Senate apportionment "has increasingly come to underweight the preferences of ideological liberals, Democrats, African Americans, and Latinos."[36] As we shall see, this bias is directly related to the contemporary correlations between and among social demographics, partisanship, and urban versus rural residency. We will deal with ideology and partisanship later. Here I will focus on race and ethnicity. Just as there are several ways to measure malapportionment, there is more than one way to assess the relative representation of whites and minority populations in the Senate.

If we divide the fifty states by their percentage of African American residents, according to 2018 census estimates, there are sixteen states with Black populations under 4 percent. These states are nearly all smaller-population states, including six of the seven states apportioned only one representative each after the 2010 census.[37] The sixteen states constitute one-third (32 percent) of the states and Senate but just under 10 percent of the national population, and not even 2 percent of the Black population. Politicians in these states simply do not have to consider the interests of Black voters. And they certainly do not elect Black members of Congress to either chamber. In the era of one person, one vote, no African American representatives or senators have been elected from these states during the forty-two years from the elections of 1968 through 2020.

Contrast that with the sixteen states with the highest percentage of African Americans, ranging from New Jersey with 13.6 percent to Mississippi with 38 percent. These states, with the exception of Delaware, have at least four representatives, and some are among the largest-population states in the country, including New York, Florida, Illinois, Michigan,

Georgia, and New Jersey. With nearly 42 percent of the national population, they represent nearly 65 percent of all African Americans. And the difference in representation is astounding, at least in the House of Representatives. In the House, during the same forty-two-year period, these states produced seventy-seven Black representatives, who served a total of 508 terms! And this level of representation in the House came despite barriers and obstacles related to social inequality and district lines that have frequently been drawn to protect incumbents, who are often white.

While Black senators have been far and few between, the sixteen states with the highest percentages of African American residents produced four of the six African American senators elected since the implementation of direct election with the Seventeenth Amendment in 1913.[38] Even if few Black senators have been elected in general, the white senators who were picked from the states with larger percentages of African Americans had to consider Black voters even if, as in some southern states during this time, they were often crucial components of the losing coalition. In most of the other states in this group, Black voters have frequently been part of winning coalitions.[39] The Senate systematically underrepresents African Americans, and a significant percentage of the Senate can, from the perspective of electoral calculation, ignore them altogether. States with significant percentages of Black residents pay attention to their interests and, as one measure of this, elect Black representatives and even senators.

This same point can be extended to minorities more generally, especially with the inclusion of the large Latinx populations in many states. The sixteen states with the largest percentages of minority populations (averaging 46 percent, and ranging from Virginia with 35.5 percent to New Mexico with 62.5 percent), as before, are about one-third of the Senate but over 55 percent of the national population. In sharp contrast, the sixteen states with the smallest percentages of minority populations (averaging just over 13 percent and ranging from Maine with 4.9 percent to Utah with 19 percent) contain less than 16 percent of the nation's total population. Lynn Baker and Samuel Dinkin broaden the point I have been making here by pointing out that the at-large nature of Senate elections (in contrast to House districts) further reduces the chances that minority populations will have an impact on Senate elections in most states.[40]

And, among other things, representation means money. Equal representation has been linked to smaller states receiving proportionally greater federal funding, even when controlling for levels of poverty.[41] In their award-winning book on the policy consequences of equal representation, Frances Lee and Bruce Oppenheimer show that "small states benefit disproportionately, receiving higher per capital allocations of federal funds than large states across a broad range of domestic distributive programs, even after controlling for differences in state needs."[42] Particularly in areas of federal spending dictated by formulas written by Congress, such as transportation and community development, small states get proportionately more than large states. Many programs, for example, are designed with minimum guarantees. Such a provision typically dictates that each state gets at least 0.5 percent of the total allocation (and in the 2010 census, twelve states had populations less than 0.5 percent of the US total population).[43] This showed up particularly clearly in discretionary grant programs designed by Congress in response to the 2009 recession. For example, in 2010, Alaska, Wyoming, and Vermont were the top three states in per capita grants, while Texas was 42 and California 27.[44] The correlation is hardly linear, and things can shift from year to year, but in that same year the top fifteen states in per capita grants had an average population of 3.3 million while the bottom fifteen states averaged 7.5 million (the average population was about 6.2 million). In response to the Great Recession starting in 2007 and 2008, "the federal government has spent hundreds of billions to respond to the financial crisis, it has done much more to assist the residents of small states than large ones. The top five per capita recipients of federal stimulus grants were states so small that they have only a single House member."[45] Even after the attacks of September 11, 2001, the flood of money that was distributed to states for state and local security projects and programs displayed the same small-state and rural bias.[46] Finally, congressional "earmarks," those special and generally relatively small funding requests that benefit one state or House district, are "distributed relatively equally among Senators," regardless of state population.[47] No matter what programs are involved, this bias in federal spending is typically cited as a problem in and of itself, which it is. But, once again, the relationship to the demographics of small versus large states looms large: smaller *and whiter states* get a disproportionate share of federal dollars compared to the larger states with, typically, far greater percentages of minority residents, whose communities are relatively impoverished and underserved by a variety of state and national programs.

## One Wyomingan, Sixty-Six *Republican* Votes: Equal Representation in the Era of Partisan Polarization

Of course, the distortions of equal representations are a problem regardless of ideology or partisanship. As just indicated, however, far more than during the *Baker-Reynolds* era, the vectors of urban versus rural, racial and ethnic identity, political ideology, and partisanship have converged. One of the signal features of contemporary American politics from the late 1980s onward has been partisan polarization.[48] As the meaning of liberal and conservative became more consistent and persistent, and as it became increasingly clear that the Republican Party was the conservative party and the Democratic Party was the liberal party, politicians and voters sorted themselves accordingly. Perhaps one of the most striking aspects of this sorting is geographic. Americans are aware of red states and blue states, but in many ways the true divide is between rural America, dominated by Republicans, and urban America, dominated by Democrats—a divide between red states and blue cities, as one account put it.[49] In an era of increasingly ideologically homogeneous parties and sorted voters, the representational consequences become increasingly stark everywhere in American politics, but particularly in the Senate.

Partisan sorting and polarization have created a very strong relationship between and among state size, urban population, and Senate elections, a relationship that was less pronounced before the 1990s.[50] One way to see this is to categorize states by their relative balance of urban and rural population. We can start by dividing the states into three nearly equal groups by their percentage urban population—the least urban, moderately urban, and heavily urban—using the Census Bureau's definition (figure 4). For each of the three groups we can determine the average state size. The group of least urban states had an average population of 2.53 million, compared to 5.44 million for the moderately urban states and 8.33 million for the heavily urban states. We can see, perhaps unsurprisingly, that state size and urban population are positively related. Each group represents almost exactly one-third of the Senate (34, 32, and 34 percent, respectively) but vastly different percentages of the total national population. The least urban states control thirty-four Senate seats but have only 16 percent of the total population, whereas the heavily urban states, which control the same number of Senate seats, have 52 percent of the total population (with the moderately urban states controlling thirty-two Senate seats and home to 32 percent of the population). The final

76    THE SENATE

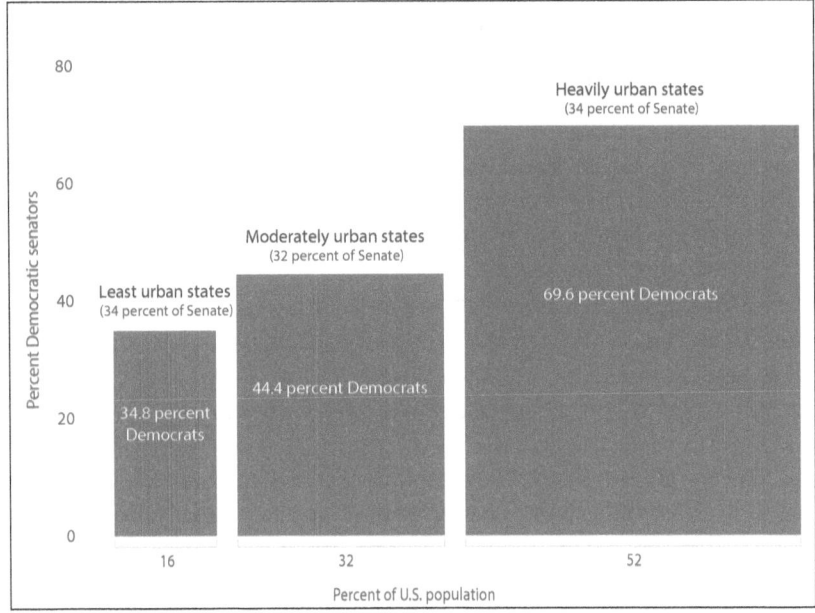

FIG. 4. Senate representation in an era of partisan polarization between urban and rural states, 1993–2019
*Note:* Least urban states average 54.5 percent urban; moderately urban states average 71 percent urban; heavily urban states average 87 percent urban.

step is to see whether there is a relationship between the state size–urban correlation and the partisanship of the senators elected from each group.

In the fourteen elections from 1992 to 2018, the seventeen heavily urban states, representing a majority of the nation's population, elected an average of nearly 70 percent Democratic senators. Reversing this, the seventeen least urban states produced just under 35 percent Democratic senators. Or, put the other way, they elected nearly 65 percent Republicans. In this way, seventeen rural states representing only 16 percent of the national population produced a full 44 percent of the Republican Senate membership during that quarter century. The 52 percent of the national population living in seventeen heavily urban states produced 47 percent of the Democratic Senate membership. Not surprisingly, the remaining sixteen states, the moderately urban group, fall between the least and heavily urban in terms of average size and the kind of senators elected. In the enduring landscape of polarized America, the Republican Party benefits from a highly efficient distribution of its voters in rural states. So it is not just California compared to Wyoming, it is across the board and involves relatively precise groups of voters with substantially different interests in government. In this way, the Senate has evolved into a nationwide gerrymander. To gerrymander is to draw "the boundaries of electoral districts in a way that gives one party an unfair advantage over its rivals," according to *Britannica,* or, with a bit of added detail in *Webster's,* "to divide (a territorial unit) into election districts to give one political party an electoral majority in a large number of districts while concentrating the voting strength of the opposition in as few districts as possible."[51] This has to be done with political force and creativity at the level of the US House of Representatives and state and local offices, especially because electoral districts beyond the Senate must be equal in population. In the US Senate, however, gerrymandering is not a political tool; it happens automatically if partisanship is correlated with geography. If ideology and partisanship did not overlap with the combination of urban–minority concentration and state size, there would be no clear Senate "gerrymander," so to speak. But they do, they have for some time, and this is likely to endure and perhaps become ever more acute.[52]

This is the very kind of systematic distortion that the Supreme Court found unacceptable in the 1960s and that would in principle be unacceptable to most Americans. In short, urban and minority voters are dramatically underrepresented in the Senate, with stark consequences for the ideology, party, and policies with the most support in the national government.

## Justifying, or at Least Excusing, Equal Representation in an Era of Democratic Equality

How can such radical disparities in representation be justified, or at least rationalized? Aside from equal representation being part of the founding bargain and part of the Constitution, which are blunt facts more than arguments, what are the contemporary justifications for two senators per state?

Equal representation is deeply ingrained in unexpected ways. For example, as a professor at the University of California, I have for decades taught classes on American politics filled almost exclusively with students from the Golden State. Whenever the Senate has been part of our considerations, I have included facts and figures about Senate apportionment and the degree of inequality it entails, mostly as a way to get students to think about something they take for granted. While generally aware that their state is large, Californians often seem surprised to learn that nearly one in every eight Americans is one of them. Few are aware how small, by comparison, the smallest states really are. Even so, almost every time this disparity suggests that a change in Senate representation might be justified, one or more students demur, asking "What about Delaware, or Rhode Island—what would happen to them?" The nature of the crimes that would be committed against these Lilliputians, once stripped of their senatorial protection, is a bit vague. When pressed, it pretty much comes down to federal funding and things like the location of the final resting place for nuclear waste. When asked, even the experts who have thought about such matters far more than my students have cannot do much if at all better. Justifications and rationales tend to trail off into excuses and pragmatics.

These justifications and rationales fall into four categories. The first line of argument invokes general *principles of good government* to which equal representation can be linked, however tenuously. For the United States, the principles of good government being invoked are a system of separation of powers with checks and balances, pretty much *the* central principle of the American system of government. This core principle is connected to equal representation through what might be labeled the Senate syllogism, which runs as follows: Bicameralism is a vital part of the system as a check on and refinement of legislative power; bicameralism is intended to prevent rash decisions and improve deliberation by dividing the legislature into two differently constituted chambers; equal representation is an important part of what makes the chambers different; therefore, equal representation preserves the benefits of bicameralism. This line of argument can acknowledge the democratic shortcomings of equal representation while asserting its value in the multifaceted Madisonian system of separated powers and checks and balances.[53] That might be true, but equal representation just happens to be one way to create strong bicameralism. The Warren Court made it clear in the *Reynolds* decision that the application of one person, one vote to both chambers need not undermine the effectiveness of bicameralism:

> We do not believe that the concept of bicameralism is rendered anachronistic and meaningless when the predominant basis of representation in the two state legislative bodies is required to be the same population. A prime reason for bicameralism, modernly considered, is to insure

mature and deliberate consideration of, and to prevent precipitate action on, proposed legislative measures. Simply because the controlling criterion for apportioning representation is required to be the same in both houses does not mean that there will be no differences in the composition and complexion of the two bodies. Different constituencies can be represented in the two houses. One body could be composed of single member districts, while the other could have at least some multi-member districts. The length of terms of the legislators in the separate bodies could differ. The numerical size of the two bodies could be made to differ, even significantly, and the geographical size of districts from which legislators are elected could also be made to differ. . . . In summary, these and other factors could be, and are presently in many States, utilized to engender differing complexions and collective attitudes in the two bodies of a state legislature, although both are apportioned substantially on a population basis.[54]

While strong bicameralism might be a vital component of a separation of powers system, equal representation is not a necessary condition for the benefits of bicameralism. This argument is a defense of bicameralism, not equal representation as such. In fact, the costs of structuring bicameralism in this way might far outweigh the benefits.

The most direct and important contemporary argument is based on *constitutional principle*. Equal representation, it is argued, protects and preserves federalism, the constitutional division of power and authority between the states and the national government. As Misha Tseytlin argues, equal representation has been justified primarily by this precept, what he labels the "sovereignty protection hypothesis."[55] There are, however, two sides to the federalism coin: the preservation of the sovereignty granted states in the Constitution and the representation of states, as states, in the deliberations of the national government. Much has changed as far as the relative sovereignty of states, and the Seventeenth Amendment severed the link between senators and states as corporate entities. So one can argue that this line of argument has lost considerable force. In chapter 2, I argued that equal representation has been less about states' rights and federalism or "sovereignty protection" and more about regional and partisan power. Senators from various states have used their voting power to advance their interests. In particular, small-state senators are rationally motivated to use their disproportionate voting power to obtain benefits and advantages for their states from the national government. That is, the "sovereignty protection" rationale is far more accurately seen, in Tseytlin's terminology, as "augmented voting power," augmented voting power that has been used at best incidentally in defense of federalism.[56]

Defense of small-state sovereignty would have involved fending off "vertical aggrandizement" by the federal government, that is, federal decision-makers taking "away the independent choice of individual states in order to increase their own power."[57] But the historical record on this is thin at best. For the most part, history records dozens of fights over material interests such as tariffs and hard versus soft money, often involving regional interests and coalitions.[58] These conflicts are about what Tseytlin labels "horizontal aggrandizement," which happens when "any subset of states" uses "federal power to impose those states' preferences on citizens in other states."[59] Even the momentous events leading to the Civil War were about the extension of slavery or fugitive slave laws, not state sovereignty as such.

Small states have not been the particular guardians of federalism any more than large states. For the most part, states of all sizes have been more interested in using their power in the Senate, whether they are under- or overrepresented, to advance a variety of interests, mostly dictated by the partisan alignments of the day rather than by a principled commitment to state sovereignty or any other constitutional tenet. It has become nearly impossible, if it was ever at all clear, to separate arguments about the principle of federalism from arguments about power.

Nevertheless, a third line of contemporary argument embraces rather than evades the idea that equal representation is about *political power.* "Without [equal representation], wealth and power would tend to flow to the prosperous coasts and cities and away from less-populated rural areas," according to political theorist Stephen Macedo.[60] "Cities already are the homes of America's major media, donor, academic and government centers," argues Gary L. Gregg II, another political scientist. "A simple, direct democracy will centralize all power—government, business, money, media and votes—in urban areas to the detriment of the rest of the nation."[61]

This argument seems to suggest that the US government can or should stem the tide of history. The movement of people and resources from rural to urban areas has happened regardless of political boundaries and systems of representation. That flow is a basic fact of modern civilization.

What, precisely, can a government—particularly an explicitly limited and federal one like that of the United States—change about that? So, to be precise, such arguments must be referring to the use of the wealth and resources distributed by the government, as opposed to the largely market-driven distribution of economic power more generally. Indeed, the implication is that rural areas are entitled to use overrepresentation to capture government power and resources to offset market forces that supposedly advantage cities in population growth and material wealth. Which is, of course, exactly what happens. Small states often get more than their proportional share of federal funds.

This small-state bias in federal funding has been a source of some bemusement and ridicule, as the ire of red state Republicans over "big government" and "welfare" from Reagan onward is somewhat at odds with the actual distribution of federal revenues to smaller Republican states. The main point, however, is that, regardless of party or ideology, it is not at all clear how this would change were Senate representation to change, except by elimination of some or all of the disproportionate advantage to smaller states. It would not affect, and should not affect, other national policies. Most federal spending, for example, is dictated by entitlement programs in the areas of health care, welfare, and veterans. Such programs are tied to individual characteristics. One is or is not, for example, a veteran who qualifies for one or more such benefits. The geographic distribution of veterans or senior citizens determines the distribution of these sorts of entitlement checks from the federal government, not the representational power of the states, which, as we have seen, does affect some other government programs.

The political power argument speaks to some general concern about representation of interests but has no standard for fair representation. At what point does overrepresentation become absurd? How relatively small, one might ask, do small states and rural populations have to get before concerns about their well-being become ludicrous? Moreover, even if all the wealth were piled into urban areas, surely that would not mean that Wall Street billionaires would have the same interests as immigrant hotel workers in New York City. Donald Trump lived in Manhattan; Warren Buffett lives in Omaha. The Heritage Foundation, Chamber of Commerce, and Club for Growth are all in the city of Washington, D.C., but, as conservative as they are, it is not clear that they represent the geographic interests of rural areas. Instead, such well-organized groups and wealthy allies in urban areas depend on the overrepresentation of conservative voters residing in those states to elect Republicans; that is what they care about and attend to.

In the end, this concern for rural interests essentially replicates the arguments that failed before the bar of the Supreme Court in the 1960s apportionment cases. Any changes wrought by one person, one vote at the state level were fair and did not result in the demise of rural areas. As well, it is not clear why the rural areas of Wyoming deserve more representation than the rural areas of California, Texas, or New York. This highlights the point that one should not conflate federalism and equal representation. A robust version of the former can exist comfortably without the latter and is not dependent on it. If states, as states, have an interest in the maintenance of a particular division of labor between states and nation, then the numerical basis of their representation is not an essential factor. If anything, their mode of selection is. That is, the selection of senators by state legislatures kept them more tied to the corporate interests of their states, but the Seventeenth Amendment took care of that.

The final line of argument in support of equal representation is the trump card of *practicality* or *pragmatism*.[62] One can concede the democratic inequities of equal representation and still deem it a "tolerable imperfection" for largely pragmatic reasons because the costs of changing it are perhaps impossibly high and the benefits that might ensue perhaps rather small.[63] Ultimately, while almost any constitutional amendment is an improbable undertaking, equal representation is especially unlikely to arouse the public passion that would be requisite even to get the Sisyphean boulder in motion. Political theorist Stephen Macedo sums up the case succinctly: "Equal representation of states in the Senate is a singularly unlikely candidate for mass political mobilization for at least three reasons: it has various respectable rationales, it is deeply entrenched constitutionally and therefore would be very costly to change, and even if it does contribute somewhat to injustice it does so without embodying and expressing direct moral insult (like racial discrimination)."[64]

Two out of three isn't bad, but Macedo is simply wrong on the last point, and it is by far the most important. As we have seen, Senate representation is a structural form of racial and ethnic discrimination that has no contemporary parallel. Short of an improbable and dramatic reversal of demographic trends and projections, equal representation will continue to underrepresent minorities substantially and systematically. This underrepresentation will continue to result in disadvantageous partisan alignments and patterns of institutional control, which in turn will lead to policy choices that fail to advance their interests. Viewed from the flip side of this coin, equal representation can be seen as "affirmative action for white people."[65] Moreover, discrimination against minorities highlights the "moral insult" of equal representation, but such disparate effects of the representational distortion are part of the more general violation of one person, one vote. The violation of that principle is so glaring that an inquiry into its actual or differential impacts is unnecessary, however important those are. In the end, this is primarily a normative question of democratic fairness, and the various arguments mustered in its favor cannot overturn the democratic indictment of equal representation. In fact, in the twenty-first century, one could argue that the distortion between equal representation and democratic values is far sharper, owing to the principle of one person, one vote and the underrepresentation of urban and minority voters, than was the clash between democratic values and state selection of senators in the early twentieth century leading to the Seventeenth Amendment. In this case, however, and perhaps unlike in the case of the Seventeenth Amendment, one could make an argument that the elimination of equal representation would have a profound impact on American politics.

Equal representation's violation of one person, one vote is bad enough. As we have seen in chapter 2 and discuss more in a later chapter, senators and others compounded the offense by transmuting equal representation into a general principle of minority rights. In turn, equal representation and minority rights have been used to defend the various forms of minority power in the Senate's rules of procedure, specifically those that allow its members to filibuster and empower a minority of senators to delay or thwart altogether what the majority seeks to accomplish. Before we get to the history and impact of the filibuster and supermajority cloture, however, we need to understand another fundamental element of the Senate's constitutionalism, one that, like equal representation, has been used to support and justify the filibuster. This feature, the Senate's self-conception as a "continuing body," links that institution's longer and staggered terms to the practice of extended debate and supermajority cloture in the Senate.

# 4

# The Right of the Living Dead

STAGGERED TERMS, CONTINUING BODIES, AND CONSTITUTIONAL MYTHS SENATORS TELL THEMSELVES AND AMERICA

> There could be no new Senate. This was the very same body, constitutionally and in point of law, which had assembled on the day of its meeting in 1789. It has existed without any intermission from that day until the present moment and would continue to exist as long as the Government could endure. It was emphatically a permanent body.
>
> —SENATOR JAMES BUCHANAN, 1841

BECAUSE ONLY one-third of the Senate is up for reelection every two years, the Senate is said to be continuing, permanent, perpetual, or undying, to the point that scholars and politicians have claimed it is the same Senate that first met in 1789. Unlike the House, "the Senate . . . is a continuing body," wrote George Haynes in his 1938 history of the Senate. From the first session, he continued, there has "never since been a time when the Senate as an organized body has not been available, at the President's summons or in accordance with the terms of its own adjournment, for the transaction of public business."[1] Staggered terms—any arrangement of terms of office so that not all members of a body are appointed or elected at the same time—are one of the constitutional provisions that distinguish the Senate from the House and are the foundation for the notion that the Senate is a continuing body. As equal representation became the foundation for the Senate's self-conception as the constitutional bastion of minority rights, staggered six-year terms were being used to add another element to the Senate's perceived exceptionalism. The Senate, with its longer term and higher age requirement, is not just the older and wiser chamber of Congress, it is immortal!

Staggered elections for the Senate, whatever their intended effect, create a continuing body in the literal meaning of the term: a body whose membership is subject to only fractional change at any point in time. This is "continuing body" as a simple adjective or descriptive fact. But senators developed the mere fact of continuity caused by staggered elections into a constitutional self-conception and set of practices, such that the actions of past senators could and should bind or restrict current members of the body. This is continuing body as constitutional doctrine and practice, which applies particularly to that body's rules.[2] If the Senate never dies, then neither do its rules. As journalist William White put it in his midcentury history of the Senate, "And since, unlike the House, the Senate is a continuing body, never ending and never wholly overturning from one Congress to the next, the Senate rules go on immutable from one Congress to another. It is not necessary to renew or continue them; there they stand as unshakable in fact, almost, as the Constitution itself."[3] With less poetry and more precision, Senator Robert Byrd said much the same thing: "The United States Senate is an unbroken thread, running from our time back to its first meeting in New York in April 1789. By this I mean the Senate is a continuous body. While the entire House of Representatives is elected every two years, only one-third of the senators run at each biennial election. Since two-thirds carry over, our rules are continuous and do not have to be readopted at the beginning of each Congress."[4]

The Senate harboring a self-conception as a continuing body as part of its tendency to institutional aggrandizement is in and of itself harmless and unobjectionable. The problem comes when the self-conception is turned into an implied constitutional restraint, such that the actions of past senators bind or restrict current members of the body. In particular, the notion of the Senate as a continuing body has been the chief reason, as the White and Byrd quotations indicate, that the Senate does not vote on its rules of procedure at the start of each Congress as the House does. In the House, the new majority votes on and sometimes modifies that chamber's rules. In the Senate, no vote is taken automatically. Once a Senate tradition, this practice of not voting on the rules at the commencement of a new Congress was in 1959 turned into one of the rules—that is, another rule that would not be voted on by future Senates. This was done as part of a compromise to appease southern Democrats wanting to protect the particular rules that allowed them to filibuster civil rights legislation. The continuing body idea is also an important part of the rationale for a supermajority threshold of two-thirds of all voting senators needed to cut off debate on proposed changes in Senate rules of procedure. This is the connection between, or leap from, continuity as mere description to continuity as doctrine. The constitutional construction of the continuing body doctrine has served as another barrier to changing the rules of the Senate generally but particularly the supermajority cloture provisions of Rule XXII after they were created in 1917. The continuing body doctrine helped to elevate Senate rules and the filibuster to the status of higher law, akin to, if not quite part of, the Constitution.

Thus, not only did the continuing body doctrine get written into Senate rules as part of the Senate's long history of filibusters in support of white supremacy, the doctrine itself is little more than a self-serving mythology based on a misinterpretation of the purpose of staggered terms in the Senate. The links between the Senate as a continuing body, the intentions of the founders, and the Constitution are, in fact, quite ironic. The debates at the 1787 Constitutional Convention make no mention of the Senate as a continuing body. "Permanency" and "duration" were used in reference to one thing only: the length of senatorial terms. And those were as often a source of apprehension as they were of celebration. Widespread concerns about a Senate aristocracy, including the fears of several delegates to the convention that a permanent aristocracy would entrench itself in a new national capital, throw cold water not only on the idea that the Senate was intended to be the bastion of minority rights but also on the notion that a continuing body was part of the founders' grand design. But that is the least of it. This chapter reveals the origins of the continuing body mythology by exposing the deliberate misinterpretation of the purpose of staggered terms, criticizes the Senate's use of this pretension, and shows how this specious concept has been used to protect and elevate the status of Senate rules, particularly the ones that allow for minority obstruction.

## Why Does the Senate Have Staggered Terms?

We take staggered Senate terms for granted, but why were they included in the Constitution? As we have seen, the structure and composition of the Senate was the most contentious matter debated and resolved at the Constitutional Convention. And staggered Senate terms are on any scholar's list of the key decisions of 1787 that made the Senate the Senate. Despite their importance in the architecture of American bicameralism, however, little scholarship exists on the origins and purpose of staggered terms for the US Senate.⁵ Instead, historians, political scientists, and journalists alike have repeated a conventional wisdom in a matter-of-fact manner that draws on assumption more than evidence. This dominant perspective portrays staggered elections as part of the framers' intent to create an insulated, stable, deliberative—and thereby continuing or permanent—Senate. For example, the authors of a recent history of the Senate claim that the framers "decided that only one-third of the senators [would] come up for election each two years, further to insulate the Senate from popular enthusiasms or turmoil."⁶ Almost ninety years earlier, historian Lindsay Rogers wrote much the same thing, as did many others in between.⁷

For example, "By requiring only one-third of the Senate to seek re-election every two years," according to one congressional scholar, "the framers hoped that short-term fluctuations in public opinion would be leveled out in the Senate, allowing only enduring shifts in sentiment to take hold."⁸ Robert Caro, in perhaps the bestselling book on the Senate, writes that "the Framers armored the Senate against the people," and that, on top of state selection and long terms, staggered elections "would be an additional, even stronger, layer of armor."⁹ Prominent American politics textbooks interpret staggered terms as "intended to make that body even more resistant to popular pressure" and part of what insulates the Senate "from momentary shifts in the public mood."¹⁰ To my chagrin, my earlier work on the creation of the Senate offers another example.¹¹ In this way, selection by state legislatures, six-year terms, and staggered elections almost always have been thought of and portrayed as a harmonious package to create a less democratic upper house. Staggered terms have typically been an implicit part of every cliché about the Senate as the "world's greatest deliberative body" that "cools the coffee" brewed by the House. And there is an ahistorical quality to many of the assertions regarding the Constitutional Convention's use of staggered elections as if they emerged ex nihilo in Philadelphia as a "solution" to the problem of complete turnover of the Senate¹² instead of seeing staggered terms as a familiar practice from early state constitutions that might have had a different or more complicated function.¹³

This conventional interpretation has, however, little basis in the origins of and intention behind the Senate's staggered terms. My argument is not that these and other similar characterizations are wrong in their implications about the *potential effects* of the combination of long and staggered terms. I show that they are misleading and inaccurate as far as the primary *intentions and political interests* that led to the inclusion of staggered terms for the Senate in the Constitution.

Where, then, did staggered terms come from, and why were they added in this specific way to the Constitution? As I lay out in detail below, staggered terms were (1) in the revolutionary era, a mechanism to ensure "rotation," or democratic turnover, (2) added to the Constitution as part of a compromise to assuage opponents of an insulated Senate and obtain a majority in support of a long term for that body, and (3) portrayed during ratification as a form of rotation that counteracted the perceived dangers of the long term and a Senate aristocracy. Whatever the effects in practice, staggered terms were intended primarily to mitigate the potential dangers of a legislative body with long individual tenure by exposing it to more frequent electoral influence.[14]

The irony is that staggered elections, a category of rotation intended to disrupt the accumulation and perpetuation of institutional power, came to be seen as part and parcel of the Senate's conservative purpose and produced the notion of an undying Senate or continuing body. More generally, seeing staggered terms as a form of electoral accountability, as a form of rotation, reminds us of the complexity of the Senate's creation. The Senate was certainly intended to be the more conservative or undemocratic of the two legislative chambers, but not every aspect of its construction fits that mold. The combination of long terms and staggered elections evinces the framers' efforts, with both abstract principles and political necessity in the mix, to balance stability with responsiveness in the design of republican institutions.

## "Rotation" in the Late Eighteenth Century

In the years leading up to the Constitutional Convention, including the wave of state constitutions written in the 1770s and 1780s, staggered terms—the phrase was not used in this period—were one of a set of mechanisms used to create what was called "rotation." In discussions of the tenure of any governmental office, the term "rotation" was invoked with some regularity to refer to the frequency with which the membership of an institution would be subject to change in whole or in part. "Rotation" was about devices that ensured regular turnover in officeholders and encompassed two approaches: provisions that limited reeligibility for office (that is, forms of what we now call term limits) and provisions that staggered the terms of membership in legislatures or other governmental bodies by dividing the membership into groups or classes to be selected in different years.[15]

In his 1776 "Thoughts on Government," John Adams endorsed rotation, in the form of term limits, but annual terms held a higher status, "there not being in the whole circle of the sciences, a maxim more infallible than this, 'Where annual elections end, there slavery begins.'"[16] Annual elections, the paramount mechanism of democratic accountability in the revolutionary era, were frequently paired with eligibility rotation as a powerful check on governmental power. For example, the Articles of Confederation restricted delegates to Congress to serving no more than three years of any period of six, in addition to annual terms. In combination, short terms and eligibility restrictions together ensured rotation.

Unlike limits on reeligibility, rotation in the form of staggered elections could be applied only to chambers with terms greater than one year, and even going into the summer of 1787, annual elections were still the norm. Along with the Congress of the Confederation, ten states had annual elections for their lower house. Two, Connecticut and Rhode Island, held elections every six months for theirs. Only South Carolina had two-year terms for its general assembly.

Nevertheless, the revolutionary and founding era saw a move away from the viselike grip of annual elections. Even many champions of annual elections for the lower house acknowledged the virtue of balancing the kind of electoral check one-year terms represented with the accumulation of wisdom and experience and at least limited insulation from popular pressure. In the colonial era most upper houses were councils—some with indefinite appointments—that combined executive and legislative functions. The new state constitutions created upper houses that were more democratic in their selection, more clearly separated from the executive, and with longer terms than the assembly.[17] The innovation of legislative senates with longer terms was tied to rotation in every case except Maryland, which also featured a system of electors to pick its senate.[18]

The scholarship on state constitutions does not spend much time on staggered elections for the new senates, but several historians imply that upper chamber rotation was to enforce turnover and electoral accountability.[19] Perhaps it was self-evident given the context. With the lower house of nearly every state elected for one year only, no rotation was required. This implies quite directly that these state constitutions, aside from Maryland's, were trying to combine a longer term in the upper house with turnover and an electoral check. In other words, the virtue of a longer term for some positions was to be balanced by rotation in the form of staggered elections.

A few state constitutions, including those of Virginia and Pennsylvania, provide contextual evidence for staggered terms as a form of rotation, but Delaware serves as a telling example. Its 1776 constitution created a "Legislative Council" composed of three councilors elected from each of the three counties that made up Delaware. These nine councilors served three-year terms, but one councilor *from each county* would be rotated out each year.[20] Insofar as the lower house, the assembly, was elected to annual terms and even the executive privy council had two-year terms with rotation and limits on reeligibility, it is difficult to see the rotation in the legislative council as anything but that, especially as it was rotation within each county's group of three councilors. In this way, the counties would be able to influence the nature and direction of their representation in the upper house every single year.

## Rotation and the Senate at the Constitutional Convention

Given this backdrop of recently formed and tested state charters, the delegates to the convention were familiar with staggered terms as a form of rotation for offices with longer terms. Its ultimate application to the proposed national Senate, therefore, is not surprising, but neither was it automatic. When the delegates added staggered terms, they did so as part of a compromise to balance the longest Senate term attainable with a form of rotation.

As I showed in the first chapter, the Constitutional Convention opened with consideration of the so-called Virginia Plan or Randolph Resolutions, which were largely the work of James Madison. He was the foremost advocate for an independent and stable Senate, one characterized by experience, knowledge, detachment, and elevated selection. If staggered elections had been part of a plan for augmenting the continuity or detachment of the second branch, it is probable that Madison would have included such a provision in the Virginia Plan, especially insofar as Virginia's state senate had a four-year term, with one quarter going out every year. Madison was, however, an avowed proponent of the Maryland senate with its term of five years—the longest of any state—and no rotation.[21]

Only two weeks into the proceedings, the convention delegates first considered the periods of service for both chambers. This discussion took place before the delegates got bogged down in the debates over equal and proportional representation and the interests of small and large states, but it followed the unanimous decision on June 7 in favor of state legislatures selecting senators. On June 12, long terms *for both chambers* won decisive initial victories, with three-year terms for the House prevailing 7–4 and seven years for the Senate by 8-1-2, with no mention of any type of rotation.[22]

The first proposal for rotation of any kind did not come until several days later, and it was for the House, not the Senate. On June 21, when the delegates reconsidered the House term, some pushed for a shorter tenure than three years, citing in some cases the annual elections that were still common at the state level. Delaware's John Dickinson favored the three-year House term agreed to earlier but argued against the "inconveniency of an entire change of the whole number at the same moment" and "suggested a rotation, by an annual election of one third." In a clear splitting of the difference, three years was struck by a decisive vote in favor of two years, which presumably did not require any rotation but was long enough to be practical, in light of the distances representatives would have to travel. It bears repeating that the first recorded mention of staggered terms occurred in a proposal for the lower chamber and in the spirit of the usual meaning and purpose of rotation.[23]

The final decision on Senate terms was more difficult and protracted. Despite the initial agreement by the 8-1-2 vote, many delegates had concerns that seven years was too long. When the delegates returned to the question of Senate terms on June 25, a few days after having reduced the House term to two years, Nathaniel Gorham of Massachusetts proposed four years instead of seven, with "1/4 to be elected every year."[24] This was countered by a proposal for seven years but also with staggered terms. North Carolina's Hugh Williamson then suggested six years as more convenient for rotation. But the delegates did not vote to add staggered terms at this point. They took the first step of striking seven years by a 7-3-1 vote. Long terms continued to do poorly, with six and five years falling short on the same 5-5-1 votes.[25]

The next day, Gorham tried to end the gridlock by proposing six years, but with the additional provision of "one third of the members to go out every second year." Delaware's George Read still favored life appointments, but "being little supported in that idea . . . was willing to take the longest term that could be obtained." And so he countered with nine years and one-third rotation.[26] Insofar as he favored life appointments to the Senate, Read's inclusion of rotation was a recognition of the political need to offset long terms with refreshment and renewal. After some debate, nine years with rotation lost 3–8, but six years with rotation won 7–4.[27] With the earlier opposition to six and even five years, it is clear that rotation helped seal the deal, and rotation was about change, not continuation. It was a way to temper long terms of service with fresh blood.[28]

Although the convention records show extensive debate about the purpose and merits of a long Senate term, only a few comments such as Read's conveyed an explicit rationale for rotation. With one exception they concern balancing a long term with electoral accountability. For example, Roger Sherman sought the shortest term feasible and argued that "the two objects of this body are permanency and safety to those who are to be governed. A bad government is the worse for being long. Frequent elections give security and even permanency. . . . Four years to the senate is quite sufficient when you add to it the rotation proposed."[29] Sherman contrasted the "permanency" of four-year terms (versus his state's annual elections) against the turnover provided by rotation.

In the last recorded speech before the final votes on Senate term length, Pennsylvanian James Wilson showed how rotation was more a compromise than a vital principle. Wilson cited the importance of some permanence or stability in the government for treaties and diplomacy (indeed, a Senate with a long term might even be a match for a foreign monarch): "The popular objection agst. appointing any public body for a long term was that it might by gradual encroachments prolong itself first into a body for life, and finally become a hereditary one. It would be a satisfactory answer to this objection that as 1/3 would go out triennially, there would be always three divisions holding their places for unequal terms, and consequently acting under the influence of different views, and different impulses."[30] The one direct reference to rotation as a way to stabilize Senate membership came from Edmund Randolph, who, just after Gorham's proposal for four-year terms with one quarter rotation, "supported the idea of rotation, as favorable to the wisdom and stability of the Corps. [which might possibly be always sitting, and aiding the executive]."[31] Randolph's comment invoked the Senate's as yet undefined but anticipated relationship with the executive, particularly in foreign affairs and the business of treaties.

Even with Randolph's invocation of wisdom and stability, the framers' deliberations and actions show that they primarily viewed and used Senate rotation as a tool for fostering this body's electoral accountability rather than institutional autonomy or insulation in the antidemocratic sense. Staggered terms became part of a compromise, a means to an end, a way to balance the merits of long terms against the threat of permanency. In short, one side, the staunch advocates of a republican Senate, got as long a term as possible, and some who feared an entrenched aristocracy or needed some degree of compensation or political cover got rotation as a check.

## Staggered Terms in the Ratification Debates

The structure and powers of the Senate were significant controversies during ratification, including the six-year term, which many conventioneers and commentators felt was too long. Staggered elections for the Senate were less of a topic, but evidence from the various debates during ratification, treated with appropriate caution, underscores that its main purpose was to offset concerns that attended long terms.

Annual elections and rotation featured in the critiques of the proposed Constitution. Some of its opponents thought two years was too long a term for representatives and still favored the provisions in the Articles of Confederation that combined annual terms for delegates to Congress with the additional restriction of serving no more than three years of any period of six, which was a different type of rotation in the form of term limits. Indeed, the length of House and Senate terms were among the more frequent criticisms of the proposed Constitution, with antifederalists often suggesting one-year and four-year terms instead.[32] And such was antifederalist fear of a detached Senate aristocracy that staggered elections were not reassuring to all. A delegate to the Massachusetts convention referred to staggered Senate terms as "but a shadow of rotation."[33] Brutus, the premier antifederalist essayist, referred to the Senate's staggered terms as a form of rotation, but condemned the absence of eligibility rotation and called for a reduction to a four-year term.[34] Yet even if some thought it an insufficient form of rotation, antifederalists neither criticized nor sought to repeal the provision for staggered terms.

In turn, advocates of ratification invoked staggered terms as a powerful check on a permanent or insulated Senate. Many pro-ratification delegates argued against term limits, the other form of rotation, and against recall, but defended staggered terms for the Senate as a different and necessary type of rotation. My search of the debates at the state conventions produced seventeen such endorsements of staggered terms by a total of eleven proponents of ratification.[35] All the references characterize staggered terms as a safeguard against a "perpetual" Senate, a Senate aristocracy. Subjecting one-third of the Senate to election every two years would keep senators attentive to their states and bring in new sentiments about government and policy.

In Massachusetts, Fisher Ames called rotation a "very effectual check upon the power of the Senate."[36] North Carolina federalist James Iredell argued that the newly elected one-third "will bring with them from the immediate body of the people a sufficient portion of patriotism and independence" to thwart any dangerous alliance between the executive and the Senate.[37] "By constructing the senate upon rotative principles," said Charles Cotesworth Pinckney to his fellow South Carolinians, "we have removed . . . all danger of an aristocratic influence" while allowing the long term of six years to provide the "advantages of an aristocracy," including wisdom and experience.[38] Finally, Alexander Hamilton endorsed staggered terms at the New York convention, arguing "that safety and permanency in this government are completely reconcilable."[39] The man who, at the center of his major speech at the Constitutional Convention, proposed life terms for senators likely would not have thought of staggered terms as a way to increase Senate "permanency." Instead, as he put it, two equally important principles—the safety of electoral accountability and the detached judgment and experience provided by "permanency"—could be harmonized by balancing long terms with rotation.

Stretching from the state constitutions through ratification, rotation in the form of staggered elections had one central purpose, ensuring the turnover of officeholders. Staggered terms were seen by some as more dimensional in their intended effects than, for example, term limits, a blunter form of rotation. In a few instances, proponents portrayed staggered terms as a form of accountability that also preserved institutional knowledge or continuity, even if this perspective rested on an implicit assumption that massive or even complete turnover would occur in bodies without staggered terms. But the argument for preservation or continuity of knowledge was not antidemocratic in the manner typically implied by the conventional view of staggered Senate elections. In light of the evidence above, the general argument that the framers added staggered terms to further insulate the Senate and further distinguish it from the democratic House is unsustainable. When joined together, however, long and staggered terms certainly had multiple effects. Even if the intentions and politics of the convention led to the addition of staggered elections to temper long terms, the combination produced a body, that in comparison to the House, never would be subject to the same degree of potential electoral change.

This chapter provides another illustration of the complexity of the Senate's origins.[40] The Senate was, of course, the object of the Great Compromise that tried to blend Madison's Senate of far-sighted statesmen with equal and direct representation of states. Placed at the intersection of several constitutional vectors or tensions—responsiveness and deliberation, legislative and executive powers, states and nation—the Senate reflects the multiple forces and goals at work in its construction. The central elements of the Senate's composition as ratified in 1789—selection by state legislatures, six-year terms, and staggered elections—were a package that embodied these various ideas and interests. By contrast, the common understanding of Senate staggered terms has tended to see and portray the Senate as a neater, more coherent package than it actually was. The fact that the founders intended the Senate to be the less democratic chamber does not mean every feature of its composition, including staggered terms, must have been intended to contribute to that goal.

## How Did Mere Description Become Constitutional Doctrine?

In light of the origins of Senate staggered terms, how and when did the idea of staggered elections as a form of rotation dissipate to be replaced, by and large, with an interpretation that conflated them with insulation, detachment, and continuity? When did the descriptive reality of continuity become a doctrine about Senate practice and procedure? That remains uncertain.

After ratification, some famous commentators, including St. George Tucker in 1803 and Joseph Story in 1833, still portrayed staggered terms as rotation.[41] Nevertheless, at some point during these years—when and how remain a bit of a mystery—senators began developing and applying the doctrine of the Senate as a continuing body. That is, at some point senators took the mere fact of staggered elections and transformed it into a broader characterization of the Senate as a legislative body. It was no longer simply that staggered elections were one aspect of the Senate's architecture, like equal representation or state selection. Instead, staggered elections made the Senate a continuing body, with certain constitutional attributes flowing from that status. And "continuing," "permanent," and "perpetual" all carried the implication of conservatism, in the literal sense, and insulation and detachment. In this way, the rise of the continuing body doctrine is inextricably linked to the interpretation of staggered elections as part and parcel of the Senate's conservative purpose.

As indicated by this chapter's epigraph, a quotation from Senator Buchanan, this understanding or claim goes back at least to 1841, and statements such as his imply that the concept was by that point a familiar one. What did Buchanan mean by asserting that the Senate "was emphatically a permanent body," that there "could be no new Senate"? It was certainly more than a mere description based on the fact of staggered terms. Buchanan emphasized the three things that would remain the core of the continuing body doctrine down to the present. First was the general conservative consequence and purpose of continuity. In his words, the Senate "was the sheet-anchor of the Constitution, on account of its permanency." Second, as the chief example of this continuity, the Senate's "rules were permanent, and were not adopted from Congress to Congress, like those of the House of Representatives." Finally, and as implied by the example of the rules, "one Senate" had the "right to bind its successors."[42] Notice that this last phrasing carries the linguistic and logical difficulty at the core of the doctrine: if it is always the same Senate, then how can one Senate be succeeded by another? And if it is the same Senate, why can't it change its mind?

Subsequent debates in the Senate invoked 1841 as the first time the Senate considered, however briefly and inconsequentially, the meaning of its self-description.[43] Coming as it did in the hotly partisan and sectional politics of the Jackson era, the debate in 1841 was hardly about the lofty and perpetual status of the Senate. And it was not about how Senate rules protect deliberation and minority rights, even though to that point, "the Senate had seen no more prolonged or partisan obstruction"[44] than during this debate, which has been cited as the first unambiguous filibuster in Senate history.[45] The matter at hand, and the object of the extended debate, was a raw and transparent partisan dispute about the Senate printer, of all things. For decades, nineteenth-century Congresses contracted private printers, typically publishers of partisan newspapers in Washington, D.C., to print public documents, including the proceedings of the House and Senate. The new majority party, the Whigs, started a special session of the new Twenty-Seventh Congress by moving to fire the printers recently hired by the outgoing Democratic majority at the end of the just expired Twenty-Sixth Congress. Filibuster or no, for several days the Democrats put up a fuss, two senators almost had a duel over their ad hominem remarks, and a few senators, as minor asides in their speeches, characterized the Senate as a continuing body.[46]

The details need not detain us except to note that, aside from the accusations of naked partisanship from both sides, the main points of dispute were about whether the Senate was acting in its legislative or executive capacity during this special session, whether the printer qualified as an officer of the Senate, and whether or in what way the contract reached with a printer could be terminated. Buchanan was the only senator to speak more than a few words in support of the continuing body concept, and it was at best a secondary argument. In fact, in the context of Buchanan's full commentary, his invocation of the Senate as a continuing body was almost a non sequitur and somewhat absurd. As part of his argument that the printer hired during the Twenty-Sixth Congress could not be fired by the Senate of the Twenty-Seventh, Buchanan claimed, as noted, an unqualified right for the Senate at one point in time to bind itself and its successors because there is never a different or new Senate. It was a declaration rather than an argument, and a point, one suspected, he would find himself disputing if the partisan shoe had been on the other foot. One senator spoke in opposition to Buchanan's characterization of what a "permanent body" implied, and two others referred to the Senate's continuity in a single sentence, each amid much longer remarks focused on the other more pertinent arguments. The rest of the debate and the final outcome—Buchanan and the other Democrats lost—suggest the status of the Senate as a continuing body was irrelevant, ignored, and certainly far from settled.[47]

This pattern of brief and desultory invocations continued through the nineteenth century. Several times, especially in the 1870s and 1880s, it came up in discussions of the status of the Senate's president pro tempore, and once in 1876 in regard to the joint rules that Congress once maintained.[48] If one surveys the occasions from 1841 through the early 1900s when the Senate discussed—however briefly—its status as a continuing body, several things are apparent. There was no unanimity, and no small part of this disagreement was partisan. Some senators argued, for example, that the House was just as perpetual, for it is always ready to meet if necessary. As well, the advocates of the doctrine could never connect mere or descriptive continuity—that is, the fact that only one-third of the Senate is up for election every two years, or the ability of the Senate to meet at any time related to its executive functions—to the implied broader doctrine, that descriptive continuity determines how the Senate should or must conduct its business, such as continuing its rules from one Congress to the next. Instead, they often referred to Buchanan's words in 1841 and—as Buchanan did—to unnamed authorities who all agreed that the Senate is the continuing body intended by the framers, who were then referenced imprecisely or not at all. For example, Senator Thomas Harkwick in 1917, whose "conviction on this subject was . . . profound," knew that the Senate "was intended by the makers of our Constitution to be a permanent body, and provision was made that two-thirds of its membership should always be in office."[49] The straw of descriptive continuity was never turned into the gold of constitutional doctrine by any sort of logic that was not, in the end, a circular reference to staggered elections.

Despite the lack of rigor and logic, the continuing body doctrine endured for a variety of reasons, and it became a commonly invoked pillar of Senate identity, as indicated by the quotations from George Haynes, William White, and Senator Robert Byrd at the start of this chapter. It is not hard to see the reasons why. The doctrine is based on a stubborn and unchanging descriptive fact stemming from staggered elections. As well, push never had to come to shove about whether the doctrine was more than a convenient if imprecise set of assumptions. Finally, the doctrine is flattering as another coat of luster on the exceptional Senate, another alleged facet of its unique status in the Constitution and American system. The doctrine just lingered pretty much as Senator Buchanan had articulated it in 1841, available for use when and where convenient.

All of this suggests the following conjecture: Could it be that the Senate began to construct itself as a continuing body based on the fact of staggered terms, and, as the doctrine of a continuing body took hold, the functional purpose of and intent behind staggered terms evolved to harmonize with this new doctrine? That is, instead of a particular interpretation of the founding purpose of staggered terms driving the idea of a continuing body, could the subsequent appeal and utility of the continuing body doctrine have created an interpretation of the founders' intent for this small but important feature of the Constitution? Senators developed a motivated bias for appealing and adhering to what became the conventional wisdom about staggered terms because it supported the attractive features of the continuing body doctrine. The Senate's self-conception and definition as a continuing and deliberative body circled back to build and reinforce the conventional wisdom about staggered terms: that the Senate is a continuing body, which the framers must have intended, and so staggered terms must have been designed to produce that result.

This motivated bias suggests that two understandable but faulty forms of reasoning contributed to the rise and power of the conventional wisdom. The first is what one might call the fallacy of coherent construction. It is hardly novel to point out how frequently and misleadingly "the framers' intent" is invoked, as though a particular facet of the Constitution were unambiguous in its construction or purpose. In some instances, such a generalization is not an abuse, but in most cases it is a distortion. And that is true of almost anything involving the Senate, which was, after all, the object of the Great Compromise that blended the oil of the Senate as the bastion of federalism with the water of the Senate as the citadel of far-sighted statesmen. Nevertheless, we tend to see and portray the Senate as a neater, more coherent package than it actually was.

The second is a version of the teleological fallacy, the familiar problem of reasoning from functional effects backward to intent and origins. Because X results in Y, X was designed to produce Y. Insofar as there is no purely functional reasoning in this instance—it has all been tainted by assumed knowledge of the founding—this fallacy rests primarily on observations about the impact of staggered terms on the Senate, especially compared to the House. As the Constitution was put into practice and concerns about long terms quickly disappeared amid a gradual process of democratization, the most obvious effect of staggered terms was the insulation of two-thirds of the Senate at every national election—rather than the opportunity to refresh one-third with new blood—even if the actual history of incumbency, turnover, and party control in each chamber complicated the impression of a volatile House and stable Senate. It also became commonplace to assume that all representatives were thinking about reelection on an ongoing basis, whereas only one-third of the Senate seemed so directly afflicted. As the average tenure of representatives and senators quickly converged, the difference in institutional knowledge and stability seemed less important than the difference in electoral cycles. These developments, along with a lack of scholarship on the origins of staggered terms specifically, facilitated the understandable conflation, by senators and scholars alike, that staggered elections with longer terms and selection by state legislatures were part of the founders' conservative intentions.

I contend that just as the origins of staggered terms for the Senate are more complex and interesting than the conventional wisdom implies, the relationship between the interpretation of staggered terms and the development of the doctrine of the Senate as a continuing body has likely been an interdependent and mutually reinforcing discursive process. Regardless of the exact relationship of staggered terms to the continuing body doctrine, the result was a conventional interpretation based more on the consequences of staggered terms in practice and discourse than on their historical origins.

## The Self-Serving Illogic of the Continuing Body Doctrine

Beyond the lack of constitutional foundation, the flaws in the logic of the continuing body as any sort of binding principle are numerous and compelling.[50] And senators have been aware of them for at least a century. It is no coincidence that the longest discussion of whether or not the Senate is a continuing body in anything more than a descriptive sense came during the special Senate session in March 1917 that produced supermajority cloture. I analyze the creation of cloture in greater detail in the next chapter, but let me say here that after several episodes of unpopular filibusters and amid the rather sudden shift toward involvement in World War I, the Senate took up a proposal to add a procedure to its rules that would end debate with a vote by a supermajority of two-thirds of senators voting. As part of these proceedings, two senators, Robert Owen of Oklahoma and Montana's Thomas Walsh, both of whom favored cloture reform, initiated the argument that the Senate is not a continuing body except for executive business. They did so in hopes of preventing a filibuster against the pending proposal to create the rule allowing debate to be terminated by a supermajority vote. On March 7, Senator Walsh took the floor and consumed the entire day subjecting the continuing body doctrine to a withering interrogation. Walsh was out to destroy the assumption that Senate rules continued from one Congress to the next. As Walsh had pointed out the day before, "The question as to whether the rules live from one Congress to the next has never been directly considered by this body, although many times incidentally it has been asserted that the Senate is a continuing body."[51] To Walsh, those assertions amounted to nothing more than the simple fact that "two-thirds of its Members remain in office at the expiration of each two-year period."[52] The Montana Democrat enumerated and explained the several problems and inconsistencies in the doctrine of the continuing body, including the paramount fact that all legislation dies at the end of a Congress. What stronger evidence could there be against the claim that the Senate is a continuing body than its own decision that its most important business, legislation, does not carry over from one Congress to the next? It if were, a bill reported by a Senate committee in an election year would still be alive for floor debate when the new Senate convened in the new year. And even if the putatively perpetual Senate passes a measure, but the House disapproves or even fails to take any action, both chambers must start over during the next Congress. This is parliamentary tradition rather than a provision in the Constitution or House and Senate rules. And yet it has never been questioned, particularly—and most tellingly—by any senator wielding the continuing body doctrine. The logic of this practice is self-evident. In his 1951 testimony before the Senate Rules Committee, Walter Reuther explained it this way: "The reintroduction of bills into the Senate of each new Congress is made necessary, of course, because a majority in favor or against a given bill may be changed by the election of new Senators to some or all of the one-third of the seats whose terms expire. A bill passed by an earlier Senate could not, therefore, be considered the will of the later Senate unless a new vote were taken."[53] With this and other examples, Walsh showed that the Senate decides when aspects of its business and organization continue from one Congress to the next; this is not determined by the consequences of staggered elections.[54]

Senator Walsh's arguments, and others I will discuss, are as good today as they were over one hundred years ago. As he implied, the conception of the Senate as a continuing body might be more compelling were it not for the fact that the Senate itself is utterly inconsistent in its application of the principle. That is, the most important elements of what the Senate actually does—its business in its legislative and executive capacities—do not carry over, or continue, from one Congress into the next. Senator Walter Mondale made this clear during a 1975 debate on the filibuster and cloture reform. Mondale noted that during the various debates about cloture, "much has been said about the Senate being a 'continuing' body." However, "The Senate is hardly a continuing body when it wipes the slate clean of bills, resolutions, nominations, and treaties at the beginning of each new Congress. Nor is it a continuing body with respect to many of its other actions."[55] Most of the key examples Mondale cited are not, like the idea of the continuing body, mere tradition or norms. They are in the Senate rules, the same rules that continue from Congress to Congress.

Nominations do not even survive beyond a single session of a given two-year Congress.[56] The memberships of Senate committees are appointed at the start of every Congress.[57] Rule XXX specifies that "all proceedings on treaties shall terminate with the Congress, and they shall be resumed at the commencement of the next Congress as if no proceedings had previously been had thereon." Treaties are not legislation requiring bicameral action. They are a shared power with the executive. As such, and as international agreements reached by the president, it would be logical for consideration of treaties to be carried over from one Congress to the next, even if the Senate were not a continuing body. Notice, however, that should the Senate decide to act on a treaty that was carried over from the last Congress, senators start from a clean slate, as if the president had been obliged to resubmit it.

As a result, the arguments for the continuing body doctrine frequently have had a circular quality. The Senate chooses to behave in a certain way because it is convenient or practical, such as having the president pro tempore serve until changed (that is, serving from one Congress to the next but at the pleasure of the Senate). Such things are clearly a choice, not a mandate determined by continuity. That behavior creates some continuity in Senate action across Congresses. The behavior is then justified by reference to the fact that it is a continuing body. But it is a continuing body because it chose, in this particular instance, to create a behavior that can be characterized as continuation. Other things do not "continue," because the Senate chose not to behave that way. The body does not have to continue its rules from Congress to Congress; it chose to, and then chose to apply supermajority protections to those rules, which in turn were rationalized by the continuing body doctrine. In short, there was no clear theory of continuation that empowered or required particular behaviors with regard to the rules, committees, treaties, the president pro tempore, or anything else. Instead, chosen behaviors served as the proof that the Senate was the continuing body implied by staggered elections.

This circularity, where arguments about continuity chase their own tail, can be seen when supporters of the doctrine invoke a Supreme Court decision that briefly mentions the differences in continuity between the Senate and the House.[58] The language in the decision did not amount to more than taking judicial notice of something as a fact, a fact that was, in any event, not central to the decision at hand. *McGrain v. Daugherty*, a 1927 decision, was about Congress's power to compel witnesses to appear and testify as part of its constitutional duties.⁵⁹ At the end of the decision, the Court, in discussing a secondary question, noted that the Senate was a continuing body, mostly because it has behaved that way. The decision pointed out that the Senate had at times specified that the work of committees could extend beyond the end of a Congress, in the interim before the new Congress commences.⁶⁰ That is the full extent of the Court's recognition of the Senate as a continuing body. Voilà: the continuing body doctrine has constitutional sanction because the Supreme Court has taken judicial notice of the fact that the Senate chooses to behave, in certain instances, like a continuing body. The Senate can choose to behave in some ways because of staggered terms—such as allowing committees to exist or function between Congresses—that make it continuing in practice by its actions rather than by mere description. Staggered terms, however, do not compel the Senate to turn description into action; they do not determine anything beyond how elections affect the membership of the Senate.

The list of important ways in which the Senate does not act according to the putative logic of a continuing body demonstrates, as Aaron-Andrew Bruhl puts it, that "the exception is, of course, the Senate's rules. What we have then is not so much a bunch of data points scattered all over the place but rather a line with an anomalous outlier representing the Senate's handling of its own rules."⁶¹ The Senate has used the continuing body doctrine to protect its rules and little else. And, as if to give final proof of this, a particular group of senators with a singular stake in protecting the rules that gave them leverage against an emerging civil rights movement got the continuing body doctrine written into those same Senate rules.

## From Doctrine to Rule: The Continuing Body Doctrine Gets Codified in Service of White Supremacy

For many decades this protection of the rules was not, as mentioned, a Senate rule but a tradition or practice justified by the continuing body doctrine. But even this telling exception to protect the rules makes no sense. Just because in theory there might be two-thirds returning senators and one-third new senators, why does that preclude majority action on a new set of rules? Even with addition of the one-third, there could easily be a new majority, as far as sentiment concerning the rules, within the new Senate. And as Walter Reuther argued as part of his 1951 testimony, this new group of senators "must be able to express its will on the rules," particularly something as important as the rule on cloture because of its potential effect on the Senate's ability to consider and decide on the substantive legislation that has to be introduced each Congress.[62]

In 1959, however, the Senate made sure that such a majority would never be able to upset tradition and attempt a majority vote on the rules, and, as with so much else about the Senate throughout its history, this action was directly connected to southern senators' attempts to protect white supremacy in their states and region.

That year Rule V was amended to include the following: "The rules of the Senate shall continue from one Congress to the next Congress unless they are changed as provided in these rules"[63]—meaning that a two-thirds supermajority would be required to shut off debate on any proposal to change the rules; a new Senate would not be afforded the opportunity to change the rules by a simple majority. Prior to Rule V, section 2, nothing in the Senate rules embodied or even implied anything about the Senate's undying nature or what it might entail for its rules. This change inscribed for the first time in Senate rules what had heretofore been only a tradition and codified what some senators took to be the principal implication of the Senate as a continuing body. However, Rule V was not written primarily to enshrine a principle of Senate continuity; it was written to protect the filibuster from future threats. The revised language of Rule V was introduced and passed as part of an attempt to protect supermajority cloture from substantial reform by drawing on and codifying the continuing body doctrine in service of southern resistance to civil rights.

Senate obstruction or filibusters of civil rights measures in the postwar era was meeting increased opposition in the late 1950s in the wake of the 1954 *Brown* decision and an increasingly liberal Senate majority. Some northern Republican and Democratic senators were pushing for reform of Rule XXII, the cloture rule that empowered filibusters by requiring a two-thirds vote of all senators to end debate. Majority Leader Lyndon Johnson sought a compromise that would placate both reformers and the southern Democrats. Johnson's compromise lowered the cloture threshold from two-thirds of all members to two-thirds of those present, and it provided that cloture could be applied to any motion to proceed to consideration of a change in the rules. This was hardly major reform. But to smooth the path to this all but meaningless change by offering further protection to southern Democrats, Johnson added the language that altered Rule V to codify that the rules continued from one Congress to the next.

The Rule V language was sought particularly by Richard Russell, leader of the southern Democrats seeking first, last, and always to preserve their ability to filibuster any and all civil rights legislation. The amendment of Rule V was not a means to the end of protecting the filibuster as a matter of principle, it was another concession to racist southern senators seeking to protect their power to obstruct or prevent even the most limited efforts by Congress to protect the rights of African Americans.[64] This divided advocates of reform by confronting them with a no-win choice: go for mild filibuster reform to show change is possible but with it get a provision that would all but preclude future rule changes, or kill reform to stave off the enshrinement of the continuing body myth (again, applied only to Senate rules, not to other aspects of its business). But in the end, the compromise passed easily.[65] By combing the two-thirds threshold with Rule V's explicit mandate that the rules continue unless changed against the extraordinary odds set by Rule XXII, the Senate entrenched cloture from alteration by even substantial supermajorities.

As the means to this end, the revised Rule V became the most prominent and powerful acknowledgment of the circularity of the continuing body doctrine and its relationship to the Senate's tortured contrast between its lofty self-conceptions and the ugly politics those conceits attempted to obscure. As the 1959 reform debate drew to a close, Majority Leader Johnson was summing up what the compromise agreement would accomplish. "This resolution," Johnson concluded, "would write into the rules a simple statement affirming what seems no longer to be at issue. Namely, that the rules of the Senate shall continue in force, at all times, except as amended by the Senate. This preserves indisputably the character of the Senate as the one continuing body in our policy-making process."[66] Once again, as Johnson's words unintentionally confirmed, the Senate is a continuing body insofar as it chooses to behave like one for certain defined purposes and because it structures its rules accordingly, not because the Constitution made it so or obliges the Senate to act one way or another owing to staggered elections.

## House and Senate Elections: Not So Different after All

But is the Senate different from the House as a result of those staggered elections? Whether or not the Senate is a continuing body in any more than descriptive terms, its membership is determined in part by its staggered six-year terms relative to the two-year terms for the House. What

I have not considered to this point is whether this constitutional distinction has made a difference as far as membership and behavior are concerned, distinct from the debate about its status as a continuing body. Some aspects of this puzzle are complicated or unanswerable. I will address briefly the question most relevant to the concerns of this chapter: whether or not staggered terms produce a more stable Senate membership compared to the House. No doubt some founders recognized the buffering effect staggered elections could have, in theory, and it is fair to view them as a potential barrier to rapid change. But the historical record of the buffer in action is less neat. For one thing, for the first 125 years of its existence, the Senate was picked not by "voters" but by state legislatures. Election by state legislature was the constitutional safeguard for picking the Senate. House elections in the nineteenth century tended to be more volatile, but the relative contributions of staggered elections versus selection by state legislature would have to be disentangled, even if one suspects that staggered elections mattered quite a bit.[67]

Regardless, after senators became directly elected, House and Senate elections came to display some remarkable and persistent similarities that from an empirical perspective make the idea of the Senate as a continuing body look rather academic or abstract. For example, from 1946 through 2014 (a total of thirty-five elections), following a presidential or midterm election, an average of 87.8 percent of the Senate had served in the previous Congress (figure 5). While this sounds like an impressive level of continuity—arguably the kind of continuity that could be credited to staggered elections—the House has averaged nearly the same level of continuity despite all 435 seats being contested every election. Over the same period, an average of 84.4 percent of every new House consisted of members from the previous Congress, remarkably close to the Senate average of nearly 88 percent. Not infrequently an incoming House has been more "continuing" than the postelection Senate that same year. Eight of the thirty-five elections from 1946 to 2014 produced Congresses with a greater percentage of continuing representatives than senators, and two were all but ties.[68] As others have shown, in modern elections Senate incumbents have been, on average, more vulnerable than House incumbents.[69] If the counterfactual alternative is simultaneous six-year Senate terms, there is little doubt—assuming the same pattern of incumbency and congressional careers—that staggered elections increase change and dynamism rather than stability.

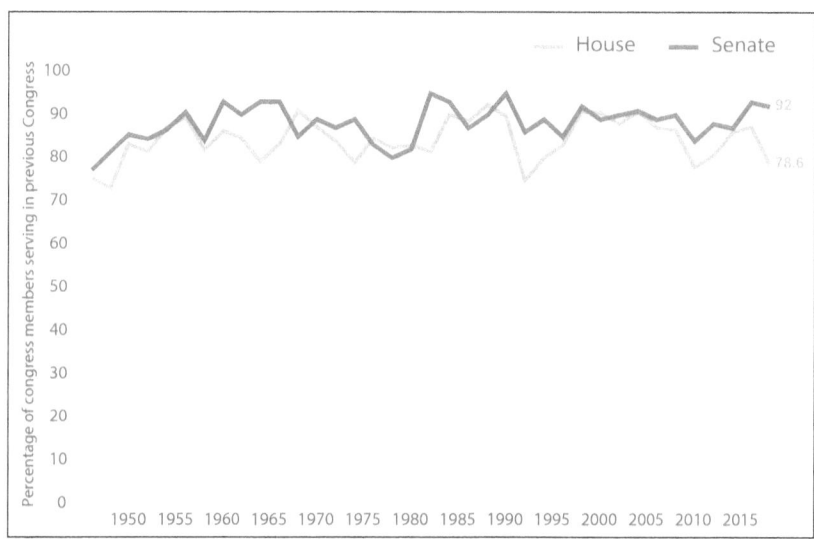

FIG. 5. Continuity of Senate and House membership, 1946–2018
*Data:* Brookings Institution, *Vital Statistics on Congress: Data on the U.S. Congress,* updated February 2021, https://www.brookings.edu/multi-chapter-report/vital-statistics-on-congress/.

Moreover, staggered elections aside, it is not clear that even the six-year term makes much of a difference in the relative behavior of senators and representatives. As I have shown, staggered terms were about rotation and change within the context of the longer term, which was the intended source of stability and conservatism. That is, if staggered elections do not result in a more stable membership in the Senate than in the House, then any behavioral differences can be attributed largely to the longer term. Political scientists have done some work on the impact of two- versus six-year terms. For example, do the one-third of senators who are up for election behave differently from the two-thirds who are not? The findings are, at best, ambiguous.[70] Effects are elusive, limited, and probably of a diminished nature in the contemporary era of the perpetual campaign, ceaseless fundraising, the 24/7 news cycle, and social media. In an atmosphere of hyperpartisanship, partisan sorting, and highly engineered districting, the partisan complexion of the state or district probably makes more difference than the electoral cycle of two- or six-year terms.

This brief dip into the empirical reality of bicameral elections and behavior cannot undermine the continuing body doctrine, which is based on the mere fact of staggered elections, regardless of their actual effects. But the historical pattern of House and Senate electoral outcomes shows that the concept, in addition to being institutionally incoherent, has almost no practical meaning.

## The Undying Body, or The Rights of the Living Dead

The irony is that staggered elections, a category of rotation intended to prevent the entrenchment or perpetuation of institutional power, produced instead the notion of an undying Senate, and are interpreted as a vital part of the Senate's conservative purpose. Senators and scholars alike will no doubt continue to debate the constitutional and institutional status of the doctrine. Let me reiterate my findings: staggered terms were for institutional accountability, not institutional entrenchment. The doctrine took a constitutional stipulation about the composition of the Senate—how it is elected—and turned it into a rule about the status and operation of the Senate, at least for the few things the Senate chooses. Again, whatever the exact mixture of motives and rationales for staggered elections, the irony is that this produced the notion of an undying Senate and is interpreted, against the grain of the records of the founding *and modern electoral history,* as a vital part of the Senate's conservative purpose. For the Senate to entrench its decisions, to protect them from the preferences of a new Senate majority, is the opposite of the main intention behind staggered terms, even if that original purpose might not deter senators' desire to apply this particular self-conception.

In fact, the continuing body doctrine takes the Senate beyond the worst fears of rotation's advocates insofar as it entrenches not simply the power of current members but also the decisions of those who are no longer in office, a majority that no longer exists.[71] As a result, the new majority—something that rotation was intended to produce—is effectively anchored to the past. Anchored to the decisions, in many cases, of the long dead and departed. Senator Thomas Walsh, as part of his all-day speech in 1917 excoriating the continuing body doctrine, lamented the Senate's reification of its rules. Walsh took a moment to both acknowledge the general wisdom of his predecessors yet poke a bit of fun at the rigidity of the Senate's adherence to the past. Quoting Lord Byron, Walsh noted of ancestral senators "that we are required . . . to salute them as: 'The dead but sceptered sovereigns, who still rule our spirits from their urns.'"[72]

It is also a case in point that the supposed Senate principle of "minority" voice or rights grates loudly against the continuing body claim. After all, if minorities have special rights or protections in the Senate, then how is it that the approximate one-third of "new" senators after any election can be denied a say in the rules by a purely hypothetical majority of the two-thirds who constitute the continuing Senate after any election? Moreover, it is not clear that the continuing two-thirds have any special status since they probably never had the opportunity to vote on the things that are being protected by the Senate's being a continuing body. Most of that continuing two-thirds were at one time in the not very distant past, as individuals, part of the new one-third. In short, what I have called descriptive or mere continuity—the continuity structured by staggered elections—is really "temporary" or "transient" continuity, and any continuity beyond that in process or action is a matter of Senate choice, based on a particular political theology.

The continuing body is there to protect the decision of a majority or supermajority that no longer exists and may not have for generations. And thanks to Rule V, the minority (or majority) might not even have the chance to debate, let alone change, the decision from long ago. Isn't it a particular egregious violation of rights, minority or otherwise, to be silenced or stymied, not by the living but by the dead?

Not if you are Senator David Turpie. In 1893, Turpie, an Indiana Democrat, used the continuing body notion to take the argument about Senate rules one step closer to the Constitution. "Is not the Constitution of the United States the will of the majority," asked Turpie during a debate over a proposed cloture rule, "a will of the majority, permanent, enduring; a law for all generations? Are not the rules of the Senate of the United States, most of them a hundred years old, the will of the majority, the permanent will?"[73] Senate rules become a form of higher law simply by their rigged or enforced endurance, the living legacy of the long departed. And no such legacy has had a more exalted status or more impact—especially on the fate of civil rights—than Senate Rule XXII, the provision that required, prior to 2013, a supermajority to close debate on any matter before the Senate.

# 5
# The Filibuster
FROM SOUTHERN CITADEL TO THE SIXTY-VOTE SENATE

Nostra Culpa: The Senate Apologizes for Failing to
Pass Antilynching Legislation and Misses the Point

On June 13, 2005, by a voice vote the Senate passed a resolution apologizing "to the victims of lynching for the failure of the Senate to enact anti-lynching legislation."[1] The resolution and apology referred to the long and bleak era from the end of the nineteenth century to the mid-twentieth during which more than four thousand African Americans were lynched and almost no one was punished by local and state authorities. Indeed, and instead, lynchings—defined as the killing of a person or persons (as by hanging) by mob action without legal sanction—were not infrequently a form of public entertainment done in broad daylight with the full knowledge of both local law enforcement and the local press.[2]

Apologies and regret for the shortcomings and failures of the United States in regard to various aspects of slavery and civil rights are not novel. What made this apology interesting was that the Senate was singling itself out. It was a Senate resolution about the Senate—not a joint or concurrent resolution to be passed by the House or possibly signed by the president. Senator Mary Landrieu of Louisiana, one of the resolution's principal authors and sponsors, put it this way:

> Without question, there have been other grave injustices committed in the noble exercise of establishing this great democracy. Some have already been acknowledged and addressed by this and previous Congresses, and our work continues. However, there may be no other injustice in American history for which the Senate so uniquely bears responsibility. In refusing to take up legislation passed by the House of Representatives on three separate occasions and requested by seven Presidents from William Henry Harrison to Harry Truman, the Senate engaged in a different kind of culpability.[3]

The speeches that preceded and continued after the voice vote focused on the horrors of lynching and related civil rights matters in US history. Many senators covered this in considerable detail and with apparent emotion and sincerity. All fine and good, except that the resolution was about the Senate's failure, not the horrors and national shame of lynching. Only a few senators even mentioned the cause—the only cause—of the Senate's failure, almost in passing, and none bothered to do more than that. The cause was the filibuster. Despite majority support in each case, the antilynching measures were, in the face of filibusters, withdrawn from Senate consideration.

The resolution does not use the word or concept. Instead, as we have seen, the resolution apologizes for the "failure" of the Senate to pass antilynching legislation, also noting that the Senate "failed" to enact such legislation on more than one occasion. Twenty-seven senators (seventeen Democrats and ten Republicans) offered remarks on the resolution covering twenty-five pages or approximately 35,000 words in the *Congressional Record*. Only six senators (four Democrats and two Republicans) invoked the filibuster as the cause of the failure.[4] And the word "filibuster" was used a total of seven times in any form. The senators who filled pages and pages of the *Congressional Record* with excruciating details of the history of lynching, including the stories and names of individual victims, barely mention the filibuster, cloture, or minority obstruction.

Only Utah Republican Bob Bennett, in the final remarks on the resolution, stated the matter plainly: "I note that it was the filibuster that made it possible for the Senate to be the body that blocked this legislation in the past. I would hope that in the future, we would all realize that the filibuster should be used for more beneficial purposes than that."[5] Bennett was alone in linking the filibuster's regrettable past to its present and future use, even if the connection he was drawing did not transcend partisanship. This resolution of apology happened to come amid a small crisis over the use of the filibuster by Democrats to block President Bush's judicial nominations. Although more Democrats than Republicans mentioned the filibuster in their remarks about the apology resolution, there is little doubt that Bennett's more precise and pointed comment was directed at current events and Democratic obstruction of the nominees.

On the one hand, senators took time for this unprecedented collective recognition of its institutional failures more than seventy years earlier, when it, hardly for the first or the last time, failed to protect the rights of African Americans. Yet on the other, even when this rare moment of bipartisanship prevailed amid the increasingly rancorous and polarized battles between majority and minority in this century, the Senate still missed the point about the filibuster and, therefore, about itself.

I would argue that instead of representing an exception, even if a particularly abject one, to the Senate's otherwise distinguished history as the world's greatest deliberative body, the sad history of antilynching legislation is much more the rule. As far as civil rights are concerned, the Senate had much more to apologize for than this one issue. Moreover, the real "failure" of the Senate lies much less in this particular case from the early twentieth century than in that institution's ongoing failure to realize and correct the dysfunction and injustice of its rules of procedure and debate that empower and encourage what we commonly think of as filibusters. The minority obstruction and vetoes those rules sanction created the "sixty-vote" or "supermajority Senate," that is, a Senate characterized by the need to attain a supermajority of sixty votes to get almost anything done.

This chapter provides a history of the rise and dysfunction of the sixty-vote Senate, making a normative argument about its purpose, value, and even constitutionality. Unlike most work on the Senate's peculiar procedures, the central objective of the chapter is not so much to describe supermajority processes and their effects as to evaluate them. Supermajority cloture, created as a way to limit filibusters and obstruction, instead and ironically became the principal cause of the Senate's political dysfunction, as exemplified by the apology. For several decades this dysfunction was closely tied to efforts to defend and maintain white supremacy. More recently, the damage to accountable and effective government has been more general, especially in an era of strong partisan polarization. Overall, supermajority cloture, aided and abetted by the mythology of minority rights and the continuing body doctrine derived from equal representation and staggered terms, distorted the Senate's constitutional purpose and place in the system of separation of powers and checks and balances. This chapter documents how that came to be, and argues that supermajority cloture is very hard to justify in theory and practice. The filibuster fails on pragmatic grounds alone. Instead of being a central element in what makes the Senate allegedly the "world's greatest deliberative body," the filibuster is counterproductive and undermines deliberation. Moreover, the supermajority Senate does not square with the republican theory of government in the Constitution. This version of the Senate is not based in the Constitution but rather violates the founding architecture of institutional power.

## Rules of Procedure, Extended Debate, Filibusters, and Cloture

How did the Senate get to this point? How did a rule of the Senate that was created as a procedure—and one that would most likely be used quite rarely—*to limit* filibusters become not only the primary mechanism *to support and facilitate* filibusters and obstruction but also the de facto supermajority decision rule for most important Senate votes? How was it that political scientists and journalists come to refer to this body as the sixty-vote Senate or supermajority Senate?

Let's start with the fundamentals. Every decision-making body sooner or later develops and codifies rules for how to proceed. Such rules of procedure, or rules of order, structure how that body considers and decides on its business. Many Americans are familiar with the title if not the details of *Robert's Rules of Order*, first published in 1876.[6] Drawing on British parliamentary procedures, Henry Martin Robert created a manual of procedures that could be used by nearly any organization that makes decisions. Despite the variations from student and city councils to state legislatures, Congress, the British House of Commons, and the UN General Assembly, these rules of procedure cover the same necessities and often in much the same way.

One necessity is the structure of what we can loosely call "debate." Who can speak, when, for how long, and what motions are allowable? In particular, how is consideration or debate brought to a close to make a final decision on the bill or motion? Legislative bodies and other decision-making organizations typically have one or more ways, governed directly or indirectly by majority rule, of ending consideration of the matter on the floor or bringing it to a vote.

Most of us, whether we have participated on student councils, school boards, or in local government, are aware that among such procedures are motions to postpone or table, which remove the matter at hand from further consideration at least temporarily. A less familiar one is referred to as the "previous question," a nondebatable motion leading directly to a vote on whether the main question should now be put to a vote. If decided in the affirmative, debate is immediately closed and the vote is taken on the main question. If the previous question motion is defeated, then consideration of the main motion continues. Indeed, the first rules written and agreed to by the Senate in April 1789 stipulated that "when a question is before the Senate, no motion shall be received unless for an amendment, for the previous question, or for postponing the main question, or to commit, or to adjourn"—all decided by simple majority votes.[7]

However, when the Senate revised its rules in 1806, it dropped the previous question. Scholars agree that the Senate felt such a provision was unnecessary in light of the small size of the body and its ability to hear from any or all senators on any issue, and the Senate retained other ways to end debate, including the motions to postpone or adjourn.[8] From 1806 until 1917, for 110 years, the Senate had no other provision to close debate if any senator wished to speak. It also had no general restrictions on how long a senator could speak or on what subject. In fact, prior to 1917, Senate rules allowed essentially unlimited debate. For obvious reasons, senators have preferred and used the phrase "extended debate." For more than a century, Senate debate was governed by forms of unanimous consent. Debate closed when no one else wanted to hold the floor, when every senator present agreed, in effect, that debate was over.

The ability of a senator to speak was protected by the right of recognition and noninterruption in what is now senate Rule XIX on debate: "When a Senator desires to speak, he shall rise and address the Presiding Officer, and shall not proceed until he is recognized, and the Presiding Officer shall recognize the Senator who shall first address him. No Senator shall interrupt another Senator in debate without his consent, and to obtain such consent he shall first address the Presiding Officer, and no Senator shall speak more than twice upon any one question in debate on the same legislative day without leave of the Senate, which shall be determined without debate."[9] The power to speak is augmented by the fact that the Senate has no general germaneness rule. That is, once recognized, a senator does not have to address the matter under consideration. Speech or amendments not germane to the issue at hand are not subject to a point of order.

These two simple principles embedded in the Senate rules, but backed as well by long tradition, norms, and precedents in the form of rulings by the presiding officer, produced the power of the individual senator to filibuster. Filibuster refers to the use of obstructionist tactics, especially prolonged speechmaking, for the purpose of delaying or preventing legislative action. It is, in the words of the Senate's own website, an "informal term for any attempt to block or delay Senate action on a bill or other matter by debating it at length, by offering numerous procedural motions, or by any other delaying or obstructive actions."[10]

Not every long debate qualifies as a filibuster, but a minority of senators can use various tactics, including holding the floor, with the obvious purpose of stopping a measure, even one with clear majority support, from receiving a final vote. The classic if somewhat mythical filibuster amounted to a physical and psychological contest of wills and endurance as the filibustering minority held the floor for as long as possible, preventing action by a frustrated but determined majority. But filibusters and obstruction were also governed by other factors, including norms that limited its use and a less busy legislative schedule that allowed for greater flexibility in debates. Moreover, filibusters and extended debate were not restricted to the Senate. Both characterized the nineteenth-century House, at times more than they did the Senate. As an early scholar of the filibuster observed, "Tactics patently obstructive, however, were characteristic of the House long before they became common in the Senate."[11] And more recent scholarship confirms this.[12] The Senate is remembered for its "golden age" of great debates in the mid-nineteenth century, featuring the likes of Clay, Webster, and Calhoun. But the House also had lengthy and sophisticated debates on the same great national questions. They just weren't noticed or covered as much as those in the Senate.[13]

But the Senate and the country changed around 1900, and those changes put some pressure on extended debate. In 1926, as part of a discussion about the regulation of debate in the Senate, Frank W. Mondell, who had been a Republican representative from Wyoming for twenty-six years, offered a nice if somewhat exaggerated summary of the original environment and the changes that made some procedure for closure or cloture (a word derived from a French term) seem logical if not universally desirable:

> There was a time when the fact that the Senate had no cloture was of little importance. Originally it had but 26 Members, and there was so little for it to do that time hung heavily on the hands of the Senators and there was no reason for hurrying anything. In those days and for a long time thereafter no one thought of conducting a filibuster or talking a bill to death. As no one thought of doing it, why have a rule to prevent it? But times and conditions and the Senate have changed. August and dignified representatives of sovereign States, chosen by carefully selected legislatures, have made way for Senators the products of primaries and of

universal suffrage. The Senate grew to a membership of 96 when all our contiguous continental territory came to Statehood.[14]

By the time Mondell offered this assessment, the United States had become a predominantly urban nation and the industrial giant of the world with greater involvement in international affairs. A larger and directly elected Senate faced a bigger and more complicated legislative agenda. While the Seventeenth Amendment, which produced direct election of the Senate, did not change everything, it did make senators more accountable to the public and perhaps more predisposed to use all the tools at their disposal to represent their constituents. In addition, the presidency and increasingly the bureaucratic executive branch were, if unevenly, showing their potential under such presidents as Theodore Roosevelt and Woodrow Wilson as the dynamic and activist branch of government.

Most of the same forces affected the House as well, which by the start of the twentieth century had 386 members. As the House grew, it tended to restrict debate and dilatory tactics, even if lengthy debate and obstruction were still possible and practiced. The House's original rules contained a "previous question" motion, but each member was entitled to speak once after its adoption; that is, debate on the main question did not automatically end.[15] In 1841, with a membership of 223 and some filibusters under its belt, the House added a notable restriction on debate to its rules, limiting members to one hour of debate on a particular matter before the House.[16] Or, in the words of the current rule, a member "may not occupy more than one hour in debate on a question in the House or in the Committee of the Whole House on the state of the Union except as otherwise provided in this rule."[17] Another rule specified that "remarks in debate shall be confined to the question under debate, avoiding personality."[18] In other words, debate had to be germane, unlike in the Senate. Other details and developments need not detain us, but by the early twentieth century, the House had instituted various rules of procedure that were providing effective majority rule and control by the party with the most seats.[19]

Meanwhile, the late nineteenth-century Senate was feeling the effects of minority obstruction. Its ability to take effective action was suffering along with its public reputation. This was an era of intense partisanship and sectional tensions, and senators were growing accustomed to the exploitation of the rules in service of the resulting battles between parties and regional interests. Summarizing this era, Franklin Burdette claimed that "the power of the Senate lay not in votes but in sturdy tongues and iron wills. The premium rested not upon ability and statesmanship but upon effrontery and audacity."[20] The *Congressional Record* is replete with filibustering by individual or small groups of senators. And many among them made no pretense about their means and end: they made clear to their colleagues that they would talk about whatever they wished and that their goal was to kill any given measure or compel a compromise the majority did not want.

Moreover, until the Twentieth Amendment in 1933, Congress met after the elections in November of even-numbered years for a "short" or "lame duck" session that expired on March 4, the date set for the inauguration of new Congresses and presidents. One well-known problem with this arrangement was that the "old" Congress had nearly four months to meet and transact business while the newly elected Congress waited its turn. Particularly in the Senate, the March 4 deadline offered the temptation to obstruct as Congress attempted to finish its business. And so this short session became a particular target for filibusters. In turn, widespread knowledge of and disgust over this tactic was an impetus for what became the Twentieth Amendment, which moved up the meeting date for the incoming Congress to early January. While the Senate occasionally had fine debates about important questions, too often the right to speak and the power to use dilatory motions were in service of less noble purposes. For example, near the end of the lame duck session in 1903, Senator "Pitchfork Ben" Tillman threatened that unless and until a $47,000 claim by South Carolina for expenses from the War of 1812 was included in a supplementary appropriation bill, he would read from a nearby pile of books until Congress was forced to adjourn. He got his way, as did others using such tactics.[21] Supporting a Republican short-session filibuster in early 1917 aimed at running out the clock on the Democratic legislative program in general and a Wilson war measure in particular, Ohio senator and future president Warren Harding held the floor for parts of two days, during which he regaled his colleagues with a story about his marital infidelity in Paris (his wife got a Parisian bonnet of her choosing for being such a good sport about his "night off without any inquiries afterwards").[22]

## Cloture: The Senate Tries to Limit Filibusters

However flip the future president's comments, his lengthy speech was part of the dramatic end-of-session filibuster that provoked a change in the Senate rules to limit such calculated obstruction. Filibusters and obstruction had been increasing. In the thirty-three years from 1880 to 1913 there had been twenty-one filibusters, significantly under one per year. In the four years from 1913 to early 1917, fifteen filibusters, or nearly four per year, occurred.[23] The consequence of such regular and persistent filibusters and obstruction was an early twentieth-century Senate often in disarray and disrepute, even if, depending on the issue, many in the nation supported particular filibusters. It took special circumstances, however, for the Senate, which had operated more or less successfully for more than a century without a procedural motion to end debate, to adopt supermajority cloture in 1917.

As with many important changes in American politics, war was involved. Woodrow Wilson, who had just been reelected president in November 1916 with the self-righteous slogan "He kept us out of the war," was just a few months later, and with even greater self-righteousness and certitude, leading the country into war, which Congress would declare on April 6, 1917. Meanwhile, Wilson was pushing a bill through Congress to arm merchant ships against attacks by German submarines (the German resumption of unrestricted submarine warfare at the end of January had been an important factor pushing Wilson to support a declaration of war). The bill sailed through the House on a vote of 400–13 only to run aground in the Senate on the shoals of a filibuster conducted by what the president labeled "a little group of willful men" who had "rendered the great government of the United States helpless and contemptible." Led by Robert LaFollette, these senators were able—with the help of Senator Harding, among many others—to run out the clock on the Sixty-Fourth Congress in the climactic example of a short-session filibuster. "Never had a filibuster," according to one scholar, "so stirred the public mind." And that public mind "was in agreement with the President: the situation had become unbearable and the Senate should at last be brought to provide the remedy."[24] Wilson then decided he had the authority to arm ships without congressional action. He nevertheless called a special session of the new Senate for the explicit purpose of amending the rules to curb filibusters.[25] The Senate was under the gun, and the vast majority of senators were ready to act.

On March 8, 1917, and after a relatively short debate, the Senate added a rule of procedure that, for the first time since 1806, provided a motion and mechanism for bringing debate to a close. Referred to as "cloture," this amendment to Rule XXII, in its original version, provided for a vote to end debate on any "pending measure" before the Senate. Rule XXII as amended that year required two-thirds of those voting to invoke cloture. Instead of a simple majority a supermajority was necessary, and two-thirds was a tall hurdle. Moreover, the rule also created the potential for a lengthy debate even after a successful vote on a cloture motion by allowing each senator to speak for a maximum of one hour after cloture was invoked.[26] The moderate nature of the proposed rule facilitated the decision. Some senators wanted majority cloture; some wanted no change whatsoever. Several senators predicted that such a high threshold would be unlikely to do much to tame obstruction.[27] This was anything but a majoritarian gag rule.

Unlike the Seventeenth Amendment, which had to scale the heights of the Constitution's amendment process, cloture was just a change in the Senate rules requiring only a majority vote of its members. Whereas the direct election amendment received considerable fanfare over the years of its long march from proposal to ratification, cloture was the result of a very brief but intense burst of political pressure. Nevertheless, these two transformations marked a sea change in the Senate, seemingly bringing it into the twentieth century of industrial democracy by creating a Senate attuned to the popular will and able to take action. Whereas the constitutional change to direct election quickly became unremarkable and unnoted, the effects of supermajority cloture grew and became increasingly, if still episodically, controversial.

Although many recognized the somewhat compromised and moderate nature of the reform, supermajority cloture was produced as a way to bring minority obstruction under control. Like the unintended consequences of many reforms, however, the effect was at first ambiguous and then quickly on its way to becoming counterproductive. Cloture evolved into a powerful tool for obstructing the Senate's business, magnifying the power of Senate minorities and even individual senators. Before Rule XXII, filibusters were more or less effective, but the responsibility—in principle and mostly in practice—was on the person or persons holding the floor to retain control.[28] The implementation of a cloture procedure did not change everything, but it did have the effect of shifting the burden more to the majority, again in both principle and practice. The majority in favor of a measure or particular action has to actively muster a supermajority to successfully invoke cloture. The burden shifted from keep going if you can to stop us if you can. You have the tool; use it.

This shift was subtle at first because the rule was not frequently used or exploited by either minorities to thwart the majority or by the majority to control the minority. As many studies have shown, not much changed in the aftermath of Rule XXII. One metric is the number of cloture motions, cloture votes, and successful invocations of cloture over time (figure 6). From 1917 through the 1950s cloture motions were rare (only thirty in forty-four years), as were votes on those motions (twenty-three total). And cloture was invoked only four times. Things picked up a bit in the 1960s, but it was not until the 1970s—with the numbers for that decade far exceeding the totals from the preceding forty-four years—that cloture became a commonplace feature of Senate proceedings.

Such statistics, however, obscure the controversy that arose periodically over filibusters, controversy almost always due to one issue: the attempts, however limited or far-reaching, by Congress to protect the rights of African Americans, and the formidable intensity of the efforts by southern senators to protect white supremacy in their states. Such legislative efforts were not the only objects of filibusters from the late 1800s through the mid-1900s but they were the most frequent and by far the most intense targets.[29] The extent to which the filibuster—whether before or after the creation of the cloture rule—was associated with white supremacy was evident even in the 1917 debate that produced supermajority cloture. Mississippi's James K. Vardaman, who is famous for opining, on another occasion, that "if it is necessary every Negro in the state will be lynched; it will be done to maintain white supremacy," revealed as much in his March 8 speech on cloture.[30] Senator Vardaman let it be known that he was in favor of the proposed cloture rule even though "unlimited debate has served the people of the South" in the past. What had changed? Not Vardaman's heart. Instead, the former animus between North and South no longer existed. The old "spirit" that sought "to put black heels upon white necks and enthrone congenital incompetency . . . no longer exists among our friends, the white people of the North." In its stead was "broad patriotism, and disposition to do the right thing—the thing needful for the preservation of the purity of the white race and the conservation of our civilization—among the northern Republicans as there is among the northern Democrats."[31] Vardaman's political assessment was

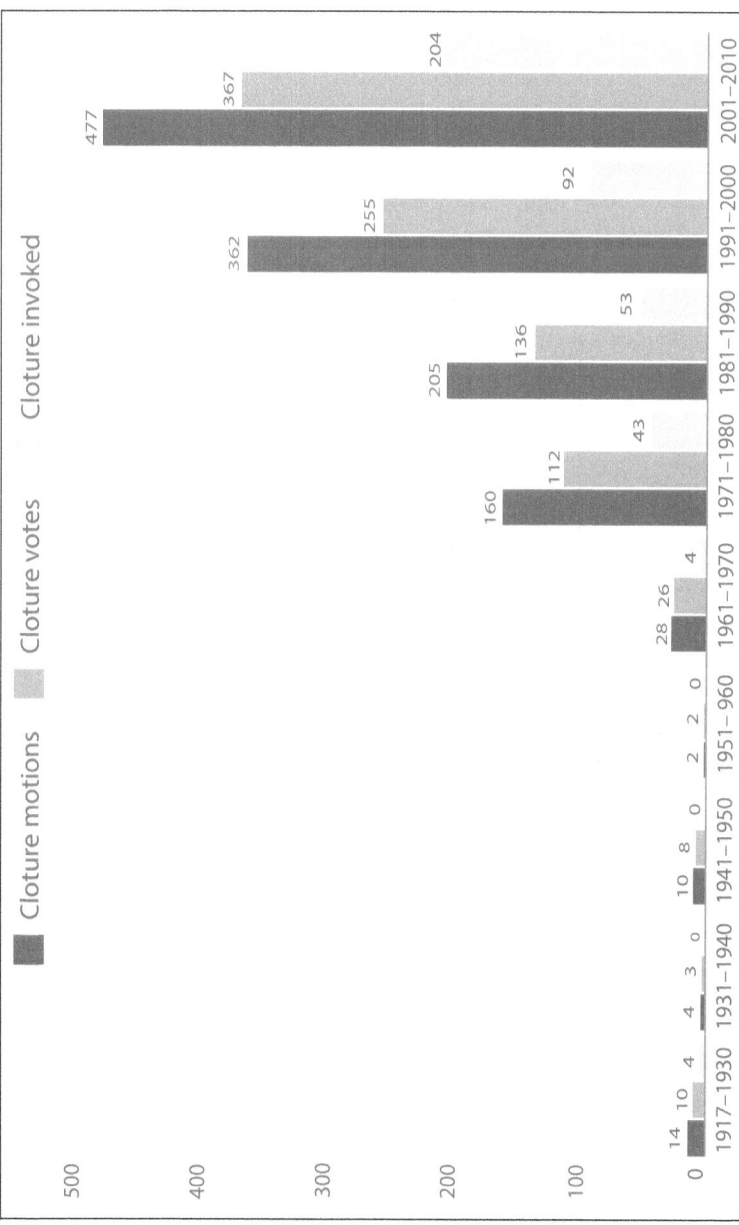

FIG. 6. Cloture in the Senate, 1917–2010
*Data*: US Senate, Legislation and Records, https://www.senate.gov/legislative/cloture/clotureCounts.htm.

in for a somewhat bumpy ride, but supermajority cloture would be there to serve white supremacy, if not the people of the South as a whole.

## The Filibuster and the Defense of White Supremacy

During the decades of the late nineteenth and early twentieth centuries the most noted—and, for some years, celebrated—filibusters targeted and destroyed the few attempts made by Congress at civil rights legislation (table 1). By the end of the nineteenth century, the Fifteenth Amendment's uncomplicated mandate that the right to vote "shall not be denied or abridged on account of race" was being systematically undermined by the Democratic parties in control of states of the former Confederacy and enforced by vigilante terrorism. When the Republicans swept the elections of 1888, putting Benjamin Harrison in the White House after four years of Democrat Grover Cleveland and six years of Democratic control of the House, they were determined to enact their agenda. Although hardly a top party priority, one element was legislation to protect voting rights in the South. The resulting federal elections bill of 1890 would have implemented indirect mechanisms for limited oversight of national elections by federal courts. The weak and likely ineffective measure nevertheless was dubbed the "Force Bill" by southerners, and the moniker stuck. Despite this opposition, the bill enjoyed President Harrison's support and passed the House. Once in the Senate, and layered in partisan and regional politics, the filibuster by southern Democrats consumed "thirty-three calendar days" from December 2, 1890, through January 26, 1891, in "the most remarkable spectacle of obstruction then known to the Senate."[32] A long and complex story, the fate of the bill involved as well a subsidiary southern filibuster of an attempt by Senate Majority Leader Nelson Aldrich to get a parliamentary ruling to end the filibuster on the elections bill. Eventually the Senate gave up, and the bill was set aside for good.[33] With the elections bill foremost in mind, and from his perspective as a US representative in 1897, Alabaman Henry Clayton lauded the Senate "as the one deliberative body of the Congress; that Senate which has in the past, when all else failed, been the last refuge of the people of my beloved Southland."[34] As late as 1917 Vardaman and other southern senators would invoke the Force Bill as the great threat thwarted by the filibuster.

As moderate as it was, the elections bill of 1890 was an explicit attempt to enforce the voting rights of African Americans. Southern senators,

TABLE 1. Civil rights legislation, constitutional amendments, and Senate rules reforms filibustered or opposed by southern senators, 1890–1975

| | |
|---|---|
| 1890 | Federal Election Bill |
| 1913 | Constitutional amendment: Direct Election of Senators (Seventeenth Amendment) |
| 1919 | Constitutional amendment: Female suffrage (Nineteenth Amendment) |
| 1922 | Antilynching |
| 1935 | Antilynching |
| 1937–38 | Antilynching |
| 1942 | Abolish Poll Tax |
| 1944 | Abolish Poll Tax |
| 1946 | Abolish Poll Tax (preemptive cloture vote) |
| 1946 | Fair Employment (FEPC) |
| 1948 | Abolish Poll Tax |
| 1949 | Cloture rule reform |
| 1950 | Fair Employment (FEPC) |
| 1957 | Civil Rights |
| 1960 | Civil Rights |
| 1961 | Cloture rule reform |
| 1962 | Literacy Test for Voting |
| 1963 | Cloture rule reform |
| 1964 | Civil Rights |
| 1965 | Voting Rights |
| 1967 | Cloture rule reform |
| 1968 | Civil rights workers |
| 1969 | Cloture rule reform |
| 1970 | Constitutional amendment: Abolish Electoral College/Direct Election of President |
| 1971 | Cloture rule reform |
| 1975 | Cloture rule reform |

*Sources:* Congressional Research Service, "Senate Cloture Rule: Limitation of Debate in the Senate of the United States" (Washington, DC: US Government Printing Office, 2011); Lauren C. Bell, *Filibustering in the U.S. Senate* (Amherst, NY: Cambria Press, 2011).

however, were on their guard for any possible opening for federal interference. As we have seen, they put up a fight against what would become the Seventeenth Amendment because direct election of senators might have created such a breach. They unsuccessfully sought a change to the proposed amendment to prohibit any additional congressional regulation of Senate elections. A few years later, when female suffrage's time finally came, southern senators resisted, largely for the same reason—the threat that such a broad expansion of the suffrage would invite intervention by doubling the number of Blacks in the South whose right to vote was denied. Whether southern senators engaged in a filibuster is less clear, but they fought the amendment and in 1918 prevented its passage in the face of passage by the House and direct support from the president, fellow southerner and Democrat Woodrow Wilson. The amendment cleared the Senate in 1919 but nearly fell short during ratification, in large measure because of the opposition of most southern states.[35] But, to be clear, southern racists did not oppose all forms of constitutional imposition or government intrusion into what had hitherto been state prerogatives, as long as they had nothing to do with white supremacy. The South readily embraced the other two "progressive" amendments produced in the same eight-year period as the Seventeenth and Nineteenth Amendments. Both the Sixteenth, allowing Congress to create a national income tax, and the Eighteenth, the national prohibition of "intoxicating liquors," received the support of southern senators and rapid ratification by their states.

The first direct legislative threat to white supremacy was taking shape as the women's suffrage movement battled toward victory. This came in the form of antilynching legislation supported by the president and the House of Representatives. The first such bill was introduced by Representative Leonidas Dyer, a Missouri Republican, in 1918. The legislation would have made lynching a federal crime punishable in federal courts and subjected states and localities to liability for damages. Making it to the House floor in 1922, the Dyer bill passed by a vote of 231–119 in the overwhelmingly Republican chamber, with only a handful of Democrats voting for the measure.[36] The Senate too was controlled by Republicans, who constituted almost 62 percent of the chamber. Despite the House vote, support from President Harding, and a favorable reporting from committee, the bill was withdrawn from Senate consideration after several days of southern filibustering following its introduction on November 27.[37] Thus defeated, similar legislation did not make a return until the early 1930s. In 1935 and 1938 antilynching bills were once again defeated by southern filibusters despite having majority support.[38]

The Senate's belated 2005 apology for its repeated failures underscores the fact that for much of the twentieth century, these early civil rights measures were explicitly or implicitly in the pantheon of supposedly ill-advised legislation stopped by the Senate filibuster. Writing in 1926, Columbia University law professor Lindsay Rogers argued that "no really meritorious measure has been defeated and some vicious proposals have been killed" by the filibuster. "Principal items" on Rogers's brief list were the elections Force Bill of 1890 and the antilynching bill of 1922.[39] In his comprehensive 1938 history of the Senate, George Haynes mentions several bills that died at the hands of Senate obstruction, including the civil rights measures, bills that otherwise "would have accorded ill with the sober second thought of the American people."[40] However dated and misguided from our perspective, such assessments both reflected and shaped perceptions of the filibuster's importance in making the Senate the world's greatest deliberative body.

Although typically supportive of the extended debate protected by the cloture rule, southern senators could themselves get annoyed by what they perceived as obstruction, with the occasional ironic result. As the clock was running out on the last day of the Sixty-Ninth Congress in 1927, Alabama senator and self-described white supremacist J. Thomas Heflin rose to denounce a filibuster—one that was derailing all Senate business—of a bill to extend the life of a select committee investigating election campaigns. In doing so at some length, Heflin perhaps unwittingly was aiding the filibuster. Spurred on by some of his colleagues, particularly George Moses of New Hampshire, Heflin vented his hatred for Catholics and Blacks while defending his earlier filibuster of the antilynching bill. Moses even goaded Heflin into a lengthy account of an incident nearly twenty years earlier when then US representative Heflin shot two people, one intentionally (a Black man) and the other inadvertently (a white man) from a Washington, D.C., streetcar after allegedly defending "a white woman against the insults and the insolence of a brutal, drunken negro." Heflin, at least by his account, then took the white man to the hospital and later paid for his medical treatment and time lost from work.[41] Heflin could not help but inject his inveterate racism even into comments originally directed against a filibuster. Unfortunately, during these decades such casual racism in Senate debate was far from the exception. Having read extensively in the *Congressional Record* of the late nineteenth and early twentieth centuries for various research projects related to the Senate, I would argue that a great deal of Senate debate and filibustering was a reflection of that era's racialized conception of manhood, the glory and honor of Anglo-Saxon manhood premised on racial superiority, which transcended party and region and was elevated still further by senatorial status. Senators invoked minority rights but were often practicing little more than manly posturing amid a prevailing consensus on racial hierarchy and social order.

If antilynching legislation was the issue of the 1920s and 1930s, attempts to abolish poll taxes were the focus of the 1940s, and the efforts in this direction were no more successful. Poll taxes were one of the central tools of disenfranchisement in the South. Every state in the former Confederacy had administered one version or another of this device, many of which were added to state constitutions or laws in the Jim Crow era.[42] Four times, in 1942, 1944, 1946, and 1948, bills to abolish poll taxes were stopped by filibusters led by southern Democrats.[43] In each case defeat in the Senate had been preceded by the bill's decisive victory in the House.[44] Even a wartime measure to temporarily suspend poll taxes for African American soldiers was a tough sell in the Senate, but it prevailed because southern senators recognized the dangers of filibustering such a limited and popular measure.[45] The problem of poll taxes would not be solved until the practice was banned by the Twenty-Fourth Amendment in 1964, with Tennessee and Florida the lone southern states supporting ratification.[46]

The years after the war saw the most intense confrontation between civil rights and the Senate filibuster. For a quarter century, postwar civil rights measures, both modest and far-reaching, were killed or obstructed by southern filibusters. Frustrations with the filibusters of civil rights measures in turn motivated the Senate majority over the years to seek adjustments to Rule XXII, efforts that were then filibustered.[47] A few senators wanted some form of majority cloture, but others sought to preserve supermajority cloture even if modified. One of the most consistent proposals, though not successful until 1975, was to lower the threshold for cloture from two-thirds to three-fifths. The results, until 2013, were a few compromises that mostly eased but sustained supermajority cloture. The many attempts and proposals produced six changes from 1949 through 1986 (table 2), with the most important and contested changes all spurred by, and subject to, southern filibusters.

TABLE 2. The evolution of the filibuster: Senate rules governing debate

| | |
|---|---|
| 1806 | The Senate omits the "previous question" motion from its rules. |
| 1806–1917 | No rule allowing a vote to end debate on a matter before the Senate and the ability of senators to hold the floor indefinitely protected particularly by Rule XIX. Only minor parliamentary precedents that restricted some obstructive tactics. |
| 1917 | Rule XXII adopted with a provision for cloture by a vote of two-thirds of the Senate present and voting. |
| 1949 | Rule XXII amended to (1) raise the threshold to two-thirds of the entire Senate membership and (2) specify that cloture can apply to procedural motions (such as the motion to proceed), except motions to consider changes in Senate rules. |
| 1959 | Rule XXII amended to (1) lower the threshold back to two-thirds of those present and voting and (2) specify that cloture can be applied to motions to consider changes in Senate rules. |
| 1975 | Rule XXII amended to lower the threshold to three-fifths of the entire Senate membership (or sixty votes) for cloture on all matters except consideration of changes in Senate rules, which retained the threshold of two-thirds present and voting. |
| 1979 | Rule XXII amended to cap post-cloture debate at 100 hours. |
| 1986 | Rule XXII amended to reduce post-cloture debate to thirty hours. |
| 2013 | Rule XXII *interpreted* to mean that the threshold for cloture for all nominations other than for the Supreme Court is a simple majority. |
| 2017 | Rule XXII *interpreted* to mean that the threshold for cloture for all nominations, including the Supreme Court, is a simple majority. |

*Sources:* Congressional Research Service, "Senate Cloture Rule: Limitation of Debate in the Senate of the United States," (Washington, DC: US Government Printing Office, 2011); Sarah A. Binder, and Steven S. Smith, *Politics or Principle? Filibustering in the United States Senate* (Washington, DC: Brookings Institution Press, 1997), 7.

Following filibusters of Truman's civil rights agenda, which included a poll tax ban and legislation to create a permanent fair practices employment committee, the Senate began in 1949 one of the longest debates and filibusters in its history, over cloture reform. In many ways, this fight over filibuster reform was a surrogate debate about civil rights. "The only reason for the effort to amend Rule XXII," Senator Kenneth McKellar of Tennessee told his colleagues, "is because of the failure to get the FEPC [fair employment practices committee] bill, the anti-lynching bill, and the anti–poll tax bill passed."[48] This monumental contest of wills culminated in the adoption of an amendment to Rule XXII that applied cloture to any business, including a motion to proceed. But this came at a price. The threshold for cloture was raised to two-thirds of all senators. And cloture would not apply at all to motions to proceed to proposed changes to the rules. Following weeks of obstruction, the application of cloture was expanded to all "matters," which closed loopholes in the original version by specifying that Rule XXII applied to such things as nominations and motions to proceed. The latter requires brief elaboration. To begin consideration of a measure in the Senate, a motion to proceed must be made and agreed to. A motion to proceed is, however, debatable. It therefore can be filibustered. Southern senators in particular had been exploiting the ostensible loophole that cloture did not apply to the motion to proceed. Thus, until the 1949 reform, minority senators could filibuster the motion to proceed without any limitations. The application of cloture did not prevent obstruction of such motions, but it at least clarified that the Senate could use cloture to limit extended debate on motions to proceed. But as part of the compromise to allow this change, the threshold for cloture was raised to two-thirds of the entire Senate, rather than two-thirds of those present and voting, which could be a significantly smaller number of senators.

Other attempts to lower the barriers to cloture followed the filibuster of the 1957 Civil Rights Act, which infamously included Strom Thurmond's record-setting twenty-four-hour-and-eighteen-minute "speech." With Majority Leader Lyndon Johnson fending off more aggressive filibuster reform, the Senate reverted to two-thirds present and voting in 1959 as part of another compromise that, as discussed in chapter 4, resulted in the Rule V provision that the rules in the Senate continue from one Congress to the next unless changed as provided for in Senate rules, the codification of the continuing body doctrine. Southerners used the filibuster to defend white supremacy and to preserve the rule that allowed them to defend white supremacy.

This filibuster reform dynamic was disrupted by the passage of the Civil Rights Act in 1964 followed by the Voting Rights Act in 1965. With a full court press by the president and large pro–civil rights majorities in the Eighty-Eighth Congress, the Senate, after weeks of debate and obstruction, overcame the southern filibuster in 1964 with a 71–29 vote, "the first time that cloture was invoked on a civil rights measure."[49] A year later, passage of the Voting Rights Act required the second such victory in a cloture vote. Combined, the two measures were the de jure end of Jim Crow segregation and political disenfranchisement. Ardor for filibuster reform abated, but did not disappear. As a reminder that things had not changed entirely, southern Democrats were central to a successful filibuster in 1970 against a proposed constitutional amendment for direct election of the president by popular vote. As Senator James Allen of Alabama put it at the time, "The Electoral College is one of the South's few remaining political safeguards. Let's keep it." Passed by an overwhelming and bipartisan margin in the House in 1969, the amendment died when the Senate failed repeatedly to reach cloture, with 75 percent of southern senators voting to not allow the proposal to come to a vote.[50]

With the constitutional and legal victories for civil rights by the 1970s having eliminated much but clearly not all of the contention around that issue, a more liberal and activist Senate was ready to make a more significant change to supermajority cloture, even if southern senators still engaged in a lengthy filibuster against it. In 1975 the threshold for invoking cloture, except for proposals to change Senate rules, was reduced from two-thirds present and voting to three-fifths of the entire Senate, or sixty votes if all Senate seats were filled. In 1986, post-cloture debate was reduced from a maximum of one hundred hours, instituted in 1979, to thirty hours. And that is pretty much how Rule XXII stood until 2013.

## From Cloture to Supermajority Decision Rule and the Sixty-Vote Senate

The triumph of civil and voting rights legislation in the mid-1960s and the reduction of the cloture requirement to three-fifths of the Senate membership did not, however, end the problems with the filibuster. As the intimate association of the filibuster with white supremacy ended, its equally close association with wider governmental dysfunction was just getting started. As Senator Walter Mondale, one of the sponsors of the reform proposal at the heart of the 1975 debate, explained, "It can no longer be said the filibuster is the tool of the representatives of one section of the country or of one political philosophy or that it is used solely against one category of legislation . . . now it is being used by Senators from all parts of the country and of all political philosophies."[51] From the 1970s onward, the Senate moved decidedly and consistently toward becoming a supermajoritarian body. Obstruction and the use of cloture as a tool to circumvent or overcome it accelerated in the 1970s and 1980s. But as figure 6 shows, the number of cloture *motions* in the 1990s nearly equaled the total from 1971 through 1990, and the number of cloture *votes* exceeded the total from the preceding two decades. Obstruction and the use of cloture motions continued to increase from there into the 2010s. The use of cloture motions is an indicator rather than a precise measure of minority obstruction or filibusters. The two are definitely related. But the relationship is complicated by the tactics and strategies available to Senate majorities and minorities.

Many factors contributed to the increase in Senate obstruction, whether measured by cloture motions and cloture votes or by other indicators, including the strategic and tactical behavior of Senate leadership. The 1970s saw a more activist and liberal government, spurred on by a new generation of politicians who, among other things, began to transform the Senate. In general, members of Congress were more responsible for their campaigns and more closely connected to their constituents, who expected action.[52] Senate elections became more competitive than House elections.[53] A more activist Congress was responding to the formidable demands of the existing welfare-warfare state created by the New Deal, the Great Society, World War II, and the Cold War, and expanding the scope and responsibilities of the government by creating even more policies and programs. Congressional workload and the resulting strains for scheduling and considering legislation grew accordingly. All this was accompanied by a steady rise in partisan polarization, especially from the 1980s onward, which solidified party voting and, in the Senate, put an increasing premium on procedural fights, especially over cloture. Norms that restrained senators from the full exploitation of procedural warfare evaporated.

Senate leadership responded in several ways. In the 1970s, Majority Leader Mike Mansfield began employing what became known as the "track system" for scheduling business on the Senate floor.[54] This practice enables the majority leader to move measures or other matters threatened by a filibuster to a side track, so to speak, while other business is considered. This allows the Senate to get other things done, but it also accommodates the obstructing minority, which does not have to hold the floor or engage in dilatory tactics. Instead, the result is one version of what is often called the "silent filibuster." As many have noted, the track system lowered the cost of threatening obstruction. Any credible threat was likely to be accommodated in some way. Meanwhile, the majority leader might be working on a way to move the sidetracked matter forward by either negotiating with whatever minority was in the way or by preparing for a cloture vote at the right time.

And, speaking of cloture, another response was the increased proactive, prompt, even preemptive use of cloture motions. There is no doubt that from the 1990s onward the Senate minority and individual members increased their willingness to use obstructive tactics to extract concessions or defeat a measure. But the majority also responded in part with aggressive use of cloture motions as a tactic to deal with perceived obstruction. Instead of waiting to see whether debate would run its course or a compromise consent agreement could be constructed, the majority leader or other members of the majority often immediately or promptly filed cloture, sometimes as soon as a motion to proceed or measure was open for consideration.[55] As noted, part of the increase in the use of cloture was a consequence of the increased willingness of members of the minority to filibuster the motion to proceed, that is, to block the bill or nomination from even being considered by the Senate. This, of course, is the opposite of extended debate or deliberation. Under such circumstances it is understandable that the majority would immediately file for cloture on the motion to proceed if there was any objection to moving forward.

One of the most discussed accommodations of supermajority cloture is what the Senate refers to as a "hold."[56] A hold is "an informal practice by which a senator informs his or her floor leader that he or she does not wish a particular bill or other measure to reach the floor for consideration. The majority leader need not follow the senator's wishes but is on notice that the opposing senator may filibuster any motion to proceed to consider the measure."[57] As the definition implies, holds are not in the formal rules and procedures of the Senate. Instead, holds are a practice that evolved from the rules that empower minority obstruction. Senators have frequently placed holds on nominations, for example. In so doing, a particular senator may have an objection to the actual nominee or may be attempting to use the leverage of a hold to bring attention to another matter, even one unrelated to the nomination. The latter have been referred to as "hostage" holds. As one example, in 2003 Idaho's Larry Craig placed holds on more than 850 promotions of Air Force officers as a protest against the Defense Department's failure to provide four cargo planes to the Idaho Air National Guard.[58] Examples of such petty holds abound. In another bit of aircraft-related parochialism, Senator Richard

Shelby in 2010 put a blanket hold on all of President Obama's executive nominations because he was frustrated with how the Pentagon was handling a procurement decision on air-refueling tankers—one that would directly affect his state of Alabama.[59] In all such cases, the majority leader must do something if he or she wishes the nomination or bill on hold to go forward. The leader can capitulate, negotiate, or call the bluff of the requesting senator or senators by ignoring the hold request and moving forward with the measure or nomination, and then seeing if those opposed are willing or able to obstruct.

The hold is another form of the "silent filibuster," like the track system but even more so. Until 2007 holds were by custom anonymous, insofar as there was no stipulation that hold requests had to be recorded and publicized in any way. Instead of eliminating holds as a practice, the best the Senate could muster was a provision included in a 2007 law, the Honest Leadership and Open Government Act, which was touted as ending secret holds. The provision required senators to provide official notification of their holds by sending a letter to the majority or minority leader within six days. The name or names attached to the request would then be published in the *Congressional Record*. But for six days the senator or senators could have a secret hold, and that might be all the time needed, especially toward the end of a congressional session. Moreover, because another like-minded senator could place her or his own hold at the end of the six days, both the hold and anonymity could be extended.[60] As a result of their often quiet and confidential nature, the effects of holds, even after the 2007 reform, are not readily recorded or systematically recognized. Regardless, the hold emerged and proliferated as another accommodation of minority power that lowers the cost of obstruction and has often resulted in some degree of success for the senator or senators behind the hold. In short, holds often cause the Senate to do what it would otherwise not have done, which is the basic definition of the effective exercise of power.

As part of all this, Senate leadership increasingly relied on the constant and creative use of unanimous consent agreements, often negotiated between the majority and minority leaders, to move legislation forward. The Senate had always done most of its business by unanimous consent, but before the 1980s, it tended to be easier to attain it. As Congress became more polarized and contentious, important business was increasingly structured by what became known as "complex" unanimous consent agreements, that is, negotiated plans for how to proceed with a measure or other matter, such as a nomination. It might include such things as the amendments that will be in order, the order and threshold for the voting on amendments, and the time for the final vote, which determines how long the matter will be considered.[61] This all makes perfect sense, but the evolution of complex unanimous consent agreements produced further Madisonian ironies as far as Senate deliberation is concerned. In the era of the supermajority Senate—fueled by hyperpartisanship—such agreements increasingly have involved an extraordinary degree of top-level centralization in the form of dealmaking by the majority and minority leaders or their staff. The resulting agreement is then ratified by their troops as the only way to break deadlocks to get at least something, anything, done.[62] This was confirmed by interviews I did with senior Senate staff, including the principal floor strategists for the majority and minority leaders. That is, for nearly any issue that divides the parties, instead of having a public debate, the leaders of the parties negotiate a deal, in the form of a complex unanimous consent agreement to structure the process on the Senate floor, and often determine the outcome on the issue. This is a strange form of bipartisanship and not exactly the kind of deliberation Madison had in mind. Instead of supermajority cloture being the rule that fosters debate by the self-styled "world's greatest deliberative body," it produces secretive bilateral negotiations among a few senators and staff.

All this to avoid threatened, or to end actual, filibusters. By and large, the effect of these strategies and accommodations—the track system, tactical use of cloture, holds, complex unanimous consent agreements—has been to empower the minority while diminishing the likelihood of anything resembling deliberation. As a consequence, supermajority cloture became so important in shaping and determining Senate action that scholars started referring to it as the "sixty-vote Senate" or "supermajority Senate."[63] And the rise of the sixty-vote Senate put cloture-related obstruction repeatedly in the national spotlight. The great filibusters of the past were often controversial for their relation to important issues, particularly civil rights, as we have seen. By the 1990s filibusters and supermajority cloture were becoming associated with divided government and governmental dysfunction in general. The threat of obstruction and a minority veto was becoming the norm rather than the exception.

In all this, what qualified as a filibuster, and did that even matter? Senate scholars have long debated how to measure filibusters. Not all extended debate or dilatory motions qualify as a filibuster. Cloture motions have been used a rough measure of levels of obstruction, but they are no more than that. Partly as a result, some scholars have gone beyond cloture motions and produced more robust measures of when a filibuster is taking place.[64] This point is well taken, but I think this approach needs to be turned on its head because the search for the somewhat elusive filibuster is beside the point. The point is minority obstruction, all the forms it takes, and its effects. If such things as the tracking system and holds produce invisible or silent filibusters, or if, as we shall see, sixty-vote thresholds are readily added to a unanimous consent agreement for votes on individual amendments, then the search for "filibusters," as such, can become somewhat of a distraction. It fails to account for much of the behavior that created and sustained, with all its controversy, frustrations, and acrimony, the supermajority Senate.

As Frances Lee has documented with insight and precision, a great deal of Senate behavior must be viewed through the prism of partisan competition rather than ideological principle. In her words, "To routinely attribute disagreement between congressional Republicans and Democrats to individual members' ideological differences is to overlook how the parties' competition for elected office and chamber control systematically shapes members' behavior in office."[65] The parties in the House and Senate often fight over issues about which liberals and conservatives might agree. In particular, "legislative partisans engage in reflexive partisanship, in which they oppose proposals because it is the opposition party's president that advances them."[66] Much of the Senate's action is geared toward partisan electoral strategy rather than lawmaking. Polarization, divided government, and a sixty-vote Senate facilitate a rational calculation by many senators that substantive legislation is unlikely to pass. The objective becomes to try to make the other side look bad. Such partisan combat feeds directly into Senate obstruction. When many senators are electorally secure—or at least highly sensitive to the constituency that matters in the primary election in their state—then obstructive behavior is often politically advantageous from an individual or partisan perspective, or both.

One result is what congressional scholar Steven Smith's calls the "Senate syndrome." What is this syndrome? It is "a pattern of behavior" created by the "combination of minority-motivated obstruction and majority-imposed restrictions."[67] The syndrome is characterized by a spiraling effect wherein exploitation of the rules by the minority engenders majority efforts to undermine or get around such obstruction. The minority then claims it is forced to obstruct because the majority acts so precipitously to restrict minority participation. This "'obstruct and restrict' pattern has dominated the Senate in recent Congresses—obstructive strategies by the minority are met by majority strategies to limit debate and amendment. 'Regular order' evaporates, and the Senate, known historically for its informality, becomes tied up in parliamentary procedure"[68] And as with some physical syndromes, what is causing what gets hard to pin down. But there is no denying that the various behaviors are logically related.

One product of the syndrome and the ironic centralization of decision-making is yet another innovation or adaptation to deal with supermajority cloture. In another procedural twist, the Senate of the twenty-first century began incorporating sixty-vote thresholds on amendments or even the bill itself into unanimous consent agreements as a way to evade the difficulties of cloture.[69] The procedural logic is pretty straightforward. If the majority seeks to advance a measure and it is clear a minority is determined to obstruct in such a way that cloture will be required, whether on the motion to proceed, the measure itself, or both, then why not speed things up by making the key thing or things at stake—the measure itself or amendments—subject to a sixty-vote threshold and bypass cloture entirely? Although examples of the incorporation of such sixty-vote thresholds into such agreements "can be found from at least the early 1990s," the practice grew amid the partisan polarization and frequent minority obstruction, especially from the mid-2000s onward.[70] One compilation of roll call votes shows forty-four such supermajority decisions on amendments or bills during the 110th Congress (2007–8), forty-four in the 111th, and 127 in the 112th.[71]

These dry statistics are telling but fail to breathe life into this practice, which can show Senate behavior—structured by its rules—at its most ineffective and cynical. On December 14, 2012, twenty-year-old Adam Lanza slaughtered twenty-six people, six teachers or staff and twenty elementary school students, at Sandy Hook Elementary School in Newtown, Connecticut. The age of the victims—the children were all first graders—and the role of the murdered teachers and staff in trying to protect their charges made Sandy Hook like no other mass shooting. For many it was the last straw in a relentless march of American mayhem. Only weeks after his reelection, President Obama seized the moment to demand action. In Republican hands, the House would not act first, if at all. Instead, all eyes turned to the Senate, which was controlled by a 55–45 Democratic majority. On Wednesday, April 17, 2013, the Senate began consideration of the gun bill, titled the Safe Communities, Safe Schools

Act. The majority leader negotiated a highly structured unanimous consent agreement to determine consideration of the bill. In this one, the focal provision was that the key amendments that would determine the core substance of the legislation would be subject to a sixty-vote threshold for approval, instead of having to reach cloture on each separately. The supermajority provision all but guaranteed that nothing of substance would be approved. Overall, five of the eight amendments achieved the simple majorities that are needed to decide ordinary legislation in the Senate but were defeated by the supermajority threshold specified in the unanimous consent agreement. As a result, it turned the entire proceeding into a bit of bipartisan political theater, of the tragic variety. That in turn certainly made a mockery of deliberation: because everyone knew what the outcomes would be, any speeches were political grandstanding.

Let's consider the two obvious implications of this practice. First, it strips bare the pretense that cloture is primarily a rule about deciding when to end debate. Instead, it has evolved into the decision rule. Second, the practice is another acknowledgment that cloture is not about voice but victory. Such agreements not only bypass cloture, they bypass debate, sometimes altogether. There is no deliberation, no persuasion; only one thing matters: sixty votes. Why waste time on anything else?

As a result, sixty-vote thresholds have become far more common and frequently required for the Senate's most consequential business. First, as to frequency, if we examine the thirty-nine sessions of Congress from 1975 through 2013 (before the Senate made an important change to cloture), we see that as a percentage of total votes the recorded votes that had a three-fifths requirement versus those requiring a simple majority increases from negligible to quite substantial (figure 7).[72] The increase seems to fall into three steps, with the sixteen-year period of the first eight Congresses seeing a slow rise to barely 10 percent, with an average of 4.2 percent per Congress. It then jumps to an average of 15 percent over the next five Congresses. Finally, from 2001 through 2013, the average skyrockets to almost 30 percent. Setting the record was the "Fighting 112th" Congress, which saw almost as many supermajority votes (234) as it did those by simple majority (244).

These overall figures underestimate the importance of supermajority votes because many uncontroversial decisions on relatively unimportant matters are achieved by simple majorities. That is, the figures represent not only the raw increase in three-fifths thresholds but also the increase

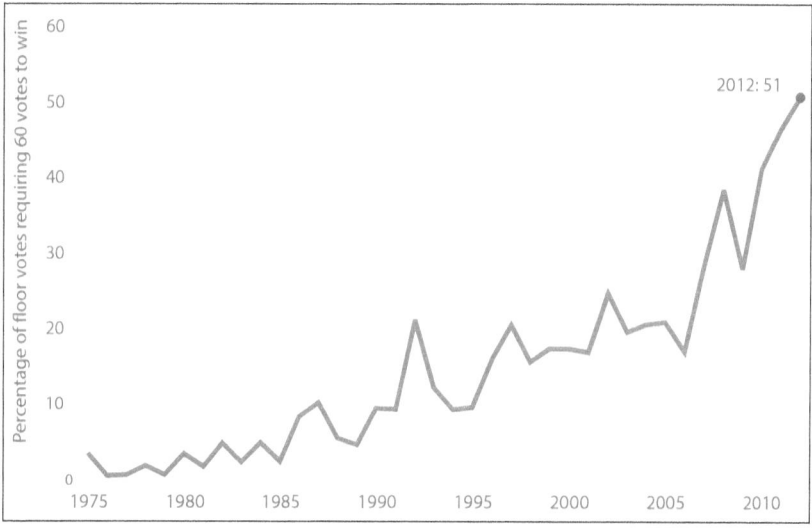

FIG. 7. The rise of the sixty-vote Senate
*Note:* Excludes votes carrying a constitutional requirement of a two-thirds supermajority, such as veto overrides and treaties.

in the proportion of important decisions made by a supermajority vote. Even in the contemporary era of extreme polarization, a good number of things in the Senate receive unanimous or nearly unanimous support, particularly presidential nominations to the executive branch and even many judicial nominations. As well, on a few important bills and resolutions, the Senate can allow for a more or less open amendment process. For example, the Senate budget resolution, which is protected from filibusters by the Budget Act, facilitates the consideration of amendments, most of which are dealt with very quickly, one after another, in what has been dubbed a vote-a-rama. As an example, in the first session of the 113th Congress in 2013, forty-six such amendments were decided by roll call votes as part of the Senate's consideration of the budget resolution. Most of these were offered by the minority and were doomed to fail. Those forty-six constituted nearly 23 percent of all the simple majority roll call votes that session.[73]

Almost by definition, the more important or controversial a bill is, the more likely it is to be the target of some level of obstruction. For example, the percentage of major legislation experiencing what one scholar terms "extended-debate-related problems" increased steadily from 8 percent in the

1960s to 51 percent from 1990 through 2006, reaching 70 percent in 2007.[74] In general, major or controversial legislation is often subject to either one or more cloture votes, or to one or more supermajority thresholds structured by a unanimous consent agreement necessary to end the procedural obstructions and allow the Senate to vote.

## The Constitutional Construction of the Fourth Veto Point in the American System

How might we think about supermajority cloture in the Senate? What is its status as a feature of the system of government? To what should we compare it? One way is to see Senate supermajority cloture as a constitutional construction.[75] The implementation of the Constitution required many decisions and actions with constitutional implications and significance but which were not specified in that document. These include the formalization of the cabinet system and creation of executive departments, judicial refusal to issue advisory opinions, the specification of the size of the Supreme Court, and the creation of the congressional committee system.[76] The Constitution does not specify the number of justices that are to make up the Supreme Court; this rather important detail was left to Congress. We now take nine to be the inviolable number, but that was not settled until well into the twentieth century. It is difficult to imagine the House or the Senate attempting their legislative responsibilities without the division of labor provided by committees, but the Constitution is all but silent on the organization of both chambers. Legislative committees were created and evolved at different rates in the House and Senate to become a fundamental part of the lawmaking process.

Many constitutional constructions have required or inspired little debate, such as the creation and evolution of the presidential cabinet, or the system of committees in both the House and Senate. Some might have seemed innovative and even controversial initially but then became routine, and now evolve with relatively little opposition. Supermajority cloture began with a brief and evanescent debate, and seemed at first to follow the same pattern of fading into the background. But supermajority cloture became more rather than less controversial over time. Rarely has a constitutional construction, let alone a congressional procedure, become so contested and contentious. All along, and especially as supermajority cloture became increasingly the source of partisan division and public frustration, arguments were mustered to support and attack its utility, merit, and constitutionality. And the arguments for and against it have been invoked over and over with increasing fervor as the sixty-vote Senate developed.

It is also a very powerful constitutional construction in its effect on the system of government. As scholars have argued, the scope and power of the sixty-vote Senate produced a fourth veto point in the lawmaking system.[77] For any proposal to become a law, it must receive majority support in the House and Senate. That means the House and Senate majorities are two veto points in the system—each can stop a proposal from becoming law. The president is the third veto point directly in the text of the Constitution. Any proposal making it past the first two veto points requires presidential approval, whether actively or passively.[78] A presidential veto presents Congress with the formidable task of mustering a two-thirds vote in both chambers to override and make the bill a law without the president's approval. Those are the three veto points specified in the Constitution as part of the normal lawmaking process.

The ability of Senate minorities, especially a united partisan minority, to use the high hurdle of supermajority cloture to kill proposals has become another veto point in the legislative process. In this way the traditional and constitutional veto points of the House majority, Senate majority, and the president have been joined by the Senate minority. The sixty-vote Senate evolved into one of the central features of a revised system of checks and balances and a focal aspect of partisan combat. Its matter-of-fact status can be illustrated by myriad quotations from senators and commentators. As just one example, it was no surprise when during a 2018 debate on immigration reform Judiciary Committee chair Charles Grassley elevated the sixty-vote Senate to constitutional status, asking his fellow senators, "Are you interested in a good bill or are you interested in getting a law passed? *That takes 60 in the Senate,* takes a majority in the House, and takes a Presidential signature."[79] No one objected to Grassley's revision of Article I of the Constitution. Indeed, "sixty-vote Senate" does not just describe the internal process that has increasingly determined Senate decision-making; that epithet captures as well the impact of supermajority cloture on the lawmaking process as a whole. Do the president and his party have the ability to overcome Senate filibusters? Should the House even act if this or that proposal is unlikely to garner sixty votes in the Senate? Or does the Senate minority have the numbers and unity necessary to thwart the president and a House majority? These are not hypothetical questions. They often dominate discussions of what might or might not happen in Washington.

Short of a highly improbable intervention by the Supreme Court, no other governing institution has any means of influencing or altering the Senate's supermajority procedure.[80] Is there another controversial feature of any other branch's institutional power that is (1) not reachable by one or more of the other branches and (2) not readily amendable by a new majority within or new occupant of (in the case of the presidency) the institution?[81] By "reachable" I mean that it is potentially subject to some level of direct intervention if not interdiction by another branch. The president may have the edge in the off-and-on struggle with Congress over war powers, but if Congress has the will it can stop presidential warmaking in its tracks. President George W. Bush's use of signing statements did not preclude congressional challenge, and Obama could have foresworn them entirely.[82] No one questions judicial review or supremacy tout court, only some of its very specific applications—and even many of those are subject to revision or even reversal. The minority party in the House might complain about that chamber's form of majoritarianism, but it is hardly constitutionally or comparatively suspect, and moreover, it is amendable by majority rule. Congress might employ ostensibly unconstitutional legislative vetoes but it does so as part of a cooperative relationship between itself and the executive branch. Only the Senate has created an internal rule of procedure that so fundamentally alters the distribution of power in the legislative process and then protected it from change by a supermajority barrier.

In recent years, many from both parties have lamented the use and abuse of the filibuster. However, a frequent refrain has been that it is the increasingly partisan behavior of senators and not the rule that is the problem, as though at some point things were better. That perspective requires, as we have seen, a distorted view of a bipartisan past that did not go so well for many Americans, a view that overlooks how successful the rules were in thwarting or pointlessly obstructing the sober assessment and determination by the majority of what the country needed to do, especially for African Americans. Instead, as represented by the politics and misdirection of the Senate apology that opened this chapter, the Senate continued to embrace the mythology that the filibuster was central to its deliberative function as intended by the founders and the Constitution.

# 6

# "Cooling the Coffee"

MORE MYTHS SENATORS TELL THEMSELVES, AND THE FILIBUSTER'S CLASH WITH EFFECTIVE GOVERNMENT AND THE CONSTITUTION

> There is a tradition that Jefferson coming home from France, called Washington to account at the breakfast-table for having agreed to a second, and, as Jefferson thought, unnecessary legislative Chamber. "Why," asked Washington, "did you just now pour that coffee into your saucer, before drinking?" "To cool it," answered Jefferson, "my throat is not made of brass." "Even so," rejoined Washington, "we pour our legislation into the senatorial saucer to cool it."
>
> —Moncure D. Conway, *Republican Superstitions as Illustrated in the Political History of America*

## Mr. Smith Goes to Washington to Cool the Coffee

In 2011 the Senate engaged in its longest floor debate about the filibuster and Rule XXII since the one in 1975 that produced the reduction from two-thirds to three-fifths to pass a cloture motion. The earlier debate took place during an era of less partisanship and polarization. This one was, instead, a direct consequence of rigid partisanship and polarization, as Democrats and Republicans fought over nearly everything using every procedural weapon in the Senate's arsenal, with the filibuster dominating the battlefield. In this case, it was the Democratic majority that was seeking to curtail obstructive tactics. During the debate, senators offered many of the usual arguments for and against supermajority cloture and its effects. One notable feature of the 2011 debate, however, was the nostalgic invocation of Hollywood mythmaking in the form of a movie from 1939. Several senators invoked Frank Capra's classic film *Mr. Smith Goes to Washington,* which features the iconic filibuster by Jimmy Stewart's character as a model of what a filibuster should be and why it needs to be preserved and protected. In fact, of the seventeen senators who spoke at least once during this debate, seven senators referenced the movie, some more than once. Even though *Mr. Smith Goes to Washington* was a popular Academy Award winner in 1939, there were no mentions of it in other much longer Senate filibuster debates in 1949, 1959, and 1975. In 2011, senators substituted cinematic fiction for their own history as an institution. No examples of real filibusters were mentioned. Perhaps senators were tempted to look to Hollywood instead of their own annals because most real "talking" filibusters to which they might have referred were not so noble. Stretching back into the nineteenth century, most had been in support of white supremacy by opposing civil rights measures or filibuster reform. Not surprisingly, there were no encomiums for Strom Thurmond's record-setter against the 1957 Civil Rights Act, for example. Instead, senators repeatedly invoked Jimmy Stewart and his character, "Jefferson Smith," in the words of Amy Klobuchar of Minnesota, "as a shining example of how individual conscience can matter because an individual can stay on the Senate floor to the point of exhaustion in order to stymie a corrupt piece of legislation."[1] Much as the Senate six years earlier consciously avoided any mention or indictment of the filibuster in its apology for its failure to pass antilynching legislation decades before, senators in 2011, perhaps unconsciously, could not defend the filibuster with its own history.[2] In 2005, the year of the antilynching apology, and during a dust-up over filibusters of judicial nominations and a threat to curtail them, then minority leader Harry Reid combined "Mr. Smith" and the framers of the Constitution in the same argument for the filibuster, mixing cinematic imagination with an equally fictional claim about the Constitution. "Some in this chamber want to throw out 214 years of Senate history in the quest for absolute power," Reid claimed. "They want to do away with Mr. Smith, as depicted in that great movie, being able to come to Washington. They want to do away with the filibuster. They think they're wiser than our Founding Fathers, I doubt that's true."[3]

## The Filibuster: Constitutional Myths and Political Realities

"We take ourselves too seriously," Senator Henry French Hollis told his colleagues. "We liken ourselves in solemnity to the United States Constitution."[4] As he addressed the Senate on March 8, 1917, the day it would vote to add a supermajority cloture procedure to its rules, little could Senator Hollis anticipate just how seriously his successors would take themselves and how solemnly they would liken this rule, and all it would entail, to the Constitution. As part of this, Hollis probably could not imagine how the rule the Senate was about to pass—a rule he supported—would become the functional equivalent of a constitutional amendment to the systems of checks and balances, a fourth veto point in the legislative process. And as supermajority cloture evolved from a rarely used procedure intended to check minority obstruction into one of the most important, frequently employed, and controversial minority veto points in American politics, the political justifications for the filibuster likewise escalated and elevated it to constitutional status as the defining feature or essence of the Senate just as, in their view, George Washington, James Madison, and Frank Capra intended.

As part of the research for this book, I read and coded every major Senate debate about reforming the filibuster and supermajority cloture from 1917 to 2017.[5] The debates prompted by the filibuster, supermajority cloture, and their reform inevitably became occasions for general expressions about the Senate's place and purpose in the Constitution and scheme of government. As senators addressed one another, they spoke directly to the relationships between and among the core concepts in this book: equal representation, the continuing body doctrine derived from staggered terms, and minority power or rights. In so doing, the debates revealed how many senators came to strongly associate, if not equate, supermajority cloture with the essence of their institutional role in the Constitution's architecture of checks and balances. Moreover, and increasingly as the decades rolled by, senators and others made erroneous connections between this essence—the filibuster and supermajority cloture—and the Constitution and founding. As supermajority cloture became increasingly associated with hindering rather than facilitating Senate business, as it became for some the problem rather than the solution, the rhetoric supporting Rule XXII increasingly cloaked it not only in the Senate's tradition of extended debate but, more important, in the founding, as an addition or enhancement that the framers either intended or would have endorsed. This chapter shows how the rhetoric in support of the filibuster became more inflated and misleading even as the historical ties to white supremacy were both undeniable and increasingly embarrassing, and even as the more general dysfunction of the sixty-vote Senate became harder to ignore. Mr. Smith and James Madison, it would seem, were brought to the rescue of the contemporary filibuster because in the face of the indelible association with white supremacy, its apologists needed to anchor its legitimacy in an unshakable foundation. And what firmer foundation is there than the founding and the Constitution?

But this institutional essence was also the core of the Senate's agony about whether it was living up to its billing as the world's greatest deliberative body. The mythology and institutional conceits of the Senate as the "senatorial saucer" and the "world's greatest deliberative body" entail considerable existential agony as the modern Senate has struggled with the rather yawning gaps between its lofty self-conceptions and the tarnished reality of its actual behavior, where fights over process supersede substantive debate and little gets done owing to arbitrary minority vetoes. In recent years, senators have had increasing trouble reconciling their constitutional exceptionalism with their institutional reality.

Depending on whose partisan ox was being gored, one could find plenty of disgust with the supermajority politics of the Senate and some strong sentiments for reform if not elimination of the filibuster. The sixty-vote Senate, however, was increasingly tangled up in the politics of partisan hypocrisy and the struggle for institutional control. After nearly each election the relative value of the filibuster changed sides, and few could separate their constitutionalism—their opinions about institutional reform—from their partisan politics long enough to have a rational debate about the costs and benefits of the outsized impact of the filibuster on Senate business. Instead, and far too frequently, senators and other commentators, even some who favored at least a degree of reform, marshalled or resorted to politically unsophisticated arguments such as the invocations of "Mr. Smith" and others based on dubious history and distortions of the founding and the Constitution.

## The Dysfunction of the Filibuster

As I have argued, the modern filibuster, as structured by supermajority cloture, collapses in practice under the weight of its persistent problems and negligible or accidental benefits. Support for supermajority cloture flies in the face of the actual behavior of the Senate and performance of Rule XXII—it does not do what it was designed to do, and in many ways it does precisely the opposite. After 1917, the Senate evolved into a less deliberative institution based on a minority veto. Supermajority cloture distorts deliberation and exacerbates collective irresponsibility. Moreover, the history of the rule in action shows the injustice done by its application and use as a de facto veto. Especially but not only in the realm of civil rights there are numerous cases where the Senate would have made a different decision if it had had some form of majority cloture, and those decisions would have made a difference. That is, in legal terms, actual "harm" was done to real individuals, not just the Senate majority but citizens who would have benefited from the alternative outcome, particularly an outcome supported by the House and president. Even so, in the face of its many dysfunctions and contradictions, supermajority cloture retains many defenders, and not just among self-interested senators.

Almost any study of or opinion piece about the filibuster or supermajority cloture lists several justifications for or arguments against it, and many are quite familiar to us. With respect to arguments in its favor, one summary from a 2012 book titled *Defending the Filibuster* is exemplary. The benefits of the filibuster "include discouraging unchecked majority control, fostering deliberation and compromise, moderating extreme outcomes and avoiding precipitous decision making, protecting the rights of minorities, discouraging more populated states from dominating the congressional process, ensuring the role of the legislative branch in oversight of the executive branch, and assuring the role of the Senate as a check and balance of the majoritarian House of Representatives in the legislative process."[6]

The catalog of positive outcomes attributed to the filibuster, and by extension supermajority cloture, is a formidable one. Indeed, one wonders how democratic government could survive without it, especially in all the democracies that have had no such thing. And this laundry list is as typical as it is analytically insufficient and politically frustrating. Not based on any explicit precepts of republican government, or a normative democratic framework, or even, in most cases, any clear constitutional analysis, the alleged positives usually come off as a random and at times contradictory package. Such lists nearly always rely on a superficial, misleading, and often implicit understanding of American constitutionalism, with loose and hackneyed references to some vague idea that the Senate was "intended to be different" or to "cool the coffee," with a quotation from the *Federalist Papers* sometimes thrown in for good measure. In almost every defense of the filibuster, the relevant terms (deliberation, compromise, moderation, minority rights, oversight, etc.) are not theorized, operationalized, or measured. For example, what does one make of the "rights of minorities," especially in the face of the Senate's rather bizarre apportionment and its extended history of resisting the legal liberation of racial minorities? Or how does one measure deliberation or compromise, as opposed to partisan obstruction and minority victory? Assertion and anecdote frequently substitute for argument and evidence.[7]

The functional rationales justify supermajority cloture as a positive, even essential feature of or addition to the system of checks and balances and to republican democracy, often regardless of Senate tradition or the founding. It is a long and at least superficially impressive list of reasons. Although each type of argument has been used by senators and commentators over the years, they are often combined and blended. In fact, that is part of the conceptual confusion and loose constitutionalism behind more than a few of the arguments. When the evidence of its costs is inescapable and its benefits are negligible, the problem is less whether a supermajority procedure is justifiable in a largely hypothetical fashion. Instead, the prior question that is almost never asked about the functional arguments is whether the Senate should be *the* institutional locus of such a tool or form of power. Many of the functional points are made with little if any justification as to why this supermajority procedure belongs in the Senate and nowhere else, at least in the national government. Instead, the location of such a feature in the Senate is often assumed or taken for granted as part of the constitutional mythology of Senate exceptionalism.

## The Essence of the Senate and Bicameralism

For many senators and commentators, supermajority cloture is not simply another bicameral difference to be added to those structured by the Constitution, such as the differences in electoral constituency and length of term. Supermajority cloture is not even *primus inter pares*. The filibuster, as structured by the provisions of Rule XXII, in this view, is the essence of the Senate and the sine qua non of the Constitution's bicameral Congress. Without the right to filibuster, senators and commentators have argued, there would be no meaningful political difference between them; indeed, the nation might as well have a unicameral or one-house legislature.

Such arguments go back at least as far as the creation of cloture in 1917, because at that time any provision for a cloture vote threatened unlimited debate. And the end of the filibuster in its traditional form meant the effective end of the Senate, in the view of some its members. As Senator Lawrence Sherman put it during his resistance to reform in 1917, the proposed cloture rule "will eventually lead to making the Senate just such a legislative body as the House of Representatives is."[8] Decades later, scholars and senators were advancing the same argument in support of supermajority cloture. In the 1980s, Senator Robert Byrd deemed the filibuster the "main cornerstone of the Senate's uniqueness," the "primary reason that the United States Senate is the most powerful upper chamber in the world." Without it, "the Senate would lose its special strength and become a mere appendage of the House of Representatives."[9] "If the Senate were to render itself a majoritarian body," aver Arenberg and Dove, "it would soon recede into the shadows of the House of Representatives. Most of the advantages of bicameralism would be done, and the Senate would suffer the fate of most upper chambers around the world."[10] Even Barack Obama, former professor of constitutional law, could not resist this convoluted linkage and its relation to bicameralism. Commenting in 2005 on the threat of a "nuclear option" by Republicans to end filibusters on nominations, Senator Obama said, "What I worry about would be you essentially have still two chambers—the House and the Senate—but you have simply majoritarian absolute power on either side, and that's just not what the founders intended."[11] As he prepared to retire from the Senate at the end of 2020, Tennessee's Lamar Alexander told an interviewer that getting rid of the filibuster "would basically destroy the Senate" because it "would be a second House of Representatives."[12] Regardless of the variations on this theme, the inescapable syllogistic logic is that supermajority cloture is the essential difference between the two bodies endorsed or mandated by the founders.

For some, the elimination of supermajority cloture would entail something even more dramatic than making the Senate just like the House. The Senate might as well close up shop. "If we are going to be reduced in our procedures to those of the House of Representatives," asked Jesse Helms during the 1975 debate, "why have a bicameral legislature? Why not save the people the enormous cost of operating the U.S. Senate?"[13] As the Senate headed toward a curtailment of the filibuster in 2017, Senator John McCain, who opposed the pending change, offered the following lament: "Benjamin Franklin is somewhere turning over in his grave. . . . Why have a bicameral system?"[14] No matter that Benjamin Franklin came from unicameral Pennsylvania and advocated for it even at the Constitutional Convention.

## The Filibuster as the Founders' Intent: Or, as Madison Would Have Put It, "You Can Never Have Too Much of a Good Thing"

Some of the comments putting the filibuster at the core of the Senate's purpose invoke the founders and their inspired design. In so doing, they join many other such statements that link the filibuster and supermajority cloture to founding intentions and even the Constitution itself, despite the indisputable fact that neither the filibuster nor supermajority cloture has any connection to the deliberations and decisions in and around 1787. As Steven S. Smith, one of the world's leading authorities on the Senate, testified before some of its members, "Defenders of Rule 22 often claim the Framers of the Constitution intended minority rights to be protected by the Senate. Taken on its face, this claim is incorrect. Nowhere in the summaries of the constitutional convention or the Federalist Papers is there an argument for allowing Senate minority factions to block action on legislation. Of course, the Senate was designed to protect the interests of small states."[15] The framers did not equate the Senate's structure and desired characteristics with minority rights, as we have seen. In general, they expressed more concern about forms of minority vetoes. And majority tyranny would be mitigated by the structure of the entire system rather than by the Senate as such. What is taken for granted as a natural fact by most of the media, many textbooks, and millions of Americans is in fact a historical construction that has almost nothing to do with the invention of the Senate and its original purpose, in theory and practice.

Even so, with increasing frequency the tradition of extended debate and the filibuster has been extended all the way back to the founding, and supermajority cloture is often mythologized into the framers' intentions for the Senate or even directly into the handiwork of the convention itself. The framers directly or indirectly intended the Senate to have some variety of supermajority rules to fit the Senate's special purpose in the system of representation and checks and balances. Some of these arguments *anchor* supermajority cloture in the founding generally insofar as the Senate was from the start the institution, they argue, of minority rights and greater deliberation. Such anchors sometimes take the form of direct *attributions* that supermajority cloture was a product of the founding and the Constitution. Finally, some have portrayed it as the essential *adaptation* to adjust the Senate's founding purpose and intent to the modern distribution of institutional power, to offset the House and especially presidential power. These quotations seem to imply, among other things, that were he alive today, James Madison, architect of our system of elaborate checks and balances, would have endorsed supermajority cloture because one of his constitutional principles must have been that "you can never have too much of a good thing."

For example, Arthur Vandenberg, one of the most celebrated senators of the twentieth century, elevated Senate rules, or at least Rule XXII, to the status of the Constitution, with the blessing of none other than George Washington. In his farewell address, which the senator quoted, Washington characterized the Constitution as "sacredly obligatory" until "changed by an explicit and authentic act of the whole people." "So far as I am concerned," concluded Vandenberg, "the Father of his Country said to us, by analogy, 'The rules of the Senate which at any time exist, until changed by an explicit and authentic act of the whole Senate, are sacredly obligatory upon all.'"[16] If he went further than some with the firmness of his analogy, Vandenberg was nevertheless tapping into a deep well of Senate sentiment, sentiment codified in the rules of the institution.

The most hackneyed link to the founding is the almost certainly mythical conversation between Washington and Jefferson—the one that opens this chapter—in which cooling saucers and hot coffee serve as a homey metaphor to simplify matters so that the otherwise brilliant Jefferson could understand why the Constitutional Convention had added a second chamber to the proposed Congress.[17] Whatever Washington, who had sweated it out at the convention, might or might not have said to Jefferson, who had been living the good life in Paris, it was clearly not about extended debate, insofar as Washington's meeting with Jefferson predated the Constitution's implementation and hence any Senate rules, norms, or practices. And as most scholars of the founding know, Jefferson spoke and wrote in favor of bicameralism. None of this has stopped senators and other commentators from employing versions of this story with great regularity and abandon as a quick and dirty QED to incorporate the after-the-fact functionalism of supermajority cloture directly into the Constitution. As a case in point, during a period of filibuster-induced tension in 1995, Republican senator Phil Gramm argued that supermajority cloture "is part of the fabric of American democracy. It was part of the process making the Senate the deliberative body of Congress that

George Washington described to Thomas Jefferson when Jefferson came back from France."[18]

Senators have made a practice of butchering this anecdote. At least one senator put Benjamin Franklin in the scene with Washington.[19] An essay by former senators Democrat Gary Hart and Republican Chuck Hagel tripped all over the story: "Based upon Thomas Jefferson's notion that the Senate was to be the saucer in which controversies cooled, Senators have, from the beginning, been at liberty to express their views at such length as they wish (Jefferson, it should be noted, was the author of the Manual of Parliamentary Procedures for the Use of the Senate of the United States in 1801)."[20] Aside from the obvious inversion of the supposed roles of Jefferson and Washington, the connection to Jefferson's work as president of the Senate is entirely misleading. There is nothing in it about saucers, coffee, or expressing "views at such length as they wish." Instead, Jefferson's manual is far better remembered for its injunction that "No one is to speak impertinently or beside the question, superfluous, or tediously."[21] Jefferson might have added "or without some degree of accuracy," a precept also ignored in Mitch McConnell's version of the anecdote. "Before giving my prepared comments," said Senator McConnell before a 2010 hearing, "I would point out that I believe it was Washington. It *certainly was one of our founders* who was quoted as saying *at the constitutional convention* the Senate was going to be like the saucer under the tea cup, and the tea was going to slosh out and cool off, and the Senate, he anticipated, would be a place where passions would be reined in and presumably progress would be made in the political center."[22] Few, however, could top Senator Pat Roberts's ramble:

> The keeper of the institutional flame was the tag I put on Senator Byrd. My wife Franki and I became very close friends of the Senator. At any rate, he recounted the story attributed to Jefferson and Washington, he would tell every incoming class about the role of the people's House and perhaps what happened, when they put the coffee pot on in regards to legislation, that the coffee was so hot it would boil over, and it was the Senate's duty to act as the saucer, as folks did back in West Virginia in the earlier days, or Kansas or Iowa or Tennessee or Texas, that they would pour the coffee out in the saucer and let it cool off a little bit so they could put their biscuit in it and actually eat it, and then the legislation would pass. The problem is, sometimes on our side maybe we want tea, maybe we want to start over.[23]

Despite all the evidence to the contrary, many continue to assert some founding connection, however implicit or explicit. To the degree that they pay attention to such things, no small number of Americans think the Senate filibuster is a constitutional provision. Professors of American politics can regale you with anecdotes of the instances in which students or others display some version of this belief. And this is not limited to average citizens. At a political science conference not so many years ago, I delivered a paper that critiqued supermajority cloture. A fellow panelist and specialist in congressional elections came up to me after the presentation and said, "But I thought the filibuster was in the Constitution."

As if to bolster this frustrating state of public belief, the Senate debates about the filibuster and other sources show that there has been a shift from largely functional arguments to ones that lean heavily on the founding and make supermajority cloture the constitutional essence of the Senate. The further in time we get from the framers and the founding, the more often they have been invoked incorrectly in support of arguments for the filibuster or supermajority cloture.[24] Summarized in table 3, the data show a pronounced increase in the percentage of comments that attribute the filibuster or supermajority cloture to the founding or founding intent or that characterize them as the essence of the Senate. The debates are not equal in size or focus, so it is difficult to make precise comparisons. Nevertheless, the trend is pretty striking. The relatively short debate in 1917 featured only one comment that connected the filibuster to the system of checks and balances created by the founders, even if somewhat indirectly. That short debate was followed by three longer ones. But even as the subsequent three debates descended significantly in size, the percentage of such arguments increased substantially. The protracted

TABLE 3. Senate debates about filibuster reform, 1917, 1949, 1975, and 2011

|  | Total words | Number of pro-filibuster arguments | Percentage of pro-filibuster arguments linked to the founding, Constitution, or essence of the Senate |
| --- | --- | --- | --- |
| 1917 | 105,000 | 27 | 4 |
| 1949 | 794,000 | 119 | 20 |
| 1975 | 333,000 | 85 | 39 |
| 2011 | 150,000 | 20 | 45 |

filibuster in 1949, which took place from February 28 to March 17, added up to nearly 800,000 words. Twenty percent of the arguments linked the filibuster directly or indirectly to the Constitution or founding, or characterized it as the essence of the Senate. Thirty-nine percent appeared in the much shorter but still lengthy debate in 1975. Finally, 45 percent of the pro-filibuster arguments were of this variety in the 2011 debate, which was less than half the length of the one that preceded it.

In the 2011 debate, the majority and minority leaders, however much they disagreed about the proposed reforms, saw eye to eye on the essence of the Senate and its roots in the founding. Majority Leader Reid, who was frustrated by obstruction but did not support the proposals that launched this debate, told his colleagues that the Senate's "ability to debate and deliberate without restraints of time limits.... is in our DNA. It is one of the many traits intentionally designed to distinguish this body from the House."[25] Making a similar insinuation, McConnell argued that "the Founders purposefully crafted the Senate to be a deliberate, thoughtful body. A supermajority requirement to cut off the right to debate ensures that wise purpose. Eliminating it is a bad idea."[26]

And Reid and McConnell were far from alone during this debate or, more broadly, during the era of the sixty-vote Senate. In 1994 testimony before the Senate Rules Committee, retiring senator Malcolm Wallop took the constitutional connection a step further by analogizing the filibuster to the Bill of Rights. "What makes the Senate such a wonderful institution," he told his colleagues, "is what also makes the Bill of Rights such a wondrous document. Like the protections enshrined in the Bill of Rights, the Senate's rules sometimes serve to frustrate or thwart the whims and passions of a free and democratic society. That is a virtue, my colleagues, not a vice."[27] The senator's analogy, however convoluted, is an example of the false equivalencies and twisted rationales that come so easily to members of the upper house, including Georgia's Johnny Isakson, who, during the 2011 debate, asked "If our Founding Fathers had not intended for supermajorities to determine certain acts of this Congress, why would two-thirds of us have to vote to pass a constitutional amendment and three-fourths of the States have to vote to ratify one? I think that showed the intent. If our Founding Fathers had not intended for minority representation to exist, I wouldn't have two Senators like California; everybody would have a proportionate number of Senators."[28]

## The Convoluted, Even Tortured, Relationship between Equal Representation, Minority Rights, and Supermajority Cloture

As Isakson's remark implies, no small part of this constitutional mythology emerged from the conceptual alchemy that links equal representation to a general principle of minority rights and in turn to the filibuster and supermajority cloture. Equal representation, the most important and divisive compromise at the Constitutional Convention, was nevertheless facilitated by the fact that having only two senators per state was one of the few ways to keep that body small, which was a central feature of a deliberative Senate and among the most widely shared values among the framers. A small and select Senate would foster a better deliberative process than the larger and democratically elected House. That better *quality* of deliberation was the core of the Senate, not any role in protecting minority rights as such. But equal representation, by definition, introduced a connection between the Senate and political minorities. The smallest state in population had the power to cancel the Senate votes of the largest state, for example. Or a coalition of smaller states comprising a minority of the nation's population could defeat the states representing the majority of the country's citizens.

Equal representation is the lone constitutional provision that gives any sustenance to the idea that the Senate's purpose was to protect minority interests, but the consequence of the Great Compromise was about one thing only: the representation of states as states, and not minority power in any other sense. As shown in chapter 2, John C. Calhoun's theory of concurrent majorities was a thinly disguised justification for southern states in the Senate having an effective veto power over legislation that affected their interests. This argument, rooted in the protection of white supremacy, helped transform a highly specific and hotly contested compromise for equal representation of the states into minority rights for any and all. In turn, equal representation and minority rights became pillars of support for supermajority cloture.

How did equal representation evolve into minority rights and thus connected to the Senate's tradition of extended debate; that is, its rules of procedure that empowered individual senators to be granted recognition and hold the floor? John Calhoun's nineteenth-century Senate—the smaller Senate that represented states equally—could afford to let debate proceed in a largely unrestricted fashion, in contrast to the rapidly growing House. This power gave individual senators the ability not only to speak at great length but to filibuster, to deliberately use this power to obstruct the majority. So the literal minority power of equal representation blended with and reinforced the notions of individual or minority power implicit in freedom of debate. Over time, the idea that the Senate was the constitutional home of minority rights took hold. This social construction was aided by the development, especially from the mid-twentieth century onward, of civil rights and civil liberties as ongoing issues in American politics. "Minority rights," whether connected to the Senate or not, were increasingly part of the political vocabulary. At the same time, extended debate and the filibuster were further institutionalized in Senate rules concerning supermajority cloture. Senators happily fused the power given to individual senators by equal representation and the filibuster or supermajority procedures. It became easy to justify their rules and behavior via a generalized notion of "minority rights" as the special province of their institution.

As a result, these two central features of the Senate, equal representation and the supermajority filibuster, became entangled through a loosely conceived notion of minority rights. The Senate debates about the filibuster show that equal representation, as such, falls away in favor of this more capacious and universalistic principle or value. One might be against the inequalities inherent in two senators per state, but who is against minority rights? This conceptual transubstantiation in turn helped obscure the fact that the democratic inequities of equal representation were enhanced by the added power of supermajority requirements to close debate. Finally, and as part of this, some senators even replaced equal representation with the filibuster as the main provision that protects small states.

Senators have had little trouble conflating equal representation with political minorities more generally in both blunt and subtle ways, and often connecting that, in turn, to the filibuster. For example, in 1949 Arkansas Democrat John McClellan argued that "the Senate was created also to give protection to the smaller States, the minority groups in political subdivisions. The House was constituted on the basis of population."[29] Fellow southerner Joseph Hill similarly cited two senators per state as an "illustration of an absolute, ironclad protection in the Constitution of the minority."[30] During the 1975 debate, John Stennis of Mississippi emphasized equal representation's special guarantee in Article V, the permanent exception to the amendment process. This, he said, made the Senate "very special as a parliamentary body," which somehow meant the Senate also "would have a rule that did protect minorities,"[31] by which of course he meant supermajority cloture. Making a similar leap in 1993, Senator Larry Craig put it this way: "I would say as it relates to cloture, our Founding Fathers designed the Senate for a unique purpose, substantially different from the House, and the cloture rule or the ability to have the Minority to cause the Majority to come to attention is an extremely valuable and important tool in the makeup of the Senate itself . . . and it is a rule like a cloture rule that substantiates what I think our Founding Fathers intended about that sense of equity [among Senators]."[32]

Implicit in this line of argument, however, is that the Great Compromise was less a limit on the representation of states regardless of population than it was a justification or license for additional enhancements of state power. From this perspective, equal representation is naturally complemented by unlimited debate or supermajority cloture; they are two sides of the same constitutional coin. Arguing in 1975 against a lower threshold for cloture, Idaho's James McClure said, "The right of speech in the Senate is particularly important because the Senate is the only institution of the Federal system in which the smaller States exercise an equal influence over the conduct of affairs of the Nation."[33] A good number of senators have seen supermajority cloture as more than just a good fit with equal representation. Instead, the protection of state sovereignty in the Senate "was undoubtedly the reason for the unlimited-debate rule," according to one participant in the 1949 debate.[34] Others, including Arkansas's William Fulbright, have totally erased the Great Compromise and the imbalance of power created by equal representation. "The distinction of the Senate depends upon unlimited debate," Fulbright argued in 1949. "That is the only reason . . . I have the slightest influence in this Government above that of a Member of the House of Representatives."[35] The southern Democrat was echoed in 1975 by Republican Hiram Fong of Hawaii, who told his colleagues that without supermajority cloture, "we will have given up the one source of protection we in the Senate were meant to afford the small states and minority population."[36] Recalling his maiden speech in the Senate, Fong's Aloha State colleague Daniel Inouye said, "I made it clear that, as someone representing a small state, it [the filibuster] was a tool I needed to ensure we were not pushed aside."[37] His colleague Claiborne Pell of Rhode Island related this protection to the literal—as in geographic or physical—size of his state. "As a Senator from the smallest State," Pell pointed out during his 1996 farewell address, "I have always been sensitive to the fact that circumstances could arise in which I would need the special protection of minority rights which is accorded by the cloture rule."[38]

Senator Chris Dodd devoted no small portion of his 2010 farewell address, mentioned in chapter 1, to defending the Senate's rules. In Dodd's oration the Great Compromise, which is sometimes referred to as the Connecticut Compromise, created bicameralism as such, which in turn was defined by the difference in chamber rules about debate, which were authored by the founders. "It was," Dodd said, "Roger Sherman and Oliver Ellsworth, delegates from Connecticut to the Constitutional Convention in 1787 who proposed the idea of a bicameral national legislature. The Connecticut Compromise, as it came to be known, was designed to ensure that no matter which way the political winds blew, or how hard the gusts, there would be a place for every voice to be heard. The history of this young democracy, the Framers decided, should not be written solely in the hand of the political majority. In a nation founded in revolution against tyrannical rule, which sought to crush dissent, there should be one institution that would always provide a space where dissent was valued and respected."[39] So beware, Dodd warned, of the temptation to reform the rules that protect minority power. As he approached the end of his final address, Dodd returned once again to "the rules," and said that senators, in coming through in times of great challenge, "have evidenced the wisdom of the Framers who created its unique rules and set its high standards." As any casual student of the founding knows, the senators from Connecticut were not the first to propose a bicameral legislature for the revised system; it was in the Virginia Plan and was basically a given. And, of course, none of the Senate's rules were written by the founders, particularly the supermajority provision added in 1917.

Such arguments are not limited to arguably self-interested senators. Allowing one bit of correct history to provide cover for a subsequent falsehood, columnist William Safire wrote that "the Senate was created to protect the minority against majority tyranny. That's why small states have the same two votes as large states and why it takes much more than a majority to cut off debate."[40] "Certainly," wrote commentator George Will in 2017, "the filibuster fits a non-majoritarian institution in which 585,501 Wyomingites have as much representation as do 39,250,017."[41] Certainly, one might argue, it is just the opposite. Some scholars have asserted the same specious connection. According to one recent history of the institution, "From this inborn mal-apportionment [equal representation] comes the Senate's embedded charter to give full and fair—and extended—expression to minority points of view. And from this arrangement flows the Senate's most distinguishing characteristic—the filibuster."[42] Legal scholars Virginia Seitz and Joseph Guerra claim that equal representation is proof that Senate was designed as a countermajoritarian body. Consequently, "entrenched Senate procedural rules reflect an affirmative exercise of the states' residual sovereign power."[43] In short, equal representation is a constitutional hunting license for states to further entrench minority power in the Senate, as opposed to equal representation being the singular constitutional provision for state sovereignty within Congress, and one that was distinctly modified by the Seventeenth Amendment. Such arguments also provide an indirect link to the founders by associating the filibuster, however loosely or directly, with state equality, as we saw earlier. The unstated corollary is that equal representation was insufficient and therefore the shortcomings of the framers—who are otherwise to be listened to and respected—must be corrected, by Senate rules, rules that are entrenched against change by subsequent Senate majorities that might prefer a different way of doing business.

The argument that supermajority cloture is a complementary enhancement of equal representation has often smacked right into the opposite argument, and both claims are as weak as they are contradictory. Across the decades, many senators have argued that supermajority cloture gives the *most populous* states, which represent a majority of the population but constitute a fraction of the votes within the Senate, a tool to avoid domination by a group of the smaller states, which can make up a majority of the Senate while representing a fraction of the nation's population. That is, a filibustering minority of senators can represent a majority of the US population. In such instances, the potentially atavistic minority rule made possible by equal representation is offset by a cloture rule that allows the senators representing the majority of the country's population to stall or stop the minority. Writing in 1926, the historian Lindsay Rogers noted that in the Senate, "a 33% minority might represent the majority of the population."[44] In other words, the still relatively new cloture rule protected populous states. During the 1949 debate on cloture reform, at least three senators, all southern Democrats, raised versions of this argument, possibly in an effort to persuade some of their large-state colleagues from the north. As Senator McClellan put it, "A change in a rule of the United States Senate which gives protection to a minority of the membership of this body ... often ... gives protection to a majority of the citizenship of this Nation."[45] Old-fashioned as that might seem, the argument lives on. Arenberg and Dove make the argument that a "minority of Senators may represent a majority of the nation" on the same page that they argue that it also is for the "protection of smaller states."[46]

It should not escape our notice that this attempt to disconnect the filibuster from the small states that are advantaged by equal representation undermines the idea that the filibuster is part of what makes the Senate the bastion of minority rights. After all, if large-state senators, who represent the popular majority, can use the filibuster to compensate for the representation their states lack in the Senate, then what, precisely, is the definition of minority? Some filibuster apologists try to have it both ways. Supermajority cloture enhances equal representation in the Senate, and that's a good thing; or it can undermine it, and that is also a good thing. Regardless, the implicit, unstated claim is the following: Senate rules can be used, should be used, to correct or improve deficiencies in the Constitution. In the case of equal representation, the filibuster improves the effect of having two senators per state by sometimes enhancing its intended effect; at other times it offsets the impact of equal representation by contradicting it. Small-state senators get to make up for what their states lack in the House and large-state senators get to compensate for what they lack in the Senate. What a remarkable institution!

Whatever the merits of such arguments, those who posit a relationship between equal representation and supermajority cloture are right about one thing: it does add to the power of smaller states. The many senators whose elections rest on massive violations of political equality enter an institution that also grants them procedural superpowers. "Rule XXII of the Standing Rules of the U.S. Senate," to quote one contemporary scholar, "gives a minority of forty-one senators, who may be elected from states that contain as little as eleven percent of the nation's population, the power to prevent the Senate from debating or voting on bills, resolutions, or presidential appointments by filibustering or acquiescing in a filibuster."[47] Even if that particular scenario is unlikely to take place, the distortions produced by equal representation—in both demography and democratic theory—are only compounded by the addition of supermajority cloture to considerations and calculations regarding its effects.[48] The current confluence of ideology and geography, as discussed in chapter 3, is a very real example of how equal representation can dramatically inflate the power of a politically coherent and cohesive population. From a political perspective, the people of the United States have never been randomly distributed, but we have been in a long period when the distribution is particularly clear and biased.

My reading of the debates and historical record leads me to conclude that the self-interested and strategic calculations of senators helped to diminish equal representation in favor of supermajority cloture as the defining feature of the Senate. An emphasis on the filibuster and supermajority cloture harmonizes with senators' electoral and partisan interests. Equal representation is inextricably tied to the representation of states or the citizens who reside in them. It does not easily translate into the individual and partisan prerogative that senators favor when talking about minority rights. For a senator, minority rights really equate to her rights, as the individual senator who just happens to represent Wyoming, California, or Minnesota. In this way, equal representation serves its purpose, however mistakenly, as a rhetorical gateway to minority rights in general, to be protected first and foremost by the power of the filibuster. The strong if socially constructed constitutional rationale supporting the filibuster provides maximum latitude for senators to use their institution's rules as they see fit. This in turn serves the political interests of senators primarily as individuals but also as partisans.

All this represents the ultimate Madisonian irony. In the *Federalist* no. 62, as we have seen, Madison starts by brushing off state equality as an obvious compromise and concession, a political necessity with self-evident potential for harmful effects. He then goes on to defend a Senate characterized by long terms and indirect selection and smaller size that would foster a different quality of deliberation. Time would pervert Madison's version of the proper relationship between the subordinate political necessity of equal representation and the primary institutional purpose of quality deliberation. Instead, state equality would come to be conflated with the idea of the rights of the minority, with the House representing the majority of population and the Senate embodying the potential power of a minority of the population residing in some coalition of states. This connection is enhanced by the Senate's rules protecting extended debate and allowing for filibusters. Without any sophisticated effort, the two—the Senate of equal representation and the filibuster—were blended together, naturalized, and harmonized as founding intent, when in the view of some, Madison included, state equality and deliberative quality were at odds with one another or at best unrelated.

## Constitutionality Reality: The Filibuster Subverts What the Founders Created

In sharp contrast to the falsehoods and insinuations about the filibuster and the founding, the stronger argument is that supermajority cloture in the Senate is not just impractical or democratically suspect, it directly conflicts with the architecture and intent of the Constitution. Can a Senate rule of procedure, created by a simple resolution, conflict with one or more explicit provisions of the Constitution such that the rule is unconstitutional? That is an interesting question, but this tour of constitutional arguments is not intended to persuade the reader one way or another about constitutionality as such. The points below constitute important arguments about sound and fair democratic practice as much as they do constitutionality. They are powerful indictments of supermajority cloture that use the governmental purpose and design of the Constitution as their democratic theory or compass point. In short, these arguments provide a sharp contrast to the typical laundry lists of pro-filibuster arguments that have no clear normative or constitutional foundation.

First, the Constitution defines specific and limited instances in which supermajorities are required, and the list is a small one. In order of appearance the five supermajority exceptions are: impeachment trial convictions (two-thirds of senators present), expulsion of members of the House and Senate (two-thirds of the relevant chamber), override of vetoes (two-thirds of both chambers),[49] treaty approval (two-thirds of senators present), and the amendment process for the Constitution itself. Moreover, the framers explicitly rejected some other supermajority options. The document does not specify that other supermajorities are not allowed, but such a provision is not necessary to make a legally sound judgment that silence means no. The common law legal principle that some have applied to this circumstance is *expressio unius est exclusion alterius,* the express mention of one thing excludes all others.[50] In this case, the careful list of supermajority provisions, by this principle, means no others are implied or allowed.

Proponents for the filibuster argue in response that there is a crucial distinction between the supermajorities in the Constitution that are all about final decisions (such as the vote on a treaty) and an internal Senate procedure that is about limits on debate, not the final decision.[51] Nothing in the Senate rules specifies that a final vote will be by a supermajority.

Even in the case where the proposal is to change one of the Senate's standing rules, if two-thirds of senators present and voting agree to close debate, the final vote on the rules change is by majority. This argument is bolstered by the emphasis others place on Article I, section 5's explicit grant of authority: "Each House may determine the rules of its proceedings." What the Constitution might take away in terms of latitude about how to make final decisions might not apply to the rules of procedure within each chamber, that is, the rules that shape but ultimately precede the potential for an ultimate decision by majority vote.

This argument ignores the realities of the sixty-vote (and even sixty-seven-vote) Senate, including the increasingly regular use of the sixty-vote threshold built into unanimous consent agreements as final votes. That crucial reality check aside, it strains credulity to argue that the rule does not fundamentally alter how or whether a majority does or does not get to vote on its preferred policy or alternative. It simply goes too far to argue that the "supermajority voting requirements to invoke cloture is *simply* a procedural rule, not a substantive one" (emphasis added).[52] Its original intent might be one thing and its actual impact quite another. Moreover, senators provide ample evidence in words and deeds that they consider it to be, and behave as if it were, the decision rule. Nevertheless, the distinction between procedures and final decisions is probably the strongest counterargument about the constitutionality of the filibuster.

As part of this counterargument, some point to other aspects of House and Senate procedure as minority veto points akin to Senate cloture, in particular the powerful role of committees. If supermajority cloture is unconstitutional, then what about the crucial role accorded House and Senate committees? One or more committees consider most legislation before the chambers as a whole do, and if the committee votes against reporting the legislation to the floor, that bill is unlikely to be revived. This is by definition a minority veto. If committees are constitutionally sound, the argument goes, then so is supermajority cloture in the Senate. Indeed, congressional committees have played a very powerful gatekeeping role in both chambers, in some eras dominating the decision-making process. While this is true, committees operate through the consent of not only the majority but the minority party as well. The House approves its standing rules at the start of each Congress, so this consent is more than implicit. Moreover, committees do not entrench in quite the same way. Whatever the committees do can be reversed by the majority in both chambers, and the House has a procedure that can be used by a majority of House members to discharge a bill from a committee and bring it to the floor.[53]

If the first line of argument relies on the Constitution's explicit list of supermajority provisions, the second is built around the several implications that both chambers of Congress would operate by majority rule in all other instances. None of the supermajority exceptions pertain to ordinary lawmaking except the override of a presidential veto.[54] Article I, section 5's stipulation that "a majority of each shall constitute a quorum to do business" is the foundation of this claim, bolstered by the incontrovertible assumption that legislatures operate by majority rule. Likewise, it can be argued that supermajority cloture conflicts with the presentment clause in Article I, section 7 by effectively requiring a minimum of sixty affirmative votes in the Senate—rather than a simple majority of a quorum—to "pass" a bill or resolution prior to its presentment to the president. Neither chamber of Congress has the constitutional latitude to disrupt the carefully constructed lawmaking process. "This balance of powers," in the view of one scholar, "would be entirely undone if it were true that each legislative chamber could define what it means for that chamber to 'pass' a bill."[55] Finally, the provision to have the vice president cast the deciding vote in the case of a tie—in a body that is perpetually composed of an even number of senators—presumes that the Senate decides by simple majority.[56] And that is one of the only jobs assigned to that office! In fact, consternation at the Constitutional Convention about the role of the vice president was eased when it was given this potentially important function.

Third, rather than being a natural extension of equal representation, the filibuster upends the politics of the Great Compromise. The superimposition of supermajority cloture on top of equal representation violates the already fraught compromise "between the interests of the majority of citizens in the more populous states and the minority living in the less populous states."[57] As noted above, twenty-one states representing less than 12 percent of the American population could form a cloture-proof block of forty-one or forty-two senators. Such a tidy coalition of the smallest states sounds unlikely. If, however, we take the twenty-one states that gave Donald Trump the greatest share of their popular vote in 2016, from Wyoming at 68.2 percent down to Ohio's more modest 51.3 percent, we see a rather more plausible coalition of forty-one or forty-two senators representing just under 31 percent of the national population.

Finally, twenty states at the start of the Trump presidency had two Republican senators. Those forty Republican senators, who were one vote short of a cloture-proof minority, represented just over 32 percent of the national population. This potential coalition was not so relevant, insofar as the Republicans were the majority party in the Senate. But this was also pretty much the situation when Republicans were the minority for part of Obama's presidency. In an era of partisan polarization, the overlap between state characteristics and partisanship is substantial and consequential.

The Great Compromise was the power given to states through equal representation. A majority of population represented in the House might be balanced or countered by a *majority* of states in the Senate, not by a minority of states using the sixty-vote threshold no matter what fraction of the population they represent, large or small. Again, the only notion of minority rights tied to the Senate is equal representation of states. It is not a gateway through which other forms of minority protection can be added to the Senate.

The final argument about the constitutionality of the filibuster is perhaps the most powerful one, even if it is the one linked least directly to any particular provision of the Constitution. Supermajority cloture violates the fundamental principle of legislative power that a legislature cannot bind its successors by preventing them from amending or repealing statutes and rules by majority vote. The term applied to any such attempt to so bind or restrict a future legislature is entrenchment.[58] Impermissible entrenchment occurs when laws "bind the public to a substantive policy judgment made by legislators who are no longer responsive to the public will or current exigencies."[59] Imagine if today's Congress by majority vote in both chambers passed a strict gun control measure banning a category of weapons and that the law included a provision that it could be repealed only by a two-thirds vote in both chambers. Certainly no one would endorse this or think it constitutional. Instead, a legislative body can only do what a future version of itself can undo by a majority vote.

This principle and practice predate the Constitution and go back at least as far as Blackstone's dictum that "acts of parliament derogatory from the power of subsequent parliaments bind not."[60] It was such a given that it there is little doubt that the framers took it for granted. Consequently there was no need to have anything explicit in the Constitution about entrenchment.[61] Higher law, as in the US Constitution, is by definition a form of entrenchment.[62] That is, the constitutional features of almost any polity are entrenched to some degree. In most cases, democratic nations such as the United States are structured by a constitution that was enacted by a supermajority procedure and can be modified only through the same or some other supermajority process. So entrenchment does exist, but it is limited to the creation or modification of higher law and is almost never the product of the legislative body alone. Higher law is the superstructure—and, yes, supermajority structure—for making ordinary or public law and policy. And it is at this point that entrenchment must end or there would be little point to having higher law or, for that matter, elections. If a legislature can entrench laws by restricting future versions of itself, then it has in effect created a kind of higher law through ordinary legislative process.

Supermajority cloture in the Senate, from this perspective, is a form of entrenchment. The first form of entrenchment is that owing to the filibuster, a future Senate majority might be unable to repeal or amend an ordinary law. Or that a new law might be unobtainable, thereby entrenching the status quo more generally. The second form of entrenchment is in Rule XXII's stipulation that debate on any changes to the rules of the Senate can be brought to a close, when any number of members object and hold the floor, only through a two-thirds vote on cloture. This is reinforced by Rule V's provision that the standing rules of the Senate continue from one Congress to the next and can be changed only through the process specified in the standing rules. The combination of Rule XXII's significantly higher threshold against changing the rules and Rule V's codification of the continuing body doctrine constitutes an extraordinary entrenchment of a supermajority procedure that often determines what the Senate can or cannot do.

As I noted earlier, we spent time with these constitutional arguments to add to the case against supermajority cloture and the exceptional Senate's self-conception. Some have argued that the federal judiciary could and should consider a constitutional case against supermajority cloture, while others make the opposite case.[63] But whether or not that is a possibility is more or less irrelevant for my purposes. And so I agree and disagree with Tonja Jacobi and Jeff Van Dam when they argue that the court is highly unlikely to rule on the constitutionality of supermajority cloture. "Consequently," they conclude, "the extensive references by both sides of the debate to constitutional arguments for and against the filibuster are essentially just political rhetoric. Although arguments can be made for constitutional support or opposition to whether a simple majority can change a supermajority rule, the constitutional legitimacy of such a change is ultimately irrelevant if the courts will not hear the case. As such, adverting to legal argumentation is theater aimed at political persuasion, not serious preparations for significant litigation."[64] Yes, court intervention is highly unlikely, but to reduce arguments about proper forms of government to "rhetoric" and "theater" is a bit much. After all, if the alternative to legal action is mere rhetoric and theater, then so much for the political process that might lead to institutional reform. While their point is well taken with regard to a strict notion of constitutionality, the arguments I have reviewed above nevertheless provide a powerful indictment of supermajority cloture on its own terms, an indictment that could be precisely the kind of "political persuasion" that leads to reform.

OVERT FILIBUSTERS against racial equality—the all too real and frequent filibusters on behalf of white supremacy—were a thing of the past by the twenty-first century. The racial bias of the Senate and the filibuster remains, however. In chapter 3, I demonstrated the very explicit bias of equal representation: the overrepresentation of smaller states inexorably entails the underrepresentation of Blacks and other minorities in larger and more urban states. The contemporary bias of the supermajority Senate is more subtle but significant nevertheless, especially when combined with equal representation. The advancement of civil rights demanded and still needs the active intervention of the government on behalf of minorities or otherwise debilitated or oppressed groups such as women. Progress toward broader social equality can require governmental programs and spending in such areas as education, employment, welfare, and health care. All this requires legislation or even a constitutional amendment in some cases. In the American government, it is far easier to veto than to pass legislation, and the Senate filibuster has been the fourth veto point in an already complex system. Yes, when the tables are turned, affected groups can use the filibuster to perhaps foil the diminution of rights previously acquired. But such rearguard actions hardly compensate for the positive power diminished by the effects of the supermajority cloture. Now add equal representation: those more likely to oppose government action in these areas, because of their greater conservatism about positive rights and governmental activism, are overrepresented in a legislative body that then further enhances their power with a potential minority veto.

This bias, however, is not the only indictment of the filibuster and sixty-vote Senate. As we have just seen, the filibuster contradicts rather than complements the constitutional system of checks and balances, separation of powers, and representational compromises. If not unconstitutional as such, the supermajority rule and behavior of the sixty-vote Senate run counter to the fundamental principles and provisions of the American system as designed and originally intended by its architects. Finally, the bias and constitutional contradictions are woven into and express themselves through the overarching practical failures of supermajority politics in the Senate. It fails by the very standards advanced by its advocates. Far from facilitating deliberation, the sixty-vote Senate undermines it by creating a veto that negates whatever purpose deliberation might serve and elevates procedural games over substantive debate. It undermines political accountability and erodes the ability of an already divided Congress to check presidential power. Rather than being a salutary check on potential missteps, the filibuster is a major cause of systemic dysfunction and, thereby, the erosion of public confidence in its government.

These three political and constitutional realities—the compound racial bias, constitutional problems, and the practical failings—would not, however, carry the day and convince the Senate to change its ways. Even as the sixty-vote Senate was being hoisted by its own procedural petard and frustrations with the filibuster were growing inside and outside the Senate during the first two decades of this century, the Senate as a whole clung to its mythology about the filibuster as its institution essence, which derived directly or indirectly from the founding or the founders' intentions. Unable to deliberate about the dysfunctions of supermajority procedures, the polarized Senate of the twenty-first century spiraled toward raw political confrontation. The world's greatest deliberative body would not draw on that alleged quality to reason its way beyond the problems of the sixty-vote Senate. Instead, heightened dysfunction combined with bitter partisan polarization to encourage both parties at different times to use brute force to change the rules by evading and violating the rules they otherwise devoted so much energy to defending. After years of partisan combat and vexation, in November 2013 and April 2017 the Senate finally took extraordinary action to reduce the scope and impact of supermajority cloture, action that was easy to construe as doing the right thing but in the wrong way, and for the wrong reason.

# 7

# The Supermajority Senate Curtailed

NUCLEAR OPTIONS AND MUSHROOM
CLOUDS OF HYPOCRISY

## Auto-Obstruction: Minority Leader McConnell Filibusters Himself

On December 6, 2012, a senator filibustered his own proposal—a first, to the best of anyone's recollection, in Senate history, a history already rich in parliamentary wonders. The senator in question was no less than Minority Leader Mitch McConnell, Republican from Kentucky. In another episode of the hyperpartisanship that had turned the institution into a free-fire zone of procedural warfare, McConnell thought he would make a proposal the Democratic majority would have to refuse, which would in turn embarrass President Obama. It did not go as planned.

The Democratic president and a Congress split between a Republican House and a Democratic Senate had been struggling over the national budget for more than a year. One part of this fight was yet another contest of partisan wills over increasing the debt ceiling, a legal limit set by Congress on the amount of debt the government can hold. Whenever the ceiling drew near, Congress tended to turn the unpalatable but unavoidable fiscal necessity of raising the limit into a surrogate for the fight over spending priorities and the deficit. One solution that had been kicking around for years, and that Obama and many Democrats supported this go-round, was to give the president the authority to raise the debt ceiling, thereby avoiding the political difficulties and partisan showmanship that accompanied every congressional effort to do this essential task. Adamantly opposed to the proposal, McConnell thought he could put the Democratic caucus in a tough position. His guess was that a majority of Democrats would vote against granting the president this kind of power, a power that might make sense but looked fiscally irresponsible.

Majority Leader Harry Reid, however, called McConnell's bluff. He knew that Democratic senators would vote to pass the proposal. McConnell had moved unanimous consent to have an up-or-down majority vote on the debt ceiling measure. Reid said, fine, let's do it. McConnell was forced to then object to his own motion. The minority leader reacted to Reid's agreement to his proposal for a vote by "reserving the right to object," adding, "Matters of this level of controversy always require 60 votes. So I would ask my friend, the majority leader, if he would modify his consent request to set the threshold for this vote at 60?"

Reid refused. In full possession of the procedural high ground, Reid described the trap McConnell had set for himself: "This morning, the Republican leader asked consent to have a vote on his proposal. Just now I told everyone we are willing to have that vote, an up-or-down vote. But now the Republican leader objects to his own idea. So I guess we have a filibuster of his own bill."

For the benefit of the media and the few Americans watching C-SPAN, Majority Whip Richard Durbin immediately summarized and simplified what had just happened. Majority Leader Reid, Durbin explained,

> said he would bring this to a vote in 20 minutes, and we would decide, up or down, whether the debt ceiling problem would be resolved once and for all under Senator *McConnell*'s proposal. Then Senator *McConnell* objected—objected—saying: No, no, we need 60 votes. For those who do not follow the Senate, 60 votes is the equivalent of a filibuster vote—breaking a filibuster vote. So this may be a moment in Senate history when a Senator made a proposal and, when given an opportunity for a vote on that proposal, filibustered his own proposal. I think we have now reached a new spot in the history of the Senate we have never seen before.[1]

This arcane bit of political circus created a small YouTube sensation and was the butt of satirical riffs on television.[2] McConnell's action was unique, but new spots, so to speak, in Senate history were getting to be a dime a dozen. McConnell's auto-obstruction epitomized the constitutional dysfunction at the core of the Senate. McConnell and even his gleeful interlocutors perhaps unintentionally confirmed the ugly truth about the Senate—the chamber had become a supermajority institution wherein sixty votes was the decision rule for nearly any important matter before it. This episode was emblematic as well of the mounting frustrations over the filibuster. Pitched partisan battles and feckless compromises over the use and abuse of Rule XXII had become a nearly ongoing feature of Senate politics in the early twenty-first century. By this point in the Obama presidency, things seemed to be heading for a showdown. And that would come less than a year later, when push came to shove over one of the most contentious uses—by both parties—of the filibuster in recent years: against presidential nominations to the federal courts.

On November 21, 2013, the Senate decided that the "vote on cloture under Rule XXII for all nominations other than for the Supreme Court of the United States is by majority vote." These few and perhaps obscure words embodied the most important change in Senate standing rules—or, to be precise, in their interpretation—since the threshold for cloture was lowered to three-fifths in 1975, and arguably since the creation of cloture in 1917. In the face of a Republican filibuster of some judicial nominations, a majority of Democrats agreed to radically reinterpret a Senate rule via a parliamentary ruling on a point of order. Just over three years later, on April 6, 2017, the Senate, under Republican control and with exclusively Republican support, voted to apply the same interpretation to nominations to the Supreme Court. Thus did the Senate remove its constitutional duty to give "advice and consent" on presidential nominations from the provisions of Rule XXII.

This was historic stuff. With these two actions an entire category of Senate business, one of its designated constitutional responsibilities, was protected from obstruction by the minority. The supermajority provisions of Rule XXII no longer applied to presidential nominations. Moreover, only a few years apart, a majority from each party voted to categorically restrict the filibuster. Finally, in each case the Democratic or Republican majority employed the same controversial method—often referred to as the "nuclear option"—to make these significant changes to a standing rule of the Senate. Instead of amending the wording of the standing rule, in this case Rule XXII, in both cases a member of the majority made a point of order to produce a parliamentary interpretation and ruling, which was then subject to a majority vote to sustain or overturn.

The so-called nuclear options were spectacular and controversial, and did bring significant change to the sixty-vote Senate. But they also highlighted an underlying reality: the Senate, often in concert with the House, had forged and used several other limitations, or "carve-outs," that protected specific congressional actions from supermajority cloture in the Senate. Over the years, Congress has structured several statutory evasions of Senate filibusters and obstruction. In all these cases there is a statutory time limit on consideration that applies to both chambers. Taken together, when these exceptions are joined with the actions of 2013 and 2017, this constitutes a major diminution of supermajority politics. The supermajority Senate remains powerful but circumscribed and curtailed. Following the second recourse to the nuclear option in 2017, many senators and observers asked whether the Senate might be heading toward the end not only of the sixty-vote Senate but of supermajority cloture entirely, as the perceived interests in supermajority cloture are modified and as the norms that supported it are eroded.

## Take Your Pick: The Nuclear, Constitutional, or Conventional Option

The creation of the supermajority cloture procedure in 1917, as we have seen, was intended to limit minority obstruction and filibusters. Before this reform, the frustrations produced by some filibusters prompted the majority to consider the use of parliamentary maneuvers to curtail what they saw as the abuse of the Senate's rules that protected the right of senators to speak for as long as they wished or could. One problem was that an ordinary simple resolution to change the rules directly by writing a new rule or revising an existing rule could be filibustered. And any proposal to add some form of majority cloture to the rules almost certainly would be subject to a determined filibuster. Could a parliamentary ruling be used to get around this obstacle?

Under Senate Rule XX, senators can pose parliamentary inquiries to the presiding officer. As the rule states, "A question of order may be raised at any stage of the proceedings, except when the Senate is voting or ascertaining the presence of a quorum." Most questions of order are routine, but some call for careful interpretation by the presiding officer, and the ruling of the chair can be, in those instances, controversial and important. Any decision by the chair can be appealed to the Senate. Such an appeal is not debatable and decided by a majority vote. In general, the presiding officer is bound by the precedents of Senate practice and so would be unlikely to make a decision that flew in the face of the clear words of a standing rule and long-standing interpretation. But if an appeal of that decision is made and a majority overturns the ruling, then existing interpretations of rules can be undone by a simple majority. This opens the possibility to do via parliamentary ruling what could not be done or would be practically impossible to do within the constraints of the existing wording or interpretations of the rules. Thousands of such parliamentary rulings have shaped Senate (and House) rules and procedures, and dozens have been made on Rule XXII alone.[3] But none of these fundamentally altered the cloture process until the nuclear option in 2013.

The idea of using a parliamentary ruling to end debate or curtail a particular filibuster goes back at least to the Senate's battle over the federal elections bill (or "Force Bill") of 1890 and 1891. As mentioned in chapter 5, this bill sought to use national authority to enforce the unambiguous command of the Fifteenth Amendment. Passed in the House and supported by the president, the bill faced a determined filibuster in the Senate by southern Democrats. In the face of this implacable opposition, the de facto leader of the Republican majority, Nelson Aldrich, introduced a proposal that would have changed Senate rules for the remainder of that session to allow cloture by majority after a reasonable period of debate had transpired. But Aldrich's proposal for a "gag rule," as his opponents inevitably dubbed it, could be filibustered too, and it was. So the Republican leader's plan was to end debate on it through a parliamentary ruling and appeal. Aldrich planned to make a point of order that the debate on his cloture amendment had gone on long enough and was in effect dilatory. Success depended on having the presiding officer rule favorably on the point of order. If the filibustering minority then appealed the ruling, the majority could table the appeal—and a tabling motion is not subject to debate—by a majority vote. The ruling would stand, and Aldrich's temporary cloture provision would have ended debate on the elections bill. This did not work out as planned. In short, enough Republican senators who opposed or preferred not to have to vote on the elections bill joined with the Democrats to displace it and move on to other business, effectively killing it.[4] The point is that this tactic of using a parliamentary ruling instead of directly changing the rule was part of the battle over the filibuster well before the creation of Rule XXII.

As that reform to limit excessive debate evolved into a powerful tool for minority obstruction, senators contemplated and acted on ways to limit or curtail the filibuster. Rule XXII has been amended several times since its creation in 1917, including the reduction of cloture on all matters except proposed changes to the rules to three-fifths. As one might expect, these changes were accomplished by compromises that led to majority votes to change the wording of the rule. Behind these successful efforts, however, were not just political compromises but also threats posed by the ongoing possibility of using the other way to change the rules, not by changing the wording but by changing the interpretation of the rule as written.[5]

Such threats were motivated in part by Rule XXII's compound frustration. First, the rule had become a tool of obstruction rather than a limitation of filibusters. Second, Rule XXII created and contained a formidable barrier to changing itself, let alone any other Senate rule. Any motion or measure to change a rule has required two-thirds of senators to invoke cloture (either two-thirds of the entire membership or, as is currently the case, two-thirds of senators present and voting). Any proposed alteration of the rules could be blocked even though sixty-six senators support it. This double frustration, with supermajority cloture itself and its entrenchment, invited senators to consider extraordinary measures to circumvent it through a parliamentary ruling.

Article I, section 5 of the Constitution specifies that "Each House may determine the Rules of its Proceedings." One interpretation of this is that at any time, a majority of each chamber is allowed to decide what its rules should be. Again, this is how the House of Representatives has operated at the start of every new Congress. Leaning on the implication that each House can determine its rules by a majority vote, one option would be for a senator to raise a point of order at the start of the new Congress asking the presiding officer if that is not the case. Whether it should or must be done at the start of a new Congress is a matter of debate, but, much as the House of Representatives adopts its rules, whether amended or unaltered, at the outset of a new Congress, it is at least a logical place to offer such a motion. The presiding officer could rule that the point of order is correct, and if necessary be sustained by a majority vote of the Senate. If instead the chair ruled against the point of order, a majority of the Senate could overturn the ruling. In either case, the result would be to open the Senate to changes in the rules by a majority vote. This is most often referred to as the "constitutional option" because of its reliance on I, 5.[6]

We can do no better than the words of Vice President Richard Nixon, who articulated the logic of the constitutional option when it arose amid concerns about civil rights reform during the Eisenhower presidency:

> It is the opinion of the Chair that while the rules of the Senate have been continued from one Congress to another, the right of the current majority of the Senate at the beginning of a Congress to adopt its own rules, stemming as it does from the Constitution itself, cannot be restricted or

limited by rules adopted by a majority of the Senate in a previous Congress. Any provision of the Senate rules adopted in a previous Congress that has the expressed or practical effect of denying a majority of the Senate in a new Congress the right to adopt the rules under which it desires to proceed is, in the opinion of the Chair, unconstitutional.[7]

Nixon was speaking as the presiding officer of the Senate at the start of the Eighty-Fifth Congress in January 1957, in one of his first actions as the reelected vice president. But it was only an answer—albeit a carefully rehearsed one—to a parliamentary inquiry from Senator Hubert Humphrey. At that time, the Republican vice president from California and the Democratic senator from Minnesota were not strange bedfellows but allies in the cause of overcoming filibusters by southern Democrats. No formal action was taken after Nixon gave his opinion, so his words—however clear and forceful—had no direct effect on Senate rules or precedents.

The constitutional option was never tested. Threat of its use resulted in or at least facilitated compromises that often got reformers only part of what they, or some among them, sought. The constitutional option was perceived to be dangerous because it could have opened the door to unrelenting parliamentary warfare, including other attempts to make significant rule changes by reinterpretation rather than by changing the text of the rule itself. The imagined conflict and chaos that might ensue would later inspire some to label this the "nuclear option." But from another perspective, such parliamentary rulings backed by majority votes have "been used throughout the history of the Senate and the House of Representatives" and could just as well be called the "conventional option."[8] In fact, Robert Byrd, that staunch defender of Senate tradition, used a ruling in 1980 to eliminate debate on the motion to proceed to nominations.[9] Such actions, based as they are on Senate rules and practice, might be more or less controversial, but even their use to dramatically alter the filibuster in 2013 and 2017 did not prove to be very explosive, let alone nuclear.[10]

## Meanwhile, the Senate Carves Out Exceptions: Legislative Restrictions on Supermajority Cloture

The threat of nuclear warfare in the Senate, however, was preceded by a series of almost uncontroversial restrictions on the reach of the filibuster and supermajority cloture. These limitations were put in place not by changing the rule itself or by the nuclear or constitutional option of a parliamentary ruling. Instead, they were written into ordinary legislation as exceptions or "carve-outs" that prevented minority obstruction of carefully specified categories of legislation or congressional resolutions. These laws contained provisions that added time limits on congressional action. These provisions—referred to as "fast-track procedures" or "carve-outs" or "majoritarian exceptions"—directly voided or restricted the rules of the Senate that allowed for minority obstruction.[11]

In 2003, as the Senate was heading into its first nuclear crisis over obstruction of President Bush's nominees to circuit courts, Majority Leader Bill Frist testified before the Rules Committee in support of restrictions on the filibuster. As part of his argument, he provided a cogent summary of the scope and purpose of the legislative exceptions:

> Mr. Chairman, the filibuster may be famous, but it is hardly sacrosanct. More than 25 statutes exist that curtail by law the right to unlimited debate. The most prominent of these is the 1974 Congressional Budget and Impoundment Control Act, which sets forth debate limitations on concurrent budget resolutions, reconciliation bills, and related amendments between Houses and conference reports. . . . The first of these debate-restrictive rulemaking statutes was enacted in 1939. Its enactment and the passage of so many provisions since, are evidence of the Senate's willingness to curb unlimited debate to further particular public policy objectives.[12]

Frist's mention of 1939 as the year of the first such exception reminds us that, in seeking the origins of many things that altered the balance of power between Congress and the president, we must go back to the New Deal. Despite a clear but essentially ignored ruling from the Supreme Court that Congress could not, in effect, delegate its legislative power to the president, Congress had gotten into the habit of at least sharing that power in novel ways.[13] One relatively innocuous version came in the Executive Reorganization Act of 1939 to allow the president to submit plans to reorganize the executive branch directly to Congress. This legislation followed a departmental logic: allow the chief executive to decide on the best architecture and arrangements for many aspects of the branch he oversees. The president's plan was privileged in several ways, including a time limit on committee consideration, a nondebatable motion to proceed, and a time limit on debate. This affected both chambers, but it directly voided all senatorial obstruction.

The Executive Reorganization Act of 1939 and its majoritarian carve-out were part of an era of increasing presidential power not infrequently facilitated and embraced by congressional action or deference. A few decades later Congress would begin to regret the powerful president it had helped create, especially in the form of Nixon's "imperial presidency." By the 1970s, it was not that the Senate was seen as particularly dysfunctional; instead, the presidency had become too dangerous and Congress as a whole too compliant or incapable of countering presidential power. As part of the reaction to the power of the presidency and to its inherent limitations in the era of the complex welfare-warfare state amid a rapidly changing world, Congress began to pass laws to facilitate its ability to act coherently and decisively by specific modifications of legislative procedure to expedite congressional action. The majoritarian carve-out could serve both purposes: to delegate power to the president and to help Congress counter presidential power.

The reaction to the imperial presidency produced, for example, the War Powers Act—enacted in November 1973 when Congress overrode Nixon's veto—as an attempt to mandate congressional participation in the decision to start or extend the use of military force. Amid the attention and controversy swirling around this resolution, coming as it did in the wake of the Vietnam debacle and as the Watergate scandal was becoming a constitutional crisis, the provisions that created timetables for House and Senate action went unnoticed or seemed like common sense. But they were there to negate minority obstruction of any resolutions Congress might attempt to pass in keeping with its responsibilities in the War Powers Act.[14] The War Powers Act was joined by the 1976 National Emergencies Act, which also tried to rein in presidential overreach. It too included expedited procedures, in this case, to consider any joint resolution to terminate a national emergency that had been declared by the president.[15]

This era produced two other major laws that circumvented supermajority cloture for specific legislation. The Budget Act of 1974 includes provisions that restrict or make exceptions to Senate rules to curtail obstruction and eliminate the possibility of veto by supermajority cloture. The goal was to bring order to what had been a fragmented legislative process, increasingly dominated by the executive branch, with little if any coordination among congressional committees. At the core of the budget act is the bicameral or concurrent budget resolution that sets revenue and spending (and deficit) targets for both chambers. An optional component is reconciliation, which mandates changes in law for direct spending programs and revenue to make the budget plan work. As part of this coordination, provisions were added to structure and limit debate and amendments on both the budget resolution and any reconciliation measures. The irony is that the reconciliation process, which was created as a circumscribed exception for purposes of passing a budget, evolved into a powerful vehicle for enacting major policy changes related to taxation and spending. The first major example of this was the Omnibus Budget Reconciliation Act of 1981, which was President Reagan's mammoth package of tax reductions and spending cuts, essentially the opening shot and signal achievement of the so-called Reagan Revolution. Every president and Congress since has used this tool, often for major initiatives, including the Health Care and Education Reconciliation Act of 2010, which was instrumental in the passage of President Obama's Affordable Care Act.[16]

Another major law from the 1970s, the 1975 Trade Act, for the most part enhanced presidential power and restricted congressional action, with the goal of reaching effective trade agreements. With Gerald Ford in the White House, the concern was less about an imperial president than about the state of the economy, including the first oil shocks and stagflation. In addition, Congress recognized that its parochialism was a problem: members of Congress were apt to play politics with any trade agreement and possibly scuttle it with amendments. Much like the budget law before it, the Trade Act put strict limits on House and Senate consideration. These restrictions in the Trade Act are commonly referred to as fast-track authority and are much like other majoritarian exceptions. These include immediate introduction of the president's proposed agreement in both chambers, a forty-five-day limit on consideration by committees, privileged access to floor consideration with nondebatable motion, a vote in each house within fifteen days after committee consideration, and no amendments in committee or on the floor.[17] The Trade Act did not make its provisions permanent, and so Congress has had to renew or extend it on several occasions. Such fast-track authority produced several trade agreements from the mid-1970s through the mid-1990s, including NAFTA. Although economic concerns and partisan politics stymied its reauthorization after the mid-1990s, George W. Bush got Congress to approve a five-year renewal in 2002, and Barack

Obama worked with Congress to get another extension in 2015, with several agreements resulting, including the Trans-Pacific Partnership, from which President Trump withdrew in one of his earliest acts in office.

As a final example, Congress tied its own hands in decisions about military base closures. Between 1977 and 1987 Congress had prevented the closure of any large bases, but as the end of the Cold War came into view, Congress passed a law that evaded the politics that kept bases from being closed by delegating the most difficult decisions to an independent commission and the president and by limiting congressional participation in the process.[18] The crucial restriction was that Congress had forty-five days after the president submitted the list of proposed closures or realignments during which a vote of disapproval could be taken, but with no changes or amendments allowed to the list. If Congress did not vote, the list went into effect automatically. The deadline and prohibition of amendments negated Senate obstruction and led to several rounds of closures and realignments.[19]

## Nominations and the Sixty-Vote Senate

While the majoritarian carve-outs did their relatively quiet work of facilitating bicameral success in some areas of public policy, the Senate nevertheless gravitated toward greater levels of supermajority politics. There were more than enough remaining targets for filibustering, including one that had been rarely exploited: presidential nominations to the executive branch and the judiciary. The rise of the sixty-vote Senate in the 1990s and early 2000s had attracted general attention to and criticism of Senate practice. Part of the more partisan supermajority Senate was the minority obstruction of executive nominations. This drew particular scorn at times, in part because the filibuster of nominations was a largely new phenomenon. In the past, a largely bipartisan deference to the president in this shared power was an important factor; in general, a qualified nominee merited confirmation. Obstruction of nominations carried a normative, even constitutional, taint. We may or may not need a new Clean Air Act, but courts have to have judges to function as courts. We might want to stop a rush to war, but the president should be able to appoint an undersecretary of defense in a timely fashion.

In fact, the special status of appointments—as a shared power that involved the ability of other branches to do the tasks assigned to them in Articles II and III—was one of the arguments against supermajority cloture.

From one perspective, presidential nominations of any variety could be seen as just another category of "measure, motion, other matter pending before the Senate" that were subject to the filibuster and supermajority cloture under Rule XXII. However, a strong case can be made—and some legal scholars and even senators from both parties have made it—that applying a supermajority procedure to nominations, particularly judicial nominations, is a rather specific violation or de facto amendment of the Constitution.[20] Does the Senate have the constitutional license to block nominations to a co-equal branch, in effect evading its "advice and consent" relationship with the executive and interfering with the judiciary's ability to function? "Advice and consent" includes, of course, the right to disapprove of a nominee. But here is a case where the Constitution is unambiguous that approval or disapproval is by a Senate majority, not supermajority. Otherwise it would make no sense to specify that treaties, the only other shared power with the executive, are to be approved by a two-thirds supermajority. The counterargument is that nothing in the Constitution mandates timely action on nominations or precludes other procedural mechanisms that might defeat a nominee short of a majority vote.[21] Even the president, in this view, is under no obligation to nominate anyone in a timely fashion. This claim might be textually plausible, but it is constitutionally specious. If the president delayed nominations endlessly and the Senate filibustered the ones that were eventually made—and we at times have not been so far from this—can one sincerely argue the Constitution is working as intended, as its words directly imply?

Regardless of the constitutional and practical arguments, prior to the confluence of partisan polarization and the sixty-vote Senate particular nominations might be controversial owing to competence or scandal, but partisan obstruction of nominations was exceptional, in part because of the constitutional norms around executive and judicial appointments. Things began to change, however. In the eighteen years from 1949 through 1966 there were no cloture motions filed on executive nominations. From 1967 through 1992, a period of twenty-five years, there were twelve. In the fourteen years from 1993 through 2006 there were fifty-five, or nearly four per year.[22] As a reminder, "Filibusters may occur without cloture being sought, and cloture may be sought when no filibuster is taking place."[23] Nevertheless, such a striking increase in cloture is a measure of the degree to which nominations had become a target of obstruction. And given the prominence in recent decades of holds, which are most often directed at nominations, cloture votes understate the rate of obstruction.

## Several Days in May: The Cuban Missile Crisis of the Nuclear Option

Obstruction of nominations was increasing from 1993 onward but did not produce a crisis until the presidency of George W. Bush, when Senate Democrats made a concerted effort to block a series of Bush's nominations to the federal judiciary.[24] The Senate of the 107th Congress started in 2001 with an historic 50–50 balance of Republicans and Democrats, with Vice President Dick Cheney holding the deciding vote if needed. Despite a few changes, it remained essentially a 50–50 Senate. The 2002 midterm elections hardly altered this, with Republicans having fifty-one seats versus forty-nine for the Democrats, including one nominal independent. Cloture was a particularly high hurdle for the majority during Bush's first term, and this resulted in a series of failed cloture attempts on six of Bush's circuit court nominations in 2003.[25] Republicans claimed that the Democrats' filibusters were the first to stop any appellate nominees and, with some debate over the exact status of Abe Fortas's nomination in 1968, produced the first successful blockage of any nomination to the judiciary that had clear support from a majority of the Senate.[26]

In the middle of this struggle, the Senate Rules Committee held hearings to consider modifications to cloture for judicial nominations. Former majority leader Trent Lott summarized the case: "What we have witnessed over the past five months in connection with the nominations of Miguel Esterada and Priscilla Owen is a hijacking of the Senate's Constitutional responsibility to advise and consent on the President's nominations. A minority of Senators have literally re-written the Constitution to engraft a supermajority rule into the confirmation process, a requirement that completely contradicts the intent, spirit and language of the Constitution."[27] Put forward by Majority Leader Frist, the main option under consideration during the hearing was one quite familiar to Senate veterans and observers: the decreasing or sliding cloture. Associated with Senator Tom Harkin, who first proposed it in the 1990s when Democrats faced aggressive Republican obstruction, the sliding cloture would restructure that procedure such that the first cloture threshold on a particular matter would be sixty, but subsequent motions on the same issue, if necessary, would decrease from fifty-seven, to fifty-four, to fifty-one, to a simple majority of those present and voting. Senator Harkin sought to apply this to all matters before the Senate; Majority Leader Frist wanted to apply it only to judicial nominations.[28] Such a change in the actual wording of Rule XXII probably would have required a two-thirds cloture vote to shut off debate on the proposed change. As a result, some Republicans had been considering the option of a parliamentary ruling all along. In fact, by early 2003 this potential tactic had acquired a new name. Senator Lott is credited with calling it the "nuclear option" because of its potentially explosive impact on Senate politics.[29] Senator Frist was at first reluctant to go down this road, in part because he believed he did not have the votes in the closely divided Senate. But the majority leader was prepared to use the nuclear option if the Republicans picked up more seats in the 2004 elections, which they did, producing a 55–45 majority.[30]

It was in this environment that Majority Leader Frist threatened in early 2005 to use the constitutional or nuclear option to allow majority cloture on such nominations. Frist's point of order would be that Rule XXII does not apply to judicial nominations because a de facto supermajority requirement flies in the face of the advice and consent provision of Article II power of executive nominations. Predictably, many GOP senators and conservative activists and pundits lauded the proposal as sensible and constitutionally necessary; for their part, many Democrats invoked the founders and the Senate's special role to defend the filibuster.

This came to an orchestrated head in May when Republicans scheduled yet another cloture vote on the nomination of Priscilla Owen. The expectation was that it would again fail and that this would lead to Frist pulling the nuclear trigger. As partisan as the Senate was becoming, there were nevertheless enough relative moderates to block movement in either direction. Five senators from the Democratic side would be enough to control cloture (getting from fifty-five to sixty) and five Republican senators could stop the nuclear option (getting to fifty-one against a parliamentary ruling in its favor). So, as with the Cuban Missile Crisis, cooler heads prevailed and averted nuclear war in part through some mutual concessions. Moderates rounded up seven from each side of the aisle to form what would be known as the Gang of Fourteen, which produced a memorandum of understanding among the participants. The fourteen signatories pledged themselves to three important commitments: to vote for cloture on three particular nominations; that in the future, "Nominees should only be filibustered under extraordinary circumstances" (the interpretation of which was left to the discernment of the individual signers); and to oppose any changes in the rules during the 109th Congress that would have the effect of evading Rule XXII in the consideration of nominations.[31]

The nominations crisis of 2005 did not solve the problem of partisan obstruction over nominations or much of anything else. Like the real nuclear crisis of 1962, it averted the immediate threat of war and produced some measure of caution, but the potential for mutually assured destruction was only increasing. The 2005 crisis did, however, seem to confirm a historical pattern of similar filibuster crises: obstruction over a particular matter produces pressure for reform; would-be reformers threaten some form of change by parliamentary ruling; compromise ensues, and the crisis abates with at best moderate reform. Despite the anger and polarization, the Senate seemed to be captured by the rules it inherited; the perceived political costs of using the simple-majority constitutional option or the nuclear option were too high at the same time that the two-thirds barrier to rewriting the rules was insurmountable.[32] There was no reason to expect a change in that quandary.

## 2013: Limited Nuclear Warfare

The 2008 election of Barack Obama as president with strong Democratic majorities in the House and Senate brought a reversal of fortunes and procedural interests to the Senate. With an initial 57–41 advantage, the Senate Democrats were joined by the independent senators Joe Lieberman of Connecticut and Vermont's Bernie Sanders, followed by Arlen Specter of Pennsylvania, who changed party affiliation in April 2009. For a few months during the first year of the 111th Congress, Democrats had nominally sixty members in its caucus and the potential to break filibusters by a straight party vote. But that limited possibility ended in January 2010 with a special election in Massachusetts to replace Ted Kennedy, who had died in August 2009. The surprising victory of Scott Brown reduced the Democratic caucus to fifty-nine. Amid these changes, the relative success of united government during the 111th Congress muted the controversy over minority obstruction.[33]

The midterm elections of 2010 upended the House by producing a large Republican majority, and Senate Democrats were reduced to a 53 to 47 advantage, counting the two independents. Filibuster reform was in the air, pushed by some consistent advocates such as Democratic senator Jeff Merkley of Oregon. Instead of any fundamental changes, the new Senate opened with a January 2011 agreement for minor reforms that rested as much on pledges to adhere to better behavior as on any revisions in the rules. As Republican Lamar Alexander put it, "We have come to a consensus about a change in behavior, which I believe in the end will be more important than the change in the rules."[34] Little changed and nothing lasted. Minority obstruction, particularly applied to nominations, was becoming such a problem that the president made a proposal for direct and meaningful reform of the Senate rules during his 2012 State of the Union address. Americans, he noted, could not be blamed for being a "little cynical" for thinking that "nothing will get done in Washington this year or next year or maybe even the year after that, because Washington is broken." "Some of what's broken," he continued, "has to do with the way Congress does its business these days. A simple majority is no longer enough to get anything—even routine business—passed through the Senate. Neither party has been blameless in these tactics. Now both parties should put an end to it. For starters, I ask the Senate to pass a simple rule that all judicial and public service nominations receive a simple up-or-down vote within 90 days."[35] The president was not asking for some form of the nuclear option. Instead, he was asking for a direct change in the language of Rule XXII such that all nominations from the executive branch would, in effect, become another majoritarian exception. The time limit of ninety days would allow extensive consideration and deliberation—even filibusters and obstruction—but with the guarantee of a majority vote within a reasonable amount of time. It was yet another reasonable proposal for cloture reform that, in the long run, would not advantage one party over the other but that would never surmount the two-thirds barrier protecting changes in Senate rules.

When the elections of 2012 gave Barack Obama a second term and slightly increased Democratic control to 55–45, more serious consideration of the nuclear option soon followed. Majority Leader Reid began the new Congress by holding open the first legislative day as a way to pressure Republicans and others less inclined toward reform into cutting a deal. A few weeks in the making, the deal was arcane and even less than what a sober realist might have expected under the circumstances. The most noted element was a change in Senate rules that created an optional new form of cloture on the motion to proceed. This was little more than a way to expedite noncontroversial measures that might be held up by just one or a few senators, empowering the majority and minority leaders to blow past this one potential obstacle.[36] The whole of this reform was pretty much less than the sum of its parts, and the compromise was pretty much dead on arrival.

## THE SUPERMAJORITY SENATE CURTAILED  183

Tension built in 2013 as Republicans continued to block many nominations. The main controversy was over the vacant seats on the Court of Appeals for the District of Columbia, often thought of as the second most important court in the country. This court was effectively split 4–4, with three seats for President Obama to fill. Senate Republicans came up with a novel and risible justification for their effort to block any appointments to that court: it had such a light workload that replacements were not necessary.[37] This was the last straw for Democratic senators, who had resisted, up to this point, any suggestions of going nuclear.[38] Once the Democratic leadership was clear that it had the necessary votes, a carefully orchestrated event was set in motion.

The showdown finally came on November 21, when Majority Leader Reid moved to reconsider the cloture vote on the nomination of Patricia Millett, which failed by a 57–40 vote.[39] When the majority failed to bring cloture, Reid raised a point of order that the "vote on cloture under rule XXII for all nominations other than for the Supreme Court of the United States is by majority vote." Following precedent and the game plan, the chair, Vermont Democrat Patrick Leahy, ruled against Reid's simple majority motion. And, as planned, Reid appealed the ruling to the floor. After Leahy asked, "Shall the decision of the Chair stand as the judgment of the Senate?," by a 48–52 vote the Senate did not sustain the chair's ruling.[40] The effect was to reinterpret Rule XXII as not applying to executive nominations except those to the Supreme Court, and that a simple majority could close debate on such nominations. Howls of protest and charges of hypocrisy ensued, but nuclear warfare never followed. What did follow that same day was a 55–43 vote to close debate on the Millet nomination. And as if to demonstrate the importance of what the nuclear option did, the next vote on the same day was a failure to invoke cloture, by 51–44, on a legislative matter, the Defense Authorization Act. Things got a little testy as the session came to a close in December and Republicans did their best to thwart the majority—they still had some tricks up their sleeves on nominations—but, given the years of polarization and obstruction by both sides, this hardly qualified as nuclear warfare. A significant number of nominations moved forward and received Senate confirmation by majority votes.[41]

Throughout the debate that led up to the nuclear option and after, senators and others were so busy pointing out their opponents' rapid constitutional pirouettes that they did not notice their own hypocrisy.

For syndicated columnist Charles Krauthammer, as an example, the 2013 Senate rule change was the latest outrage in an "outbreak of authoritative lawlessness" by Democrats and the Obama administration more generally.[42] "What distinguishes an institution from a flash mob," the columnist lectured, "is that its rules endure. They can be changed, of course. But only by significant supermajorities. That's why constitutional changes require two-thirds of both houses plus three-quarters of the states. If we could make constitutional changes by majority vote, there would be no Constitution." It might have surprised the House of Representatives and the nation of Great Britain to learn that they were flash mobs and that the latter had no constitution. Krauthammer employed, like so many filibuster apologists, the trompe d'oeil of equating Senate rules with the Constitution through his facile equation of institutions in general with supermajority procedures, which in turn implied that the Senate's rules were the equivalent of the Constitution, deserving Article V–level protection from amendment. The argument was bad enough without adding the fact that Krauthammer made the diametrically opposite constitutional argument about exactly the same potential means and end in 2005, when Republicans were preparing to use the nuclear option. Back then the pundit argued the Democrats must "be stopped by a simple change of Senate procedure that would do nothing more than take a 200-year-old unwritten rule and make it written. What the Democrats have done is radical. What Frist is proposing is a restoration." The Republicans "have a perfectly constitutional, perfectly reasonable case for demanding an up-or-down vote on judicial nominees."[43]

Aside from the recriminations and general debate about its merit and impact, the Democrats' recourse to the nuclear option in late 2013 had a fatal flaw. The argument that Rule XXII did not apply to nominations was weak enough; the argument that Rule XXII did not apply to nominations except for the Supreme Court was nonsensical.[44] The result of a political compromise to ensure that the Democrats had enough votes to execute the nuclear option, the Supreme Court exception implied that this tactic was mostly a way around the rules to achieve a particular outcome, a matter of power over principle. When the tables turned, there was no principled basis for opposition because there was no justification for the exception.

And so, on April 6, 2017,[45] the Republican Senate majority would invoke the nuclear option a second time, three years, four months, and one presidential election after the Democrats dropped the first bomb. As fate and irony would have it, this second use in the Senate was precipitated by a Supreme Court vacancy and President Donald Trump's nomination of Neil Gorsuch to be the 101st associate justice to the Supreme Court. To start there, however, would be to skip the constitutional crisis—provoked by senate Republicans—that preceded that nomination, and the presidential election that made it possible.

## Justice Antonin Scalia: May His Seat Be Wrested in Peace until 2017

Justice Antonin Scalia died unexpectedly the night of February 12 or very early the morning of February 13, 2016. Any Supreme Court nomination, especially during an era of partisan polarization and a deeply and closely divided Supreme Court, elicits intense interest and concern. Coming just nine months before a presidential election, with the campaign already in full swing, and involving the replacement for a historically important conservative justice, this nomination was expected to be as intense as any in American history. What surprised many ordinary Americans was that the Senate proceedings would turn out to be utterly unprecedented before Obama had even announced a replacement, even before Scalia had been buried—in fact, by the end of the day his death was discovered.

The very day that Scalia's sudden passing shocked the country, Senate Majority Leader Mitch McConnell announced that the Senate should not confirm any nominee from Obama. In the words of one report: "The swiftness of McConnell's statement—coming about an hour after Scalia's death in Texas had been confirmed—stunned White House officials, who had expected the Kentucky Republican to block their nominee with every tool at his disposal, but didn't imagine the combative GOP leader would issue an instant, categorical rejection of anyone Obama chose to nominate."[46] No such gauntlet had ever been thrown before a nomination to the Supreme Court, especially with nearly a year left in the term of the president who made the nomination. Moreover, McConnell soon made it clear that he would push for the nominee to not even be considered by the Senate; that is, the candidate would receive no consideration by the Judiciary Committee, let alone the nomination receiving debate and a vote on the floor of the Senate. Why? Partisan power is the obvious and only answer, but McConnell had a politically transparent justification. The Senate would not consider President Obama's nominee because that decision and nomination should be left to whoever won the upcoming election.[47]

This produced a constitutional crisis—a crisis that, owing to the temper of the times, would be interpreted by the public in strictly partisan terms. Polling just after Scalia's death revealed the extent to which Americans' partisan and polarized interpretation shaped answers to nearly any question about government. While independents split down the middle, and 77 percent of Democrats thought President Obama should appoint the next Supreme Court justice, 82 percent of Republicans thought the choice should be left to the next president.[48]

The partisan assessments of the history of appointments and what the Constitution mandates were supplemented by vigorous public and scholarly debate about whether the Senate was obligated to consider and act on the nomination.[49] Whatever the merits of the constitutional arguments, the only thing that mattered politically was Republican solidarity, which held firm. Obama's nominee—the relatively moderate and supremely qualified Merrick Garland—was never considered by the Senate Judiciary Committee, let alone by the Senate as a whole. The controversy faded, at least for many Americans, as the presidential campaign and primary season went into full swing, with Donald Trump having emerged as the front-runner even by the time of Scalia's death. But Democratic senators would not forget the Republicans' unprecedented action, the refusal to even consider a presidential nomination for the Supreme Court. Less noticed was that the Republican majority had essentially shut down the confirmation process for nearly all judicial nominations to federal courts.[50] Partisan ire was stoked further when, once Trump became the nominee and it looked like Hillary Clinton would win the election, some Republicans talked about blocking any and all of her judicial nominations.[51] The principle of "letting the people speak" applied only if the people spoke correctly on November 8, 2016. By electing Donald Trump on that day, the people spoke in a historic fashion that no doubt surprised even many of the Republican senators who had staked such a bold if duplicitous claim on behalf the voters.

## The Logical Conclusion: The Gorsuch Nomination and the Second Nuclear Option

On January 31, 2017, just eleven days into his presidency, and less than two weeks before the anniversary of Scalia's death, Donald Trump nominated Neil Gorsuch, a federal appeals court judge, to fill the Supreme Court vacancy that Republican Senators had kept open for eleven months for the new president to fill. As anticipated, the nomination set the stage for one of the first major tests of Democratic resistance to the new president's agenda and the unity of the Democratic minority in the Senate, especially in response to what the Republicans had done to Merrick Garland, Obama's nominee. A filibuster of the Gorsuch nomination was a near inevitability, and with only a two-seat majority the Republicans had no hope of reaching cloture if only a few of the more moderate and electorally vulnerable Democrats defected. Use of the nuclear option by Senate Republicans looked nearly as inevitable as the Democratic filibuster. Indeed, Majority Leader Mitch McConnell and other Republicans threatened its use if the Democrats would not allow a vote on the nomination.

As the Senate moved in early April toward the evident showdown, forty-four Democratic senators were counted as supporters of a potential filibuster against the nominee, meaning they would vote against cloture.[52] Democrats evinced their unity and determination when on April 4 the forty-four voted against the motion to go into executive session to consider the nomination. The motion to proceed to executive session is not debatable, which means it cannot be filibustered and is decided immediately by a majority vote.[53] This vote made it clear that there were forty-four votes to oppose cloture on the consideration of the nomination, and so the filibuster was under way. Majority Leader McConnell allowed a day of debate before bringing forward the cloture vote that would trigger the nuclear option. The lone highlight of that debate was another symbolic "Mr. Smith Goes to Washington" effort, this one by Oregon's Jeff Merkley, who spoke for more than fifteen hours against the Gorsuch nomination on April 4 and 5, "from 6:46 p.m. Eastern Tuesday to 10:13 am Wednesday."[54] Otherwise several senators made rather predictable statements for and against the nominee, and Democrats such as Minority Leader Schumer insisted that sixty votes should be the threshold for approval of such a vital nomination (thereby admitting, as senators are wont to do without any sense of irony, that supermajority cloture is not a rule about debate but about power and coercion). In turn, Republicans had decided not to tolerate such obstruction beyond this rather modest length of time. In light of the precedent set a few years earlier and the illogic of the Supreme Court exception, there was no attempt at compromise, and Republicans did not spend much time wringing their hands over Senate traditions.[55]

Nor did they waste much time in finishing the job. On April 6, when the majority failed to reach cloture in a 55–45 vote with party unanimity on both sides, Majority Leader McConnell immediately raised "a point of order that the vote on cloture, under the precedent set on November 21, 2013, is a majority vote for all nominations."[56] Adhering to Senate precedent and the majority leader's plan, the presiding officer ruled against McConnell. Following exactly in the steps of his predecessor, Harry Reid, McConnell then appealed the ruling of the chair. And by the same 48–52 margin as in 2013, the Senate did not sustain the chair's ruling. The effect was to reinterpret Rule XXII as not applying to Supreme Court nominations, and that a simple majority could close debate on such nominations. Which is what then happened, by the same 55–45 vote that was insufficient only minutes before. The confirmation of Neil Gorsuch followed the next day, with fifty-four Republicans opposed by all forty-five Democrats.[57]

## "The End of the Senate": Mushroom Clouds of Hypocrisy and the Senate's Extraordinary (and Extraordinarily Fragile) Self-Conception

True to form, some Republicans referred to this use of the nuclear option, echoing Krauthammer's words from the 2005 crisis, as a restoration rather than a revolution. In the words of Senator John Cornyn, who was first to speak following the cloture vote, the Senate had just restored "an almost unbroken tradition of never filibustering judges." The veracity of this claim, like many others made that day in the Senate, was open to inspection. Cornyn, however, had not finished his point. It was, he continued, during the early years of George W. Bush's administration "when some of our friends across the aisle, along with some of their liberal law professor allies, dreamed up a way of blocking President George W. Bush's judicial nominees, and that was by suggesting that 60 votes was really the threshold for confirming judges, rather than the constitutional requirement of a majority vote." While correct in pointing out the inaccuracy of any implication that sixty votes was the de facto requirement, or consensus threshold, for confirmation, Cornyn had trouble adhering to this perspective even in his short speech. "Later, in 2013," Cornyn pointed out, "when there was a Democrat in the White House and it suited them to do so, they decided to do away with the same tool they used and went nuclear, lowering the threshold from 60 to 51 majority vote for circuit court nominees and district court nominees."[58]

Rhode Island's Jack Reed responded by harking back unconvincingly to what he maintained was the Democrats' principled nuclear option four years earlier. "Even in 2013, at the height of Republicans' partisan attacks on President Obama," Reed argued, "Senate Democrats believed the Supreme Court was too important to subject to a simple majority vote. The Supreme Court is a coordinate branch of our government, and its lifetime appointees have final authority to interpret the Constitution. We understood then—as we do now—that the traditional 60-vote threshold to conclude debate on the highest Court in our nation was too important to the consensus-driven character of this body to sacrifice."[59]

Some combination of hypocrisy and amnesia pervaded nearly every speech that day. "While it was always clear," lamented John Thune, "that some Democrats would oppose any Supreme Court candidate the President nominated, I had hoped that partisanship would be at least somewhat limited. I had hoped the Democrats would want to preserve the Senate's nearly 230-year tradition in confirming Supreme Court Justices by a simple-majority vote."[60] Richard Blumenthal tried to remind his Republican colleagues that the "obstruction of Merrick Garland's nomination was . . . 'the filibuster of all filibusters.'"[61] Blumenthal knew, of course, that Garland's nomination was not filibustered. Instead, he was pointing out the hypocrisy of the argument of his Republican colleagues: extolling as they were a 230-year tradition of not filibustering Supreme Court nominations while having only recently participated in an unprecedented partisan refusal to even consider a nomination, even before it was announced, with nearly a year left in a president's term. As with the aftermath of the 2013 nuclear option, there were scattered lamentations and dire predictions about the future of the Senate if the filibuster was further restricted or eliminated altogether. Lindsay Graham warned that if the Senate went "down this road of doing away with the 60-vote requirement to pass a bill . . . that will be the end of the Senate."[62] Johnny Isakson, who had just voted to implement the second nuclear option, told his colleagues, "If we move toward a body that is a rubberstamp of the House or a unicameral government of legislation, we will never be the United States of America our Founding Fathers intended us to be."[63] The end of the filibuster would be not just the end of the Senate but perhaps of the nation as well, at least the nation supposedly desired by men who lived more than two hundred years ago, during slavery and before democracy, the Civil War, electricity, and the internet, to name just a few things.

## Adding It All Up: The Senate in the Wake of Carve-Outs and Nuclear Warfare

What do the historic actions of the Senate taken in November 2013 and April 2017 tell us about supermajority cloture as a constitutional construction? Both votes were close, but each party demonstrated its willingness to take such an extraordinary step and categorically decrease the scope of potential filibusters. Even if partisan politics was front and center in the "nuclear options" that resulted in the elimination of nominations from the provisions of Rule XXII, Senate majorities from both parties—the Democrats in 2013 and the Republicans in 2017—embraced, even if implicitly, the principle that the Constitution did not countenance supermajority cloture for executive nominations. The extraordinary character of these events raises questions about why they happened when they did, and why in this manner, and aspects of this puzzle have been explored by political scientists.[64] For our purposes, a precise explanation is not necessary. Both long-term and short-term forces were at work, just as in the start of the international wars studied by historians and political scientists. The levels of frustration over the gridlock had been building for decades, with nominations becoming a particular point of frustration amid the constant dueling between Reid and McConnell during the Obama presidency. At some level one reaches the unavoidable and perhaps tautological conclusion that the costs of doing business as usual came to outweigh the benefits, but that tells us very little about the decision-making of the leaders and rank-and-file in the Senate, particularly among the Democrats in 2013. What is clear is the historic and blunt restriction of the reach of supermajority cloture, and with it the loss of some of the luster and mythology attached to it.

With the nuclear option of 2017, constriction of Rule XXII by point of order had apparently reached its political and perhaps practical limits. Ending his speech prior to the April 6 ruling, Minority Leader Chuck Schumer said, "Let us go no further on this path."[65] A letter dated April 7 and signed by a bipartisan group of sixty-one senators implored the majority and minority leaders to help them preserve supermajority cloture for legislation.[66] While senators showed little appetite for further curtailment of supermajority cloture, the president was ready to go all the way. Following the Republicans' nuclear option in support of his Supreme Court nominee, President Trump more than once tweeted, with characteristic imprecision, his support for an end to all sixty-vote thresholds in the Senate, which is the first time a president had taken such a stance.[67] The Senate, especially with Democrats in the minority, showed little interest in following the president's lead. At the start of the Biden presidency and the 117th Congress, the Senate was split 50–50 between the two parties, but with Vice President Harris presiding, the Democrats exercised majority control. Before the new House had passed its first bill, concerns abounded about the Senate filibuster thwarting the agenda of the new administration and Democratic House and Senate, as did predictions about the likelihood of another nuclear option to further limit or end the filibuster.[68] But with firm opposition to any such actions coming from at least two Democratic senators, meaningful filibuster reform seemed unlikely, even as support for further restrictions if not elimination built within the Democratic Party, aided by pressure from progressive groups and sectors of the media.[69] The partisan politics of reform notwithstanding, the Senate of the filibuster and equal representation was standing out as the sore thumb of American democracy in need of fundamental change.

CONCLUSION

# Constitutional Repair and Reparations

THE US SENATE remains an extraordinary institution, but extraordinary does not mean excellent or even functional. The Senate is extraordinary for the combination of its structure of representation, its constitutional tasks, and its internal procedures. The Senate of equal representation of states by two members with long and staggered terms is also the institution that shares authority with the president over appointments and treaties, while still having equal power with the House over normal legislation. Created by the Senate itself are rules of procedure that established minority power so substantial that it became the fourth veto point in the legislative process.

As I stated at the outset, the contemporary Senate is neither here nor there. It is neither as the framers intended it to be, nor does it meet the requirements of contemporary American government, whether one conceives of it as a republic or a democracy. No small part of the institution's dysfunction is because it claims to be operating as the founders wanted, when in fact it is not. Likewise, the Senate's architecture, self-conception, and resulting behavior distort rather than complement or complete modern republican government. Smaller membership, equal representation, six-year staggered terms, and the relative power of political minorities in the Senate are all facts. The interpretation of each, however, developed to create a kind of constitutional mythology about the Senate. And, to different degrees, the three have evolved, separately and in combination, to produce profound and irreconcilable conflicts with contemporary notions of democratic equality and practice and even with the Constitution itself.

This mythology of Senate exceptionalism both grew out of and served to obscure that institution's singular relationship to white supremacy, its perpetuation and long-delayed demise in law and policy. One of the central arguments of this book is that the Senate has been uniquely related to the history of race in America, from the depravity of slavery, through the protracted era of racial subjugation, to the post–civil rights decades of inequality and underrepresentation. Prior to the

Civil War, the South used its power in the Senate created by equal representation and state admissions to protect slavery. After that conflict, especially as the Jim Crow regime emerged, equal representation was replaced by the filibuster and later supermajority cloture. That weapon would delay civil rights for the next several decades. Even after the triumph of civil rights legislation, the combination of equal representation and the filibuster continues to significantly diminish the representation and power of minority votes and voices. The Senate cannot be reduced to white supremacy, but for most of American history and in different ways across the centuries, the Senate has been uniquely burdened by its close and evolving relationship to it.

Equal representation is the Constitution's seemingly permanent roadblock to political equality; supermajority cloture is the Senate's self-imposed revision of the Constitution's checks and balances. Together, equal representation and supermajority cloture, compounded by the continuing body doctrine, add up to constitutional incoherence. Equal representation cannot be justified in contemporary democracy. Supermajority cloture is an unwarranted enhancement of minority power that distorts rather than advances the Senate's deliberative process. Separately and especially in combination they should not be tolerated in a twenty-first-century representative democracy. Both equal representation and supermajority cloture (until recently) have been impervious to change, and yet should either, or, more to the point, would either—if we were to start over—ever be allowed into a constitutional framework rewritten for contemporary America?

The United States has dealt with and debated its flawed and at times chaotic governance for many years while changing nothing significant about the governmental process, only the officials who inhabit it. At the core of the on-and-off crisis of governance is the inability of our institutions to address and solve problems, creating a vicious cycle, as failure produces frustration and more polarization. Whatever the controversies and shortcomings that attend the other branches, the Senate sticks out as the sore thumb of democracy and the constitutional system. It is lauded and special but perpetually flawed, burdened, and disappointing. In short, the organism as a whole is dysfunctional, but the Senate embodies and exacerbates some of the core symptoms of that systemic illness. My point is not that the Senate is a sham. The Senate functions. But at what cost? The arrogant and fragile self-conceptions of the exceptional Senate are built on multiple democratic dysfunctions.

Given the combination of the Senate's problems in principle and in practice, one could argue there should be far greater public concern about the Senate, akin if not equal to the public concern that coalesced around the direct election amendment in the early 1900s. Indeed, the comparison raises a broader parallel between these eras separated by a century. The contemporary era of governmental dysfunction, which is not limited to the Senate, should have produced the twenty-first-century equivalent of the progressive movement of the early twentieth. Progressive era efforts focused in large measure on reform of the political process at national, state, and local levels, with the Sixteenth, Seventeenth and Nineteenth Amendments their major national achievements in that regard.[1] Citizens confronted institutional shortcomings and were aroused by and involved in structural reform, but even here, many reforms were about changing the number and powers of the voters (who could vote and for what), not so much the institutions of governance. In fact, many were as motivated by a principle of justice (such as votes for women) as by any desire for better government. Some of the most important, such as the Seventeenth and Nineteenth Amendments, cut across party lines at a time when partisanship was strong by some measures but not characterized as much by ideological divisions.[2] The level of contemporary dysfunction, however, has not generated a coherent movement for constitutional reform. The election of 2000 uncovered the democratic flaws of the presidential system of elections, but ultimately became more about how votes are counted than about the problems of the Electoral College itself. Direct election of the president went nowhere as partisanship determined constitutionalism and the policies of the new Bush administration overwhelmed any efforts toward institutional change. The perceived injustice or failures of institutions can provoke indignation and initiate efforts at reform, but both are usually short-lived and often undermined by partisan interests. And that brings us to one of the most understandable but frustrating dilemmas in politics.

## Constitutionalism, Politics, and the Evaluation of Our Governing Institutions

One problem with making normative arguments about political institutions, such as the Senate (or the Electoral College, or the Supreme Court), is that most citizens, whether consciously or not, allow their politics to determine their constitutional philosophy or constitutionalism. By politics

I mean an individual's particular mix of policy and partisan preferences. Am I a liberal or a conservative, a Republican or a Democrat? And am I for or against gun control, an increased minimum wage, or preventative war against terrorist groups? By constitutional philosophy or constitutionalism, I mean one's opinions about how the power and authority to make decisions should be distributed within and among the branches and levels of government. Should the Supreme Court be able to decide constitutional questions by a 5–4 vote? Does the president have the authority to use military force without congressional authorization? Can the House impeach a president for malfeasance short of an indictable crime? Is equal representation in the Senate still justifiable?

For citizens and elected officials alike, politics often shapes or dictates constitutionalism. One is for or against presidential power depending on whether Barack Obama or Donald Trump is in the White House; one lauds or disparages the Supreme Court's activism depending on the particular issue or issues on which it is deciding. People hold theories of impeachment based on nothing more than one's knowledge of the president's party affiliation. Opinions of the Supreme Court's proper role in the election of 2000 magically aligned with party allegiance. Theories of presidential war power after September 11, 2001, derived less from the Constitution and more from one's feelings about President Bush and his responses to the attack. Is the Electoral College the best system for selecting the president? Far too often the answer depends largely on who won last time and which party is projected to be advantaged by that system in the future.

Indeed, in this century the Electoral College took center stage as the most controversial constitutional construction. Discrepancies between the popular vote and Electoral College outcomes in 2000 and 2016 raised eyebrows and outrage. Once upon a time—indeed, during decades without any such discrepancies—direct election of the president had solid bipartisan majority support. Since 2000, however, the issue has developed a decidedly partisan cast, with Democrats overwhelmingly in favor of direct election and Republicans giving majority support to the current system.[3] In the second decade of this century, the filibuster and equal representation joined presidential election as targets of reform, with a similar partisan inflection. Especially at the elite level, support for the filibuster is subject to partisan flip-flopping depending on who is in control of the Senate after any given election. For example, liberal public interest groups started campaigns to end or abridge supermajority cloture when both Clinton and Obama were hindered by Republican obstruction in the

Senate. But those campaigns disappeared when Republicans took control of the Senate. Public knowledge of the filibuster is fairly weak even during controversies surrounding its use or abuse, such as the fight over judicial nominations in 2005 or the nuclear option in 2013. In a 2010 Pew survey, only 26 percent knew how many votes are needed to end a Senate filibuster, while in a 2018 survey 41 percent were able to pick the correct option.[4] Overall however, political scientists have found that partisanship has a strong causal effect on individuals' positions on the filibuster.[5]

Recent survey data indicate that public support for equal representation is deeply ingrained even in this era of stark divisions. When reminded "that the Constitution requires all states have two U.S. senators regardless of how many people live in the state," 75 percent agreed that "all states should continue to have two senators regardless of population," versus 24 percent who felt the "Constitution should be amended so larger population states have more senators." Even among the respondents who were prompted with a reminder of the vast population differences between the largest and smallest states, and how much that has changed since the founding, 68 percent supported the continuation of two senators per state. Support was significantly stronger, however, among Republicans (83 percent) than among Democrats (59 percent).[6] This contrasts sharply, for example, with the increased partisan division over the system for electing the president, as measured by the same 2018 survey. Seventy-five percent of Democrats but only 32 percent of Republicans favored scrapping the Electoral College in favor of direct election. Positions on equal representation are probably influenced to some extent by the state in which one resides. Californians, when prompted, are probably less supportive on average than Wyomingites, though polling with this specificity is hard to find. While not uncontroversial, equal representation retains solid bipartisan support. As with the filibuster, partisan opposition has grown at the elite level, but unlike the filibuster, that opposition is unlikely to change owing to the durable demographic advantage Republicans have in rural states. In particular, the boycott by the Republican Senate majority of Obama's nomination of Merrick Garland to the Supreme Court and the Senate votes to confirm the appointments by Trump of Neil Gorsuch and Brett Kavanaugh honed the partisan edge on this issue and spurred a slew of essays that drew attention to the distortion of equal representation and ways to fix it.[7]

On such questions of governmental process, one should be able to assess existing features and proposals for reform separately from their probable or imagined partisan impact. Citizens should be for or against direct election of the presidency regardless of who they anticipate might win or lose. One should be for or against the filibuster regardless of which party controls the Senate. You should even be able to assess the justice of equal representation regardless of the size of your state of residence. Minds can change, of course. Facts and new circumstances—beyond party fortunes—can and should keep the deliberative process open. But a certain consistency is not a hobgoblin.

The real test is the following. It is not that hard, even with bad history and flimsy logic, to justify an existing procedure such as the Electoral College or equal representation, usually because it benefits you at the moment and everyone knows change is improbable regardless. But it would be another thing altogether to propose the same feature if it did not exist. Imagine that the United States had direct election of the president from the start, and someone proposed an Electoral College to replace it. Imagine a public campaign to force a Senate that, let's say, had operated for more than two centuries by simple majority to adopt a rule that mandated a three-fifths or two-thirds majority for any important decision. It would get as far as the short-lived effort by tea party activists and others, starting in about 2011, to repeal the Seventeenth Amendment—the one that made senators popularly elected. Most Americans likely missed the opportunity to even consider that evanescent cause.

I think it is safe to claim that nearly all citizens are interested in politics or drawn into political participation by one or more of the myriad problems we face at the local, national, or global level. In turn, much frustration with politics in government comes from being on the losing side in the search for solutions to whatever problem or problems are of concern. That said, much frustration and anger also stem from the inability of the American government to take decisive action—any action—on nearly any problem, except through the use of military force. I would argue that no small part of the American turn against government is motivated, somewhat ironically, by governmental gridlock and ineffectiveness, rather than by a theoretical love of liberty as such or by antipathy to government in general.

The typical reaction to being on the losing end of policy fights or to governmental failure is for citizens (the principals) to get angry at the officeholders (their agents) and seek better agents at the next election. But the agents are sent to populate and operate through a set of institutional structures that, in the case of the United States at least, minimizes the chances for success and maximizes the chances of a repeat of the nearly inevitable disappointment, leading to the next electoral ritual of temporary but feckless renewal.

If we hope to solve any of numerous formidable problems that confront this country, reform of our governmental institutions is necessary. Never has the gap between public problems and institutional capacity been more apparent. The fundamental purpose of government is to offset and modify private or external power, whether that power comes in the form of a burglar, the KKK, a polluting industry, predatory lenders, al-Qaeda, ISIS, or China. We require government that can both compete with and assist, depending on the circumstances, a powerful and globalized system of economic activity based largely on private property and capital. The problems we face are difficult and fast-moving; we need institutions that, if not nimble and efficient, are at least capable of taking decisive action.

In short, Americans must realize that it's not the people, it's the institutions.[8] In a democracy, the principals can always find new agents, but those agents are essentially the same actors elected for the same reasons under the same political circumstances. Why do we expect them to behave differently or be able to deliver? Much behavior of the American electorate exemplifies the aphorism that insanity is doing the same thing over and over again but expecting different results. In effect, there are not new or better people or politicians out there, but there might be better institutional arrangements for getting the same agents to produce different outcomes. This is hardly a new thought; it was essentially the political philosophy exemplified in the deliberations at the Constitutional Convention.

And this relationship between constitutionalism and politics is part of another complication. Because constitutionalism is so often subordinate to politics, it follows that concern for and passion about institutional reform is also secondary at best. Most people are rightfully concerned about policy and bash away at elections, ever hopeful that they will produce the changes, when it is the governmental process rather than the result of the election that is preventing the change. Procedure will often trump principle and majority preferences, but there is rarely the energy or focus on institutional reform, reform that might be the essential prerequisite for policy change. The Senate, as structured by equal representation, staggered terms, and the filibuster, is a great example of this fundamental dilemma of politics.

## The Basic Choice: Washington versus Westminster

The admonition about politics and constitutionalism reminds us that it is essential to separate our constitutionalism from our politics to arrive at some notion of consistent and durable reform. It is just as important to remember, for the same reason, that the Senate—which is sometimes examined as though it existed in a vacuum—can only be understood and evaluated as part of a system of interrelated institutions. And that system, in turn, is best understood by comparison to what it is not—that is, to other forms of democratic design.

As far as democratic constitutional design is concerned, the world of choice, and therefore the intellectual basis for consistency, is not that large or complex. In the universe of contemporary democracy, despite the variations in detail, there are two models of governmental responsibility and decision-making, Washington and Westminster. "Washington" refers, of course, to Washington, D.C., and to the system of separation of powers and checks and balances, including federalism, that has been the focus of this book. "Westminster" invokes the British seat of government and its parliamentary system based on an inextricable relationship between the prime minister and the House of Commons, with no real checks and no federalism.[9]

The fundamental distinction is between systems that rely on responsibility and accountability enforced by a strong electoral check and those that rely on separation of powers, checks and balances, and federalism. In the former, the results of the elections determine the trajectory of policy in a direct fashion; in the latter, elections produce majorities and minorities, but not necessarily the same ones across all policymaking branches, and the separation of powers and checks degrade the link between elections and policy outcomes. Elections in a strong parliamentary system often leave little doubt as to who will control the process. In the Washingtonian system, the election is often just the opening kickoff in a long game.

In a parliamentary system, if the governing institutions fail to produce, or, to be specific, if the prime minister loses control of the partisan majority or majority coalition, then something has gone wrong and the time has come for new elections, which will be scheduled for the near future. In a separation of powers system failure by the majority—assuming there is one—to enact policy is not a constitutional crisis; it might be par for the course. In recent American history, it is often difficult to refer to a governing majority insofar as control is split between and among the institutions. The common perspective is to assign some degree of policy responsibility to the president, whose party typically controls at least one chamber of Congress. But presidential failure, as long as it is not of the impeachable variety, triggers no remedy. The country must await the next regularly scheduled elections, elections in which some elements of the system—either the president, two-thirds of the Senate, or both—do not participate and are not held accountable.

The US Constitution invented the world's first codified separation of powers system. And because of James Madison's central role in theorizing and creating those features of the Constitution, the Washington system is often called the Madisonian system. American political development has added to the strength of the system, even if the Seventeenth Amendment can be seen as one obvious modification that diminished the difference between the House and Senate. The rise of presidential power and the power and reach of judicial review have sharpened the divisions between the branches. And within Congress, the Senate came to be directly elected, but the different trajectory of House and Senate rules of procedure separate the chambers in behavior and policy outcomes.

Among other characteristics, American exceptionalism is characterized by an often uncritical reverence for the Constitution and the system it created. But no small number of experts and democratic theorists think Madison and company went overboard. The most common criticism of Madisonian democracy even before the advent of the filibuster was that the founders overcompensated with the original matrix of checks and balances.[10] The Madison system is tilted too far toward veto points, minority power, and potential gridlock. As Robert Dahl concluded, "However laudable their ends, in their means the framers were guilty of overkill."[11] Or, in the words of then senator Joseph Clark, "The fact is our whole form of government, the tripartite constitutional system itself already has built-in all the checks and balances to tyranny that a modern government can afford without being incapable of action."[12] Even its most ardent supporters concede that the American system is complicated if not convoluted.[13] Few would argue directly that the founders did not go far enough.[14]

Whether or not the original Madisonian system bent too far in the direction of division of power and responsibility and away from efficiency and accountability, the contemporary Senate is another big step in that direction. And, once again, excessive or not, it is the Madisonian or constitutional system that affords us the protection, not any single institution such as the Senate.

## Deliberation in Contemporary Government: Distributed and Democratized

What about the Senate's deliberative function? If the filibuster were reformed, could the Senate's smaller size be used once again for its intended purpose? Is the American government in need of "the world's greatest deliberative body"? Once upon a time, the claims that Senate deliberations educated public opinion and shaped the preferences of senators might have been plausible if rarely compelling. From the start, however, deliberation was extended both inward and outward until Senate debate was rendered largely superfluous. Committees were the initial and vital internal innovation even early in the nineteenth century. Committees were supplemented with capable staff in the second half of the twentieth century. Oversight hearings became a significant part of congressional workload. In such hearings Congress receives expert testimony about the implementation and impact of laws, and what else might be needed to address particular problems. As part of this and the legislative process more generally, Congress has created several organizations whose sole purpose is to provide expert analysis. The Congressional Research Service, Congressional Budget Office, and Government Accountability Office furnish information and analysis on nearly any subject. Even if it is true that many senators are at least initially a "mile wide and an inch deep" on the subjects they confront, debate on the floor of their chamber does not seem to be where they seek edification and direction.

Deliberation was also extended outward with news media, the spread of education and its products, particularly scholarship, other forms of professional expertise, social movements, interest groups, public opinion polling, and so forth. Decades ago, legislators might have been among the small number of experts on the relationship between problems and solutions in public policy. Over time that changed dramatically, well before the arrival of the information age.

All of this has affected the other governing institutions as well. Although it has no formal role in the legislative process, the judiciary is a deliberative institution with a profound impact on the policy and the lawmaking branches. The Supreme Court has always been the Constitution's purest deliberative body, though much of the deliberation is not public. Its small size and secrecy facilitate authentic deliberation, that is, efforts to use reasoned arguments to persuade colleagues on the merits of a particular position. Although we live in an era of rather important 5–4 decisions, the court has historically been biased toward a greater level of consensus. Even if ultimately unattainable in a particular case, justices would prefer, and often seek, a supermajority, if not a literal consensus, for the court's rulings.

In addition, the court embodies more than a rather robust form of internal deliberation. The judiciary was always "deliberative" in the formal and intra-institutional sense, but its deliberations in the original constitutionalism were typically thought of as at least a step removed from policymaking. As the court became increasingly entangled in constitutional questions that upheld, vetoed, or even mandated policy changes both great and small, it became in effect one of the three policymaking branches, with often large effects on the president and Congress. This is not just because it came to call more "balls and strikes" on constitutional issues, sustaining or overturning actions by states, Congress, or the president. In addition, the language the judiciary used came to shape our notions of good policy, rights, liberties, and regulations. The opinions that accompany a ruling become part of our collective deliberations over policy, informing the public, Congress, and the president. We do not simply follow the court's orders, so to speak. We debate and, more often than not, absorb the various arguments at the heart of those opinions. One of which—that "legislators represent people, not trees or acres"—was a prominent part of chapter 3's analysis of equal representation. Even if less pithy than that classic from *Reynolds,* or "Separate educational facilities are inherently unequal" from *Brown v. Board,* the decisions of the court and the reasoning used become part of public discourse that affects the future actions in many cases of all the branches of government. As the breadth of topics and policies affected by the court has expanded, so has its deliberative impact on the American system, including the Senate.

Finally, and less self-evident, is the evolution of the deliberative executive. The presidency has become, perhaps contrary to the founders' expectations, not only more powerful but also deliberative. George W. Bush famously characterized himself as "the decider" as an affirmation that, as president, he might listen to various perspectives but he alone would make the final decision.[15] This notion of the decisive role of the president hews closely to the true notion of the unitary executive propounded by

Hamilton in *Federalist* no. 70. The unitary executive is one controlled by a single person, not a committee. It is thereby a more responsible and efficient executive for being managed by and accountable to one person. In this original sense, the president as chief executive or efficient administrator was almost antideliberative in its essential conception. Nevertheless, the president may be the unitary decider, but the president hardly decides in isolation. Elements of this were in place early on with the cabinet and embodied most directly in the towering figures of Hamilton and Jefferson in Washington's administration. With such variations as Jackson's Kitchen Cabinet and Lincoln's war cabinet, even the early presidents deliberated.

Even so, one must consider the contrast between the nineteenth-century president with limited access to outside information—picture Lincoln often all but alone in the White House—and the modern administrative presidency. The modern president is inundated with information and advice and is in direct and constant contact with staff and the cabinet. The idiosyncrasies of each president's personality and management style aside, the executive branch has become a vast consultative information-processing apparatus. The modern presidency has greatly expanded and institutionalized the deliberative presidency. Congress created the National Security Council for just such a purpose. The joint chiefs often play an important role in the same policy arena. The departments and agencies are machines for analyzing problems and generating solutions. Within the White House, the number of people involved and the kind of conversations they have are much more in line with what the founders considered deliberation than what the hundred-person Senate pretends to do, at least during floor debate. The presidency is also characterized by often private deliberation coupled with public accountability. This degree of secrecy is how the Constitutional Convention operated and it is how the Senate started. Executive privilege might be abused at times, but the fundamental value of a president free to consult and hear the most frank and well-informed opinions—in confidence—has never been challenged. Moreover, congressional delegation has exported important policy problems and decisions to institutions even beyond the president and courts, notably the Federal Reserve, which through its deliberations and votes governs a good bit of the economy.

Finally, we need to include federalism and the states, which have often been referred to as "laboratories of democracy." The various actions and reactions of state governments are part of our collective deliberations on a range of issues, particularly domestic policy options. Excluding the Senate, the United States has developed three deliberative policymaking institutions, with unique and overlapping qualities. In effect, the House, the president, and the judiciary as a whole compose a tricameral policymaking process of deliberative institutions with different but formidable authorities and sources of influence. How many such entities does one country need?

## Fix or Finish? A Senate for a Twenty-First-Century American System?

Building on the argument that the design and performance of the US Senate should put it front and center—but not alone—in any assessment of the crisis of American government, this chapter has argued three things so far. First, any attempt to reform the system, or even to assess the arguments in this book, requires us to separate our constitutionalism from our politics on questions of institutional power and process. Second, with the basic choices among democratic systems in mind, it is persuasive that the United States could afford fewer veto points and tilt more toward effective democratic accountability rather than toward intragovernmental checks and dispersion of power, in addition to assuring electoral equality. Third, political deliberation does not live or die with the Senate. As the Senate's deliberative status has declined, effective deliberation about policy choices has been distributed and democratized.

With these three things in mind, how might we think about reforming the Senate, along with the system as a whole? The United States is often characterized as a republic instead of a democracy, at least when it suits the speaker's purpose, owing to its multiple levels of representation and complicated architecture of governmental power that fragment both democratic input and constitutional authority. But just as the concept of democracy evolved in theory and practice, so should republicanism—it is not frozen in time with the *Federalist Papers*. Rethinking the separation of powers requires recognizing the contemporary roles of each branch within the existing Constitution. In many ways, the United States has created a more modern republicanism through the evolution of its political institutions and the constitutionalism around them, particularly in the forms of presidential and judicial power. In concert with Senate reforms, how might we change the other institutions? Setting the Senate aside for the moment, this updated republicanism embraces both greater democracy and concentration of power without abandoning separation of powers and a system of checks and balances. Modern republicanism has embodied, even if implicitly, the principles of political equality (specifically, one person, one vote), electoral accountability, majority rule, and the role of the executive and judiciary as deliberative policymaking institutions. We should recognize and enhance this development in a coherent fashion. There has been no shortage of proposals to change the arrangement of institutions and powers in the Constitution.[16] Many potential reforms are one-offs that have an ad hoc quality, such as the quadrennial spasms over the Electoral College. They fix one element in a much larger system of intertwined institutions and powers. This is understandable, given the amendment process. But even if we are limited to doing things one at a time, we should do so with an eye toward their systemic effect and what would be complementary reforms. Aside from direct election of the president, there are proposals to restructure presidential power by giving the president the constitutional power of universal fast-track authority, that is, the power to submit legislation directly to Congress and have it voted on in a timely fashion. Another proposal would change the tenure and selection of the Supreme Court. Both would enhance effective government and accountability and reduce the collective action problems of Congress and the Senate.[17]

While it is tempting to offer a comprehensive plan for constitutional reform, this is a book about the Senate and, as I have argued, the Senate should be near the top of the list. So I will focus on that. Amid the partisan polarization that has informed or afflicted evaluations of our governing institutions, some have called for eliminating the Senate altogether.[18] Do we need the Senate at all, in any form? Do we need a bicameral legislature? Perhaps not, given the development and power of the other deliberative institutions, and depending on one's preference for a more parliamentary form of power and accountability. A unicameral national government would focus attention and responsibility on the House of Representatives and president, preferably with the addition of such changes as universal fast-track authority. In light of what I have argued about the merits of tilting the American government toward Westminster-style efficiency and accountability, a unicameral Congress combined with an enhanced role for the president in the legislative process would do just that without completely abandoning the separation of powers and checks and balances of the Washington system. As well, a Senate-less system—especially if combined with other reforms cited earlier—harmonizes with my argument about the decentered and democratized nature of deliberation. Even so, it is feasible to fix rather than finish off the Senate.

Two of that institution's sources of democratic dysfunctions, the continuing body doctrine and supermajority cloture, are under control of the Senate, and the nuclear options from 2013 and 2017 have substantially diminished both. But, as noted, the Senate did the right thing for mostly the wrong reasons and in the wrong way. The Senate can and should formally repudiate any procedural implications of the continuing body doctrine, including Rule V.2. The extent to which Senate business, including the rules, continues or carries over from one Congress to the next is a choice and has nothing to do with long and staggered terms.

Along with abandoning the continuing body doctrine, the Senate should rewrite Rule XXII to end supermajority cloture but guarantee a minimum but generous period of debate (which by definition would include the ability to offer amendments) on any issue. This minimum period could be either shortened or extended by unanimous consent. As one option, the current cloture rule allows for thirty hours of debate following a successful cloture motion. This could be transformed into the period of debate allowable before a simple majority cloture motion is in order. The Senate could attempt the creation of majority cloture through a conventional process of passing a simple resolution under current rules, which would almost certainly necessitate being able to muster two-thirds of senators present and voting to close debate, as mandated by Rule XXII. The improbability of such bipartisan cooperation to end the filibuster means that the far more likely route would be through use of the "constitutional option" discussed in chapter 7. Having twice used the nuclear or constitutional option, the Senate laid the foundation for a more far-reaching point of order and ruling, one it had flirted with in the past. That would come in the form of a point of order to the effect that each Senate has the right to change its rules by a majority vote. As I noted earlier, the underlying argument is that the Rule XXII provision for a supermajority to end debate on any proposed change to the rules is unconstitutional in the face of the explicit provision of Article I, section 5, that "Each House may determine the Rules of its Proceedings." A senator could raise a point of order that the Senate has the right at any point to decide on its rules by a majority vote. The ruling of the presiding officer would then have to be sustained or overturned by the senate majority to obtain that right. A motion would follow to amend the wording of Rule XXII to allow majority cloture on any matter before the Senate after a specified period of debate, and the amendment to the rule would be decided by a simple majority. Majority cloture could, in fact, lead to greater and more effective deliberation than had become the norm within the partisan and procedural warfare surrounding supermajority cloture. With such a change, debate and deliberation might return to being more about substance than about procedure, more about voice than about victory. For too long the Senate has gotten away with—but also paid a heavy price for—lauding the filibuster as the safeguard of deliberation while behaving as though it were a decision rule and a form of minority veto, all while trying to fudge the stark difference and even blatant contradictions between the two. It has not worked, and the nation has suffered for it. The Senate should deliberately finish in the right way—that is, by voting to rewrite the actual rule instead of lying about what its words mean—what it began in the wrong way. The Senate and the country will be better off for it.

A starker choice is what to do about equal representation. In short, should the nation tolerate the massive violation of political equality inherent in having two senators per state regardless of population? I believe we should not, even those of us who live in Wyoming or Rhode Island. Do Wyoming's resident want an effective national government from which they would benefit in many ways? Or do they want to retain two senators mostly so the state can get the extra bit of bacon for Warren Air Force Base while otherwise contributing to gridlock? As we saw in chapter 3, the arguments on behalf of equal representation are remarkably insubstantial when measured against the massive, and massively irrational, violation of political equality. Unlike the continuing body doctrine and supermajority cloture, equal representation is not under the Senate's control, although senators would be part of the only process that has been used so far to amend the Constitution. The solution to the problem of equal representation is anything but straightforward even without consideration of its likelihood. One approach would be to reallocate Senate representation proportionately to each state's population.[19] Another would be to create special Senate "districts" of roughly equal population by dividing larger states and combining smaller ones. Or follow the model of the House of Representatives and allocate one per state and the rest by population, a plan that would greatly diminish but not eliminate Senate malapportionment.[20] Partisan frustrations during the Trump presidency, and hopes fostered by Democratic control under the Biden administration in 2021, revived proposals for creating new states, starting with the District of Columbia, as a way to mitigate the Republican bias of equal representation.[21] The addition of new states, including Puerto Rico, could be combined with dividing existing large states, such as California, into smaller new states. This would have the merit of bypassing the process of constitutional amendment but the downside of having a limited impact and reinforcing rather than eliminating equal representation.

Another reason to eliminate equal representation in favor of Senate representation based on one person, one vote—however that might best be done—emerges from my central historical argument documenting the Senate's deep and long connection to white supremacy and the underrepresentation of minority votes and interests. In the twenty-first century, reparations for American slavery and its legacies have been a significant if still episodic topic of discussion and debate.[22] Since the emergence of the Black Lives Matter movement, interest has grown, and reparations were even a topic during the Democratic presidential primary debates in 2020.[23] Various forms of reparations have been proposed and much of the literature is more about making the case for some sort of reckoning than about the form it would take. Some forms of reparation focus on material compensation for past wrongs, while others are more about public recognition and reconciliation.[24]

Another element in reparations could be the elimination of forms of institutional or systemic racism as a way not just to atone for the past but to remove barriers to present and future progress. And some forms of institutional racism are part and parcel of the American government—the thing that would be creating and issuing any reparations. Whatever else one might add to the list, I have made the case that the Senate, in both its form of representation and its rules of procedure, can be seen in this unflattering light, not just by looking backward at its history but also by examining its present constitution and effects.

The elimination of equal representation (along with the filibuster) would fulfill some of the important goals of the reparations movement. Reparations are not just about compensation for past wrongs. The movement is also about recognition and acknowledgment, and the production of a different future. And what greater recognition than the acknowledgment that one of the basic governing institutions must be changed because it is so tied to and corrupted by that history and its ongoing distortions? The elimination of equal representation, however, would be far more than symbolic: it would be both similar to and yet go very far beyond the removal of offensive if inert relics, such as statues of Confederate leaders and generals, however important that process is in its own right. The elimination of equal representation would be the most fundamental change in our governing structure since the Constitution was ratified. The symbol would have ongoing substance. The change in the Senate would most likely produce material and substantial changes in governmental programs from health care to education, to the enduring benefit of historically disadvantaged communities. And all Americans would benefit from having produced a system that is more democratic, fair, and equal for all.

The nation might need or want a bicameral Congress; Americans may want to retain most of the Madisonian system. But the inescapable implication of the argument in this book is that we do not need or want the Senate as currently constituted. The Senate was born with perhaps the inescapable but ultimately unjustifiable constitutional flaw of equal representation. It added a de facto constitutional amendment in the form of supermajority cloture. In and around all this, the Senate constructed itself as the exceptional political institution in the exceptional nation. We might be well served by a bicameral Congress, but it is time to bring the Senate back down to Earth, into the twenty-first century, and integrate it into a coherent architecture for a contemporary democratic republic. Americans—Republicans and Democrats alike—would be better off if the Senate were changed to end its undemocratic composition, rules, and pretensions and start anew with a vital but limited role in a revised system of separation of powers and checks and balances.

# NOTES

## Introduction

1. Another work has used the term "Senate exceptionalism," but in mostly a different way and for a different analytical purpose: Bruce I. Oppenheimer, ed., *U.S. Senate Exceptionalism* (Columbus: Ohio State University Press, 2002). The essays contained therein adhere to empirical investigations (elections, committees, representation, floor proceedings, and so forth) of how the Senate is or is not different from the House of Representatives, or what difference the Senate makes.
2. This is distinct from the academic study of what makes the United States, from a comparative perspective, empirically or historically different from, or exceptional when compared to, other democracies. See, among others, Seymour Martin Lipset, *The First New Nation: The United States in Historical and Comparative Perspective* (New York: Norton, 1979).
3. Alexis de Tocqueville, *Democracy in America*, edited by J. P Mayer (Garden City, NY: Anchor Books, 1969), 374.
4. On the concept of civil religion applied to the United States, see Robert N. Bellah, "Civil Religion in America," *Daedalus* 96, no. 1 (1967): 1–21.
5. Works on or critiques of American exceptionalism include Deborah L. Madsen, *American Exceptionalism* (Jackson: University Press of Mississippi, 1998); John D. Wilsey, *American Exceptionalism and Civil Religion: Reassessing the History of an Idea* (Downers Grove, IL: InterVarsity Press, 2015); Godfrey Hodgson, *The Myth of American Exceptionalism* (New Haven, CT: Yale University Press, 2010); Anatol Lieven, *America Right or Wrong: An Anatomy of American Nationalism* (New York: Oxford University Press, 2004); and Paul T. McCartney, "American Nationalism and U.S. Foreign Policy from September 11 to the Iraq War," *Political Science Quarterly* 119, no. 3 (October 1, 2004): 399–423.
6. Partisan use or exploitation of the exceptionalism concept can be traced to Ronald Reagan's 1980 campaign for the presidency. Among other things, Reagan invoked the Puritans' imagery of America as a "shining city on a hill." After the attacks of September 11, 2001, President George W. Bush used the vocabulary of American exceptionalism in support of his decision to take the nation to war. During these years, Republicans came to use the term nearly as a code word for a largely unquestioning belief in American superiority, supposedly in contrast to the less orthodox civic religion of Democrats and liberals such as Hillary Clinton

and Barack Obama. For example, "2016 Republican Party Platform," *The American Presidency Project,* https://www.presidency.ucsb.edu/documents/2016-republican-party-platform.

7. In 1998, Secretary of State Madeleine Albright added the phrase "indispensable nation" to the vocabulary of exceptionalism: "But if we have to use force, it is because we are America; we are the indispensable nation. We stand tall and we see further than other countries into the future, and we see the danger here to all of us" (https://1997-2001.state.gov/statements/1998/980219a.html).
8. *Annals of Congress,* March 2, 1805, 71, https://memory.loc.gov/ammem/amlaw/lwac.html.
9. Daniel Webster, "Second Reply to Hayne, January 26 and 27, 1830 (In the Senate)," Senate.gov, https://www.senate.gov/artandhistory/history/resources/pdf/WebsterReply.pdf.
10. *Congressional Record,* September 23, 1893, 1702.
11. W. E. Gladstone, "Kin beyond Sea," *North American Review* 127, no. 264 (1878): 191–92.
12. William S. White, *Citadel: The Story of the U. S. Senate* (New York: Harper, 1957), ix.
13. From Byrd's 1996 orientation speech to new senators, reprinted in the *Congressional Record,* January 7, 1997, S21–23. The senator also referred to the Senate as the "anchor of the Republic" and the "morning and evening star in the American constitutional constellation."
14. Needless to say, legislative studies in political science have devoted plenty of attention to the Senate, even if the upper chamber took a back seat to the House for many decades in the study of Congress, especially in the heyday of behavioralism. When the so-called new institutionalism highlighted the importance of rules, naturally the peculiarities of decision-making in the upper house drew empirical attention. Collectively much of this work investigates aspects of what is often thought of as "Senate exceptionalism." See Oppenheimer, *U.S. Senate Exceptionalism.* The characteristics that set the Senate apart from a comparative standpoint become the focus of analysis, whether separately or in combination: from the constitutional fundamentals of equal representation and longer and staggered terms to the various effects of its rules and norms. See, among others, Sarah A. Binder and Steven S. Smith, *Politics or Principle? Filibustering in the United States Senate* (Washington, DC: Brookings Institution Press, 1997); David W. Brady and Craig Volden, *Revolving Gridlock: Politics and Policy from Carter to Clinton* (Boulder, CO: Westview Press, 1998); Keith Krehbiel, *Pivotal Politics: A Theory of U.S. Lawmaking* (Chicago: University of Chicago Press, 1998); Gregory J. Wawro and Eric Schickler, *Filibuster: Obstruction and Lawmaking in the U.S. Senate* (Princeton, NJ: Princeton

University Press, 2006); Gregory Koger, *Filibustering a Political History of Obstruction in the House and Senate* (Chicago: University of Chicago Press, 2010); Lauren C. Bell, *Filibustering in the U.S. Senate* (Amherst, NY: Cambria Press, 2011); and Steven S. Smith, *The Senate Syndrome: The Evolution of Procedural Warfare in the Modern U.S. Senate* (Norman: University of Oklahoma Press, 2014). The normative dimensions of the Senate's unusual features are generally undisturbed. Such analysis tends to be strictly empirical and unconcerned about questions of constitutionalism, narrowly or broadly construed. Little if anything is borrowed from democratic theory and linked to an evaluative or normative argument about whether equal representation can be justified or whether the sixty-vote Senate serves a constitutional purpose or is valuable in some other way. One exception is an ardent if flawed defense of the Senate filibuster: Richard A. Arenberg and Robert B. Dove, *Defending the Filibuster: The Soul of the Senate* (Bloomington: Indiana University Press, 2012). Another, from the opposite perspective, is Adam Jentleson, *Kill Switch: The Rise of the Modern Senate and the Crippling of American Democracy* (New York: Liveright, 2021). And there has been no sustained argument about the relationship between equal representation and supermajority cloture.

15. A great deal of democratic theory has been normative and evaluates such things as deliberation, majority rule, and the relative merits of liberal, communitarian, or republican forms of government. And yet democratic theory rarely confronts existing institutions, preferring instead to compare and contrast abstractions rather than actual constitutional forms and practices, especially hybrid ones such as the Senate. This has changed to some degree with the addition of some theoretical work that often blends historical and normative analysis, frequently grounding its normative arguments on examples and analysis of real institutional arrangements, past and present. If not directly on constitutionalism, much of this can inform a critical analysis of institutions and practices that have been more or less taken for granted. See, among others, Bernard Manin, *The Principles of Representative Government* (New York: Cambridge University Press, 1997); Melissa S. Williams, *Voice, Trust, and Memory: Marginalized Groups and the Failings of Liberal Representation* (Princeton, NJ: Princeton University Press, 1998); Ian Shapiro, *The State of Democratic Theory* (Princeton, NJ: Princeton University Press, 2003); Melissa Schwartzberg, *Counting the Many: The Origins and Limits of Supermajority Rule* (New York: Cambridge University Press, 2013); and Jeremy Waldron, *Political Political Theory: Essays on Institutions* (Cambridge, MA: Harvard University Press, 2016).

16. Charles Stewart III, "Responsiveness in the Upper Chamber: The Constitution and the Institutional Development of the Senate," in *The Constitution*

*and American Political Development,* ed. Peter F. Nardulli (Urbana: University of Illinois Press, 1992), 63–96; C. H Hoebeke, *The Road to Mass Democracy: Original Intent and the Seventeenth Amendment* (New Brunswick, NJ: Transaction Publishers, 1995); Elaine K. Swift, *The Making of an American Senate: Reconstitutive Change in Congress, 1787–1841* (Ann Arbor: University of Michigan Press, 2002); Daniel Wirls and Stephen Wirls, *The Invention of the United States Senate* (Baltimore, MD: Johns Hopkins University Press, 2004).

17. I cite the law review literature on supermajority cloture and the continuing body question in the sections of the book that deal with those directly. For an example on state equality in the Senate, see Lynn A. Baker and Samuel H. Dinkin, "The Senate: An Institution Whose Time Has Gone?," *Journal of Law and Politics* 13 (1997): 21–103.

18. Bateman, Katznelson, and Lapinski make a related argument about Congress as a whole, focusing on the period from the late 1870s through the 1920s. David Bateman, Ira Katznelson, and John S. Lapinski, *Southern Nation: Congress and White Supremacy after Reconstruction* (Princeton, NJ: Princeton University Press, 2020). Jentleson, *Kill Switch,* makes a similar argument focused on the filibuster and the contemporary Senate, while giving only passing attention to equal representation.

19. There are two other notable features of the Senate's original constitutional design, but those will be part of this story only incidentally. Indirect election (selection by state legislatures) was a founding and fundamental feature of the Senate's design and constitutionalism until ended by the Seventeenth Amendment passed in 1913. Selection by state legislatures was intended to foster a more insulated and deliberative institution. This feature of the Senate's original architecture produced one of the strongest and most persistent movements of constitutional reform and resulted in the only amendment to change one of the basic design features of Congress, the president, and judiciary. From a comparative perspective, the other core feature of the Senate is its constitutional authority relative to the House's. That is, the Senate has essentially the same legislative power as the House (except for the nearly irrelevant revenue bill origination clause) and has sole authority over appointments and treaties.

20. Arenberg and Dove, *Defending the Filibuster.*

21. Charles E. Lindblom, *Politics and Markets: The World's Political Economic Systems* (New York: Basic Books, 1977), 356.

## 1. Creating Something Exceptional?

1. This chapter draws in part from my earlier co-authored work on the creation of the Senate. Daniel Wirls and Stephen Wirls, *The Invention of*

the *United States Senate* (Baltimore, MD: Johns Hopkins University Press, 2004), 76–79, 82, 91–92, 113, 133–34. Portions reproduced with permission of Johns Hopkins University Press.

2. For discussions of unicameralism, relative power within bicameral legislatures, and modern senates and second chambers in the world, see Nicholas Baldwin and Donald Shell, eds., *Second Chambers* (New York: Routledge, 2016); Arend Lijphart, *Patterns of Democracy: Government Forms and Performance in Thirty-Six Countries*, 2nd ed. (New Haven, CT: Yale University Press, 2012); and Samuel C. Patterson and Anthony Mughan, *Senates: Bicameralism in the Contemporary World* (Columbus: Ohio State University Press, 1999).

3. Article III begins with the overall structure of the judiciary and that judges will be compensated and serve during good behavior, but the method of selection, being a power shared by the Senate and executive, is detailed in Article II, section 2, regarding the general appointment power.

4. Max Farrand, ed., *The Records of the Federal Convention of 1787*, rev. ed., 4 vols. (New Haven, CT: Yale University Press, 1966), 1:339.

5. Farrand, *The Records of the Federal Convention of 1787*, 1:254.

6. Farrand, *The Records of the Federal Convention of 1787*, 1:18–20.

7. Farrand, *The Records of the Federal Convention of 1787*, 1:48.

8. Farrand, *The Records of the Federal Convention of 1787*, 1:36–37.

9. Wirls and Wirls, *The Invention of the United States Senate*, 78–82.

10. Comments ranged from brief allusions to one characteristic or goal to lengthy commentaries that referred to three or four. Most of the comments are clear and direct in reference. Others, of course, are open to interpretation. I tried to judge on the basis of the full commentary and context.

11. Jacob Ernest Cooke, ed., *The Federalist* (Middletown, CT: Wesleyan University Press, 1982), 342.

12. Farrand, *The Records of the Federal Convention of 1787*, 1:20.

13. Farrand, *The Records of the Federal Convention of 1787*, 1:375.

14. Farrand, *The Records of the Federal Convention of 1787*, 2:216, 230–31, 235–39, 251, 268–69, 272. The delegates' concern about the influence of strangers on legislative counsels extended to their fellow citizens. The August 8 vote to raise the House citizenship requirement from three to seven years was immediately followed by a debate over whether to require seven years of residence within the state as an eligibility requirement. As Rutledge put it, "An emigrant from N. England to S.C. or Georgia would know little of its affairs and could not be supposed to acquire a thorough knowledge in less time." Read "reminded him that we were now forming a *National* Government and such a regulation would correspond little with the idea that we were one people." Though any specific period

of residence was defeated, the debate evinced that the concerns about strangers was not limited solely to foreigners, and again was not by any means a concern exclusive to the Senate (Farrand, *The Records of the Federal Convention of 1787,* 2:217–19).
15. Farrand, *The Records of the Federal Convention of 1787,* 1:321.
16. Farrand, *The Records of the Federal Convention of 1787,* 1: 322.
17. There is much more to say about the motives of the small-state delegations, including their practical concerns for approval of the final product by the states. On this and the effect of each state having one vote at the Convention, see, among others, John P. Roche, "The Founding Fathers: A Reform Caucus in Action," *American Political Science Review* 55, no. 4 (December 1, 1961): 799–816; and Frances E. Lee and Bruce Ian Oppenheimer, *Sizing up the Senate: The Unequal Consequences of Equal Representation* (Chicago: University of Chicago Press, 1999), 32–43.
18. Farrand, *The Records of the Federal Convention of 1787,* 1:149, 155–56.
19. Farrand, *The Records of the Federal Convention of 1787,* 1:51.
20. Farrand, *The Records of the Federal Convention of 1787,* 1:487.
21. Wirls and Wirls, *The Invention of the United States Senate,* 71–103.
22. Farrand, *The Records of the Federal Convention of 1787,* 2:94–95. These two issues surfaced again briefly on August 9 in debate on the dilution of the money bills restriction. But neither the number of senators per state nor per capita voting was ever threatened (Farrand, *The Records of the Federal Convention of 1787,* 2:232–34). As is indicated in Charles Pinckney's remarks after the convention, delegates with experience in the Confederation Congress wished to avoid the difficulties caused by state voting (Farrand, *The Records of the Federal Convention of 1787,* 3:252).
23. This analysis parallels Elaine Swift's idea of a "watchdog on a long leash." Swift argues that after the apportionment compromise, many small-state delegates joined with the large states to ensure that the Senate, though tied to the states through state selection and equal representation, would retain some independence through long terms, national pay, and rotation. The per capita voting decision is one of the strongest indicators of this. Elaine K. Swift, *The Making of an American Senate: Reconstitutive Change in Congress, 1787–1841* (Ann Arbor: University of Michigan Press, 2002), 39.
24. Wirls and Wirls, *The Invention of the United States Senate,* chap. 5.
25. Howard Baker, "Rule XXII: Don't Kill It!," *Washington Post,* April 27, 1993.
26. Sam Stein and Ryan Grim, "Harry Reid: Filibuster Reform Will Be Pursued in the Next Congress," *Huffington Post,* November 7, 2012.
27. I also searched the term "majority" to capture other comments that might be expressing something about the minority without using that precise term. It should be noted that I would never rely solely on a digital term

search to reach any conclusions. My work on the Senate and other issues related to the founding has caused me to read volumes 1 and 2 of Farrand's *Records of the Federal Convention* twice in their entirety.

28. John Patrick Coby, "The Long Road toward a More Perfect Union: Majority Rule and Minority Rights at the Constitutional Convention," *American Political Thought* 5, no. 1 (2016): 37–38.
29. Coby, "The Long Road toward a More Perfect Union," 38n19.
30. Farrand, *The Records of the Federal Convention of 1787*, 1:135, and see 1:421–23 as well.
31. Farrand, *The Records of the Federal Convention of 1787*, 2:224, 273–74, 362–63.
32. "As soon as the Southern & Western population should predominate, which must happen in a few years, the power wd. be in the hands of the minority, and would never be yielded to the majority, unless provided for by the Constitution." Farrand, *The Records of the Federal Convention of 1787*, 1:586.
33. See, for examples, Farrand, *The Records of the Federal Convention of 1787*, 1:86, 198–99, 252, 318, 322, 494–96, 527–29, 584, 605–6; 2:4, 9, 254, 255, 536, 540, 548.
34. Farrand, *The Records of the Federal Convention of 1787*, 2:251–53.
35. Farrand, *The Records of the Federal Convention of 1787*, 2:549.
36. Farrand, *The Records of the Federal Convention of 1787*, 2:255.
37. Farrand, *The Records of the Federal Convention of 1787*, 2:585.
38. Cooke, *The Federalist*, 57.
39. Cooke, *The Federalist*, 60.
40. In the words of Senate scholar Steven Smith, "Defenders of Rule 22 often claim the Framers of the Constitution intended minority rights to be protected by the Senate. Taken on its face, this claim is incorrect. Nowhere in the summaries of the constitutional Convention or the *Federalist Papers* is there an argument for allowing Senate minority factions to block action on legislation. Of course, the Senate was designed to protect the interests of small states." Congress, Joint Committee on the Organization of Congress, *Floor Deliberations and Scheduling*, 103, 1st, May 18, 20, 25, 1993, p. 225.
41. Farrand, *The Records of the Federal Convention of 1787*, 1:456–57.
42. Farrand, *The Records of the Federal Convention of 1787*, 1:483.
43. Farrand, *The Records of the Federal Convention of 1787*, 2:450.
44. *Congressional Record*, November 30, 2010, S8278.
45. Willi Paul Adams, *The First American Constitutions: Republican Ideology and the Making of the State Constitutions in the Revolutionary Era* (Chapel Hill: University of North Carolina Press, 1980).
46. Peter Charles Hoffer, William James Hoffer, and N. E. H. Hull, *The Supreme Court: An Essential History* (Lawrence: University Press of Kansas, 2018), 16.

47. Edmund S. Morgan, *Inventing the People: The Rise of Popular Sovereignty in England and America* (New York: Norton, 1989), 267, 270–71.
48. Farrand, *The Records of the Federal Convention of 1787,* 1:133.
49. Peverill Squire, *The Rise of the Representative: Lawmakers and Constituents in Colonial America* (Ann Arbor: University of Michigan Press, 2017), 57–84.
50. Wilson was the only unequivocal advocate for direct popular election of the executive, but that did not spare the convention considerable difficulty in finding the most agreeable or least objectionable method of selecting the president. It proved to be one of the most troublesome issues following the Great Compromise on Senate representation.
51. Cooke, *The Federalist,* 347–48.
52. "Note to his Speech on the Right of Suffrage," in Farrand, *The Records of the Federal Convention of 1787,* 3:451.
53. Daniel Wirls, *The Federalist Papers and Institutional Power in American Political Development* (New York: Palgrave Macmillan, 2015).
54. Farrand, *The Records of the Federal Convention of 1787,* 2:6–7.
55. The only subsequent change to the substance of the proposed constitution came just before its final approval on September 17 when the convention agreed unanimously to lower the ratio of representation in the House from a maximum of one representative for every 40,000 persons to one for every 30,000. Farrand, *The Records of the Federal Convention of 1787,* 2:644.
56. Farrand, *The Records of the Federal Convention of 1787,* 2:629–31.

## 2. Equal Representation

1. Only the Twelfth Amendment in 1804 and the Twenty-Sixth Amendment in 1971 enjoyed quicker ratification. Tennessee was the lone state of the former Confederacy to ratify the Twenty-Third.
2. Michael Barone and Richard Cohen, *The Almanac of American Politics* (Washington, DC: National Journal Group, 2004), 368.
3. Democrats held sixty-one seats (or sixty-two, if you count an independent senator who caucused with the party) in the Senate and 292 House seats (just shy of the postwar record of 295 during the Eighty-Ninth Congress following the 1964 landslide).
4. See the website at https://statehood.dc.gov/. See also Tessa Berenson, "Mayor Wants Washington, D.C. to Become 51st State.," *Time,* April 15, 2016, 1–1; Kris Hammond, "This Unconventional Proposal for D.C. Statehood Could Use Some Trumpian Dealmaking," *Washington Post,* February 16, 2017.
5. Lawrence M. Frankel, "National Representation for the District of Columbia: A Legislative Solution," *University of Pennsylvania Law Review* 139,

no. 6 (1991): 1659–709; Philip G. Schrag, "The Future of District of Columbia Home Rule," *Catholic University Law Review* 39, no. 2 (1990): 311–72.
6. Emily Cochrane, "In Historic Vote, House Approves Statehood for the District of Columbia," *New York Times,* June 26, 2020.
7. Frankel, "National Representation for the District of Columbia: A Legislative Solution," 1660n6.
8. Max Farrand, ed., *The Records of the Federal Convention of 1787,* rev. ed., 4 vols. (New Haven, CT: Yale University Press, 1966), 1:321.
9. Alexander Hamilton, James Madison, and John Jay, *The Federalist,* edited by Jacob Ernest Cooke (Middletown, CT: Wesleyan University Press, 1982), 416–17.
10. There were no reliable census counts in use at the convention. The original apportionments were based on estimates. Virginia was the largest, with ten seats, while the smallest, Delaware and Rhode Island, had one seat each. The average number of seats was five, and New York was given six. The 1790 census made New York the fifth largest of the thirteen states.
11. Such a centralized system—far more than an amendment of the Confederation—took them, as they saw it, outside the scope of the authority granted to them in their appointment to the convention. Max Farrand, *The Framing of the Constitution of the United States* (New Haven, CT: Yale University Press, 1913), 105.
12. Rosemarie Zagarri, *The Politics of Size: Representation in the United States, 1776–1850* (Ithaca: Cornell University Press, 1987). One expression of this view at the Constitutional Convention came from Gouverneur Morris, who noted, "It has been said that N. C. S. C., and Georgia only will in a little time have a majority of the people of America." Farrand, *The Records of the Federal Convention of 1787,* 1:604.
13. Farrand, *The Records of the Federal Convention of 1787,* 1:201.
14. Although Pennsylvania did not vote to support the Great Compromise, one of its delegates might have been expressing a latent sentiment when he lamented that "he shall be obliged to vote for ye. vicious principle of equality in the 2d. branch in order to provide some defence for the N. States agst" domination by the South in the legislature (Farrand, *The Records of the Federal Convention of 1787,* 1:604).
15. The 7–5 figure includes border state Delaware in the group of states without significant enslaved populations. Delaware's enslaved population was small and becoming less important to the state's economy as the state moved away from slavery in law and practice. Its slave population rapidly diminished as a percentage of its total population (from 15 percent in 1790 to 6 percent by 1810), whereas the other border state, Maryland, retained a significant slave population for decades (32 percent in 1790 and 29 percent in 1810).

16. Leading the way were South Carolina, with 47 percent of its census count enslaved, and Georgia, with nearly 42 percent.
17. Leonard L. Richards, *The Slave Power: The Free North and Southern Domination, 1780–1860* (Baton Rouge: LSU Press, 2000).
18. The congressional act to enable the admission of Kentucky was passed just prior to that for Vermont in early 1791, but Vermont beat Kentucky to admission because it had a state constitution ready to present as part of admission and had ratified the US Constitution.
19. These counts typically include Delaware as a slave-holding state because, while unimportant to its economy and overall interests, slavery was still legal in that state.
20. For one comprehensive account among many studies of this era, see William W. Freehling, *The Road to Disunion: Secessionists at Bay, 1776–1854* (New York: Oxford University Press, 1990).
21. Barry R. Weingast provides a good summary of House actions in "Political Stability and Civil War: Institutions, Commitment, and American Democracy," in Robert Bates et al., *Analytic Narratives* (Princeton, NJ: Princeton University Press, 1998), 168–69.
22. Gregory Wawro, "Peculiar Institutions: Slavery, Sectionalism, and Minority Obstruction in the Antebellum Senate," *Legislative Studies Quarterly* 30, no. 2 (January 7, 2011): 163–91.
23. Gregory Koger, *Filibustering a Political History of Obstruction in the House and Senate* (Chicago: University of Chicago Press, 2010); Daniel Wirls, "The 'Golden Age' Senate and Floor Debate in the Antebellum Congress," *Legislative Studies Quarterly* 32, no. 2 (2007): 193–222.
24. John C. Calhoun, *A Disquisition on Government and Selections from the Discourse* (New York: Bobbs-Merrill, 1953), 28.
25. On Calhoun's and antebellum southern political thought, see James H. Read, *Majority Rule versus Consensus: The Political Thought of John C. Calhoun* (Lawrence: University Press of Kansas, 2009), and Jesse T. Carpenter, *The South as a Conscious Minority 1789-1861: A Study in Political Thought* (New York: New York University Press, 1930).
26. Read, *Majority Rule versus Consensus*, 12. More generally, William W. Freehling, *Prelude to Civil War: The Nullification Crisis in South Carolina 1816–1836* (New York: Oxford University Press, 1965).
27. Carpenter, *The South as a Conscious Minority 1789–1861*, 4.
28. Calhoun, *A Disquisition on Government*, 28.
29. Calhoun, *A Disquisition on Government*, 30.
30. Sarah A. Binder and Steven S. Smith, *Politics or Principle? Filibustering in the United States Senate* (Washington, DC: Brookings Institution Press, 1997), 56.

31. On the southern use of the filibuster before the Civil War, see Wawro, "Peculiar Institutions."
32. Michael Wayne Bowers, *The Sagebrush State: Nevada's History, Government, and Politics*, 3rd ed. (Reno: University of Nevada Press, 2006), 17–26.
33. Charles Stewart and Barry R. Weingast, "Stacking the Senate, Changing the Nation: Republican Rotten Boroughs, Statehood Politics, and American Political Development," *Studies in American Political Development* 6, no. 2 (1992): 223–71.
34. South Dakota (348,600) and Washington (357,232), for example, were bigger than Delaware, Rhode Island, Vermont, Oregon, and Nevada.
35. C. Vann Woodward, *The Strange Career of Jim Crow* (Oxford: Oxford University Press, 2001); J. Morgan Kousser, *The Shaping of Southern Politics: Suffrage Restriction and the Establishment of the One-Party South, 1880–1910* (New Haven, CT: Yale University Press, 1974).
36. Stanley P. Hirshson, *Farewell to the Bloody Shirt: Northern Republican & the Southern Negro, 1877–1893* (Bloomington: Indiana University Press, 1962); Richard Franklin Bensel, *Sectionalism and American Political Development, 1880–1980* (Madison: University of Wisconsin Press, 1984); Richard Franklin Bensel, *The Political Economy of American Industrialization, 1877–1900* (New York: Cambridge University Press, 2000); David Bateman, Ira Katznelson, and John S. Lapinski, *Southern Nation: Congress and White Supremacy after Reconstruction* (Princeton, NJ: Princeton University Press, 2020).
37. Richard E. Welch, "The Federal Elections Bill of 1890: Postscripts and Prelude," *Journal of American History* 52, no. 3 (December 1965): 511–26.
38. The strongest manifestation of this belief was in the doctrine and practice of instruction. For a few decades before the Civil War, some state legislatures developed the practice of "instructing" their senators and "requesting" their representatives to support or resist a measure. This distinction mirrored the ambivalent nature of instruction: as an order and as a petition. As the controllers of senatorial elections, state legislatures could attempt to command their senators—but not representatives, who were selected by the people directly. On the rise and fall of instruction, see William H. Riker, "The Senate and American Federalism," *American Political Science Review* 49, no. 2 (June 1, 1955): 452–69; Roy Swanstrom, *The United States Senate, 1787–1801* (Washington, DC: Government Printing Office, 1988), 159–72; Elaine K. Swift, *The Making of an American Senate: Reconstitutive Change in Congress, 1787–1841* (Ann Arbor: University of Michigan Press, 2002), 44–45, 57–58, 120–21, 164–65; and Daniel Wirls and Stephen Wirls, *The Invention of the United States Senate* (Baltimore, MD: Johns Hopkins University Press, 2004), 193–98.

39. For a short overview, see Richard Ellis, *The Development of the American Presidency* (New York: Routledge, 2012), 27–40. For more detail, see Sean Wilentz, *The Rise of American Democracy: Jefferson to Lincoln* (New York: Norton, 2006).
40. Riker, "The Senate and American Federalism," 463.
41. Riker, "The Senate and American Federalism," 465.
42. Wendy Schiller and Charles Stewart III add considerable detail to this picture. Their work reveals a variety of ways in which parties affected this process in the late nineteenth century. Primary elections, when and where instituted, were also often effective in producing a candidate to be later ratified by a legislative vote, but intraparty competition within the state legislature sometimes produced a selection different from what the primary put forward. They also catalog the variety of party mechanisms, forms of party caucuses, that were employed to structure the selection of senators. Wendy J. Schiller and Charles Haines Stewart, *Electing the Senate: Indirect Democracy Before the Seventeenth Amendment* (Princeton, NJ: Princeton University Press, 2015).
43. S. E. Moffett, "Is the Senate Unfairly Constituted?" *Political Science Quarterly* 10, no. 2 (June 1, 1895): 248.
44. Moffett, "Is the Senate Unfairly Constituted?," 256.
45. Wallace Worthy Hall, "The History and Effects of the Seventeenth Amendment," Ph.D. diss., University of California, 1936; Daniel Wirls, "Regionalism, Rotten Boroughs, Race, and Realignment: The Seventeenth Amendment and the Politics of Representation," *Studies in American Political Development* 13, no. 1 (1999): 1–30.
46. Schiller and Stewart, *Electing the Senate*; Sara Brandes Crook and John R. Hibbing, "A Not-So-Distant Mirror: The 17th Amendment and Congressional Change," *American Political Science Review* 91, no. 4 (December 1, 1997): 845–53; William Bernhard and Brian R. Sala, "The Remaking of an American Senate: The 17th Amendment and Ideological Responsiveness," *Journal of Politics* 68, no. 2 (May 1, 2006): 345–57; Sean Gailmard and Jeffery A. Jenkins, "Agency Problems, the 17th Amendment, and Representation in the Senate," *American Journal of Political Science* 53, no. 2 (April 1, 2009): 324–42; Ralph A. Rossum, *Federalism, the Supreme Court, and the Seventeenth Amendment: The Irony of Constitutional Democracy* (Lanham, MD: Lexington Books, 2001); Wendy J. Schiller, "Building Careers and Courting Constituents: U.S. Senate Representation 1889–1924," *Studies in American Political Development* 20, no. 2 (2006): 185–97; Vikram D. Amar, "Indirect Effects of Direct Election: A Structural Examination of the Seventeenth Amendment," *Vanderbilt Law Review* 49, no. 6 (1996): 1347–405.
47. Riker, "The Senate and American Federalism."

48. Carroll H. Wooddy, "Is the Senate Unrepresentative?," *Political Science Quarterly* 41, no. 2 (June 1926): 219–39.

## 3. Equal Representation's Inexorable Clash with Political and Racial Equality

1. Harry S. Truman, "Message to the Congress on the State of the Union and on the Budget for 1947," https://www.presidency.ucsb.edu/documents/message-the-congress-the-state-the-union-and-the-budget-for-1947. Truman also urged consideration of the same for Puerto Rico if the people of that territory desired it, and for some level of enfranchisement for the District of Columbia.
2. Before Alaska and Hawaii became states, the former states of the Confederacy produced 23 percent of the Senate. If united, those senators needed only eleven allies to prevent the closure of debate.
3. On Alaska and Hawaii, see, among others, John S. Whitehead, *Completing the Union: Alaska, Hawai'i, and the Battle for Statehood* (Albuquerque: University of New Mexico Press, 2004); Roger J. Bell, *Last among Equals: Hawaiian Statehood and American Politics* (Honolulu: University of Hawaii Press, 1984); Ann K. Ziker, "Segregationists Confront American Empire: The Conservative White South and the Question of Hawaiian Statehood, 1947–1959," *Pacific Historical Review* 76, no. 3 (August 2007): 439–65; and Terrence Cole, *Fighting for the Forty-Ninth Star: C. W. Snedden and the Crusade for Alaska Statehood* (Fairbanks: University of Alaska Foundation, 2010).
4. Because each state gets one representative regardless of its population, the apportionment can never be perfectly proportional or fair in that way. As well, a state on the margins of what the apportionment formula dictates might not get another seat even though it is close to having the population needed for an additional seat. As a result, there can be some significant differences among the small states in the relative power of their electorates' vote for the House. As the US Census Bureau explains, "It is impossible to attain absolute mathematical equality in terms of the number of persons per representative, or in the share each person has in a representative, when seats are to be apportioned among states of varying population size and when there must be a whole number of representatives per state" (https://www.census.gov/topics/public-sector/congressional-apportionment/about/historical-perspective.html). For a detailed analysis of this issue and its impact, see Jeffrey W. Ladewig and Mathew P. Jasinski, "On the Causes and Consequences of and Remedies for Interstate Malapportionment of the U.S. House of Representatives," *Perspectives on Politics* 6, no. 1 (2008): 89–107.

5. US Census Bureau, Apportionment Legislation 1840–1880, https://www.census.gov/history/www/reference/apportionment/apportionment_legislation_1840_-_1880.html.
6. Glendon Schubert and Charles Press, "Measuring Malapportionment," *American Political Science Review* 58, no. 2 (1964): 302–27; Arthur L. Goldberg, "The Statistics of Malapportionment," *Yale Law Journal* 72, no. 1 (1962): 90–106. For the deeper roots of this in the nineteenth century, see Peter H. Argersinger, "The Value of the Vote: Political Representation in the Gilded Age," *Journal of American History* 76, no. 1 (1989): 59–90.
7. Frances Fox Piven and Richard Cloward, *Poor People's Movements: Why They Succeed, How They Fail* (New York: Vintage, 1978); Nicholas Lemann, *The Promised Land: The Great Black Migration and How It Changed America* (New York: Vintage, 1992); Isabel Wilkerson, *The Warmth of Other Suns: The Epic Story of America's Great Migration* (New York: Vintage, 2011).
8. Stephen Ansolabehere and James M. Snyder, *The End of Inequality: One Person, One Vote and the Transformation of American Politics* (New York: Norton, 2008), 23–67.
9. Ansolabehere and Snyder, *The End of Inequality*, 64–67.
10. Justice Clark concurring in *Baker v. Carr*, 369 U.S. 186 (1962).
11. *Colegrove v. Green*, 328 U.S. 549 (1946).
12. *Baker v. Carr*, 369 U.S. 186 (1962); Jo Desha Lucas, "Legislative Apportionment and Representative Government: The Meaning of *Baker v. Carr*," *Michigan Law Review* 61, no. 4 (1963): 711–804.
13. *Gray v. Sanders*, 372 U.S. 368 (1963).
14. *Wesberry v. Sanders*, 376 U.S. 1 (1964).
15. *Reynolds v. Sims*, 377 U.S. 533 (1964), 568.
16. *Reynolds*, 562.
17. *Reynolds*, 567.
18. In his dissent, Justice Harlan put this slightly differently: "Whatever may be thought of this holding as a piece of political ideology . . . I think it demonstrable that the Fourteenth Amendment does not impose this political tenet on the States or authorize this Court to do so." *Reynolds*, 590.
19. Earl Warren, *The Memoirs of Earl Warren* (Garden City, NY: Doubleday, 1977), 306.
20. Barry Friedman, *The Will of the People: How Public Opinion Has Influenced the Supreme Court and Shaped the Meaning of the Constitution* (New York: Farrar, Straus and Giroux, 2010), 268–70.
21. Lucas A. Powe Jr., *The Warren Court and American Politics* (Cambridge, MA: Belknap Press of Harvard University Press, 2000), 255.
22. Jack Harrison Pollack, *Earl Warren: The Judge Who Changed America* (Englewood Cliffs, NJ: Prentice Hall, 1979), 209. Pollack does not give

a source for the quotation. In a 1969 interview Warren said something quite similar when asked whether the most important decision reached by his court was school desegregation or reapportionment. He replied that apportionment "is perhaps the most important issue we have had before the Supreme Court" because "most of these problems that we are now confronted with would be solved through the political process rather than through the courts." "Excerpts from Interview with Warren on His Court's Decisions," *New York Times*, June 27, 1969, 17. From the question he is responding to, it seems clear that the "problems" he has in mind are primarily the racial ones invoked by the school desegregation cases.
23. Ansolabehere and Snyder, *The End of Inequality*, 146. Justice Black's comment is according to notes made by Justice Douglas on the conference deliberations. On the connections between the apportionment cases and racial discrimination more generally, see Robert M. Crea, "Racial Discrimination and *Baker v. Carr*," *Journal of Legislation* 30 (2004): 289–304.
24. *Reynolds*, 573.
25. *Reynolds*, 574.
26. Lynn A. Baker and Samuel H. Dinkin, "The Senate: An Institution Whose Time Has Gone?," *Journal of Law and Politics* 13 (1997): 22.
27. Powe, *The Warren Court and American Politics*, 252.
28. *Reynolds*, 576.
29. Hawaii was apportioned two House seats at the outset.
30. Neil Malhotra and Connor Raso, "Racial Representation and U.S. Senate Apportionment.," *Social Science Quarterly* 88, no. 4 (December 2007): 1038.
31. Frances E. Lee and Bruce Ian Oppenheimer, *Sizing up the Senate: The Unequal Consequences of Equal Representation* (Chicago: University of Chicago Press, 1999), 10–11.
32. For 1790 I include the three states that were added during the 1790s: Vermont, Kentucky, and Tennessee. The ratio of top five to bottom five of the original thirteen was 4.5 to 1.
33. All figures are based on the 2010 census and data from the US Census Bureau (http://www.census.gov/population/apportionment/data/2010_apportionment_results.html).
34. As well, in the 2010 apportionment, each of the four smallest states, with their collective eight senators, is smaller in total population than the average size of the districts for the US House of representatives nationwide, which is 710,767 for the 435 seats.
35. John D. Griffin, "Senate Apportionment as a Source of Political Inequality," *Legislative Studies Quarterly* 31, no. 3 (August 1, 2006): 405–32; G. Ross Stephens, "Urban Underrepresentation in the U.S. Senate.," *Urban Affairs*

*Review* 31, no. 3 (January 1996): 404–18; Malhotra and Raso, "Racial Representation and U.S. Senate Apportionment."

36. Griffin, "Senate Apportionment as a Source of Political Inequality."
37. Alaska, Montana, North Dakota, South Dakota, Vermont, and Wyoming. The median state population in the 2018 census estimates was just over 4.5 million. The average population in this group of sixteen was just over two million, with only Washington above that median, with around 7.5 million.
38. The four are Carol Moseley Braun, Barack Obama, Tim Scott, and Cory Booker. The other two are Edward Brooke of Massachusetts and Kamala Harris of California. Hiram Revels and Blanche Bruce were selected by the Mississippi state legislature in the 1870s during the Reconstruction era.
39. For a parallel discussion of the impact on African Americans, though based on the 1990 census, see Baker and Dinkin, "The Senate," 43–47.
40. Baker and Dinkin, "The Senate," 43.
41. Cary M. Atlas et al., "Slicing the Federal Government Net Spending Pie: Who Wins, Who Loses, and Why," *American Economic Review* 85, no. 3 (1995): 624–29; Cary M. Atlas, Robert J. Hendershott, and Mark A. Zupan, "Optimal Effort Allocation by U.S. Senators: The Role of Constituency Size," *Public Choice* 92, no. 3/4 (1997): 221–29; Baker and Dinkin, "The Senate"; Lee and Oppenheimer, *Sizing up the Senate*, 158–222; Stephen Ansolabehere, James M. Snyder Jr., and Michael M. Ting, "Bargaining in Bicameral Legislatures: When and Why Does Malapportionment Matter?," *American Political Science Review* 97, no. 3 (August 1, 2003): 471–81; Gary A. Hoover and Paul Pecorino, "The Political Determinants of Federal Expenditure at the State Level," *Public Choice* 123, no. 1 (April 1, 2005): 95–113; Brian Knight, "Legislative Representation, Bargaining Power and the Distribution of Federal Funds: Evidence from the US Congress," *Economic Journal* 118, no. 532 (2008): 1785–803; Adam Liptak, "Smaller States Find Outsize Clout Growing in Senate," *New York Times*, March 11, 2013.
42. Lee and Oppenheimer, *Sizing up the Senate*, 14.
43. Lee and Oppenheimer, *Sizing up the Senate*, 191–92.
44. See the website of the US Census Bureau at http://www.census.gov/prod/2011pubs/cffr-10.pdf.
45. Liptak, "Smaller States Find Outsize Clout Growing in Senate."
46. Dean E. Murphy, "Security Grants Still Streaming to Rural States," *New York Times*, October 12, 2004.
47. Jeffey Lazarus and Amy Steigerwalt, "Different Houses: The Distribution of Earmarks in the U.S. House and Senate," *Legislative Studies Quarterly* 34, no. 3 (2009): 365.
48. To cite just a sample of work on this subject: James E Campbell, *Polarized: Making Sense of a Divided America*, 2016; Matthew Levendusky, *The*

*Partisan Sort: How Liberals Became Democrats and Conservatives Became Republicans* (Chicago: University of Chicago Press, 2010); John Sides and Daniel J. Hopkins, eds., *Political Polarization in American Politics* (New York: Bloomsbury Press, 2015); Bill Bishop and Robert G. Cushing, *The Big Sort: Why the Clustering of like-Minded America Is Tearing Us Apart* (Boston: Mariner Books, 2009); Morris P. Fiorina and Samuel J. Abrams, *Parties at War: Partisan Sorting and the Contemporary American Electorate* (New York: Routledge, 2016); "Political Polarization," Pew Research Center, n.d., http://www.pewresearch.org/packages/political-polarization/.

49. David Graham, "Red State, Blue City," *Atlantic,* March 2017.
50. Franco Mattei, "Senate Apportionment and Partisan Advantage: A Second Look," *Legislative Studies Quarterly* 26, no. 3 (August 2001): 391–409.
51. See *Britannica Encyclopaedia,* online edition, sv. "gerrymandering" (www.britannica.com/topic/gerrymandering), and *Merriam-Webster Dictionary,* 17th ed., online, sv. "gerrymander" (https://www.merriam-webster.com/dictionary/gerrymander#h2).
52. Following the one person, one vote revolution, gerrymandering of House and state legislative districts gradually became a national issue and the subject of several Supreme Court cases. For one thing, information technology allowed those drawing the district lines to get ever more precise in locating voters in predictable ways. Another factor involved the intersection of the Voting Rights Act with how racial majorities and minorities were divided. Overall, the accusation became that legislators were picking their voters rather than the other way around. The controversy became especially prominent following the elections and apportionment of 2010. Subsequent elections seemed to show that creative districting was capable of reliably producing a majority of seats for a party in, say, Pennsylvania or North Carolina that would win only a minority of the statewide vote.
53. Adrian Vermeule, "Second-Best Democracy," *Harvard Law & Policy Review* (blog), Harvard Law School, 2006, https://harvardlpr.com/online-articles/second-best-democracy/; Stephen Macedo, "Our Imperfect Democratic Constitution: The Critics Examined," *Boston University Law Review* 89 (2009): 609–28.
54. Reynolds, 576–77.
55. Misha Tseytlin, "The United States Senate and the Problem of Equal State Suffrage," *Georgetown Law Journal* 94 (2006): 859–88.
56. Tseytlin, "The United States Senate," 867–68.
57. Tseytlin, "The United States Senate," 875.
58. Such as those described by, among others, Richard Franklin Bensel, *Sectionalism and American Political Development, 1880–1980* (Madison: University of Wisconsin Press, 1987); and Peter Trubowitz, *Defining the*

*National Interest: Conflict and Change in American Foreign Policy* (Chicago: University of Chicago Press, 1998).
59. Tseytlin, "The United States Senate," 875.
60. Quoted in Liptak, "Smaller States Find Outsize Clout Growing in Senate."
61. Gary L. Gregg II, "Keep Electoral College for Fair Presidential Votes," *Politico*, December 12, 2012.
62. Noah Feldman, "Revamping the Senate Is a Fantasy," *Bloomberg*, October 10, 2018.
63. Macedo, "Our Imperfect Democratic Constitution," 627.
64. Macedo, "Our Imperfect Democratic Constitution," 612.
65. David Leonhardt, "The Senate: Affirmative Action for White People," *New York Times*, October 19, 2018.

## 4. The Right of the Living Dead

1. George Henry Haynes, *The Senate of the United States: Its History and Practice* (New York: Russell and Russell, 1938), 341.
2. Richard S. Beth, "'Entrenchment' of Senate Procedures and the 'Nuclear Option' for Change: Possible Proceedings and Their Implications," Congressional Research Service, March 28, 2005; Aaron-Andrew P. Bruhl, "Burying the 'Continuing Body' Theory of the Senate," *Iowa Law Review* 95, no. 5 (2010): 1401–65.
3. William S. White, *Citadel: The Story of the U.S. Senate* (New York: Harper, 1957), 59.
4. Quoted in Michael J. Gerhardt, "The Constitutionality of the Filibuster," *Constitutional Commentary* 21, no. 2 (2004): 464.
5. This claim is based on an extensive bibliographic search. Nearly one hundred works were examined for any reference to or characterization of staggered terms or rotation related to the Senate. In addition to existing bibliographies of Senate scholarship, the author's collection of works on the origins of the Senate, and electronic library catalog searches, twelve separate searches were done using JSTOR and Google Scholar. No articles or books were found on the origins of staggered terms. Instead, any claims about why staggered terms were applied to the US Senate, if mentioned at all, are part of broader studies: books, dissertations, and articles on early state constitutions, the Constitutional Convention, the revolutionary and founding eras, ratification, Senate history, and the US Congress generally.
6. Neil MacNeil and Richard A. Baker, *The American Senate an Insider's History* (New York: Oxford University Press, 2013), 15.
7. According to Rogers, "The terms of the major branches . . . are so arranged as to raise effective shields against gusts of popular passion. . . . Senators serve for six years . . . and one-third of the membership is renewed every

two years." Lindsay Rogers, *The American Senate* (New York: Knopf, 1926), 15.
8. Charles III Stewart, "Responsiveness in the Upper Chamber: The Constitution and the Institutional Development of the Senate," in *The Constitution and American Political Development*, ed. Peter F. Nardulli (Chicago: University of Illinois Press, 1992), 62.
9. Robert A. Caro, *Master of the Senate: The Years of Lyndon Johnson* (New York: Vintage Books, 2003), 9–10.
10. Theodore J. Lowi and Benjamin Ginsberg, *American Government: Freedom and Power* (New York: Norton, 1990), 49; Samuel Kernell and Gary C. Jacobson, *The Logic of American Politics* (Washington, DC: CQ Press, 2000), 164.
11. Daniel Wirls and Stephen Wirls, *The Invention of the United States Senate* (Baltimore, MD: Johns Hopkins University Press, 2004), 210.
12. Fred Barbash, *The Founding: A Dramatic Account of the Writing of the Constitution* (New York: Simon and Schuster, 1987), 135.
13. The literature, based on the same comprehensive search and review mentioned above, contains four variations on the conventional wisdom. In order of decreasing frequency, first are assertions without evidence of any kind. Second, this interpretation is offered and supported by brief and casual evidence unrelated to staggered elections. In such cases there is a general quotation about the Senate's difference, such as the common "cooling the coffee" anecdote or a quotation from *Federalist* no. 62, even though the quotation is unrelated to staggered terms. Third, selective or very limited evidence, typically in the form of one or two quotations from the records of the Constitutional Convention, is offered to support the usual claim (and sometimes with misleading or inaccurate information). Finally, a few suggest that staggered terms blended the goals of electoral accountability and institutional continuity, with almost no evidence or analysis; see, for example, Paul Eidelberg, *The Philosophy of the American Constitution: A Reinterpretation of the Intentions of the Founding Fathers* (New York: Free Press, 1968), 143. Few and far between are claims or implications that staggered terms were added to the Senate's architecture to offset the antidemocratic implications of a long term; see, for example, Elaine K. Swift, *The Making of an American Senate: Reconstitutive Change in Congress, 1787–1841* (Ann Arbor: University of Michigan Press, 2002), 40; or Akhil Reed Amar, *America's Constitution: A Biography* (New York: Random House, 2005), 144. These claims are offered with no more evidence than is the conventional wisdom.
14. For somewhat greater detail on the three eras of evidence, see Daniel Wirls, "Staggered Terms for the US Senate: Origins and Irony," *Legislative Studies Quarterly* 40, no. 3 (2015): 471–97.

15. On the importance of rotation (in general, and in both forms) as part of revolutionary era constitutionalism, see Jackson Turner Main, *The Upper House in Revolutionary America, 1763–1788* (Madison: University of Wisconsin Press, 1967); Gordon Wood, *The Creation of the American Republic: 1776—1787* (Chapel Hill: University of North Carolina Press, 1969); and Willi Paul Adams, *The First American Constitutions: Republican Ideology and the Making of the State Constitutions in the Revolutionary Era* (Chapel Hill: University of North Carolina Press, 1980). On forms of rotation extending back to Athenian democracy, see Bernard Manin, *The Principles of Representative Government* (New York: Cambridge University Press, 1997).

16. John Adams, "Thoughts on Government," 1776, http://www.masshist.org/publications/adams-papers/index.php/view/PJA04dg2.

17. Main, *The Upper House in Revolutionary America, 1763–1788*; Adams, *The First American Constitutions*; Marc W. Kruman, *Between Authority & Liberty: State Constitution Making in Revolutionary America* (Chapel Hill: University of North Carolina Press, 1997).

18. Maryland voters picked electors, who then gathered in the capital to nominate and select state senators. I have not found anything in the records of the 1776 Maryland Constitutional Convention that explains the choice of five years without rotation beyond the desire for an independent and conservative body, which is also evident in the use of the two-stage election (see Main, *The Upper House in Revolutionary America, 1763–1788*, 101–14, 189). South Carolina had the same two-year terms for both its chambers.

19. Main, *The Upper House in Revolutionary America, 1763–1788*; Adams, *The First American Constitutions*; Kruman, *Between Authority & Liberty*.

20. Constitution of Delaware, 1776, https://avalon.law.yale.edu/18th_century/de02.asp.

21. In a 1785 letter outlining ideas for constitutional reform in Virginia, Madison went into considerable detail on the form of the legislature and suggested a term of four or five years for the "other branch" (and up to three for the lower house), and endorsed the Maryland Senate. He did not mention staggered terms, and moreover argued against limits on reeligibility, the other type of rotation. Just prior to the convention, in letters to Edmund Randolph and George Washington, Madison provided "some outlines of a new system" he had been contemplating. As part of this he mentioned as an option staggered terms (rotation) for the smaller second branch of a bicameral legislature with longer terms, features that were, again, part of the Virginia constitution; James Madison, *Papers*, edited by William T. Hutchinson, William M. E. Rachal, and Robert Allen Rutland (Chicago: University of Chicago Press, 1962), 354, 370, 384–85. Based on a comment about the Maryland Senate in a Madison letter from 1786, Greg

Weiner argues that Madison saw staggered terms as part of what Weiner calls "temporal republicanism." But there is no evidence that Madison wanted to include staggered terms in the Virginia Plan or proposed them at the convention. Greg Weiner, *Madison's Metronome: The Constitution, Majority Rule, and the Tempo of American Politics* (Lawrence: University Press of Kansas, 2012), 50.

22. Max Farrand, ed., *The Records of the Federal Convention of 1787*, rev. ed., 4 vols. (New Haven, CT: Yale University Press, 1966), 1:214–19. Three and seven years were likely inspired by British practice. A few delegates made reference, mostly negative, to the "Septennial Act" of 1716 that changed the maximum parliamentary term from three to seven years. Owen C. Lease, "The Septennial Act of 1716," *The Journal of Modern History* 22, no. 1 (March 1, 1950): 42–47.
23. Farrand, *The Records of the Federal Convention of 1787*, 1:360–62, 365.
24. Yates's notes record Gorham as proposing "that the senators be classed, and to remain 4 years in office; otherwise great inconveniences may arise if a dissolution should take place at once" (Farrand, *The Records of the Federal Convention of 1787*, 1:415). "Inconveniences" without more context is ambiguous. But it is worth remembering that Gorham's Massachusetts held annual elections for every level of its state government, including its senate.
25. Farrand, *The Records of the Federal Convention of 1787*, 1:396, 415–16.
26. Farrand, *The Records of the Federal Convention of 1787*, 1:421.
27. Farrand, *The Records of the Federal Convention of 1787*, 1:421–26. Although there was no discussion of this, it was probably clear that rotation would give each state a shot at having least one senator on an interim basis, that is, that senators from the same state would be staggered.
28. For further analysis of the voting patterns of the state delegations on this issue, see Wirls, "Staggered Terms for the US Senate," 481–83.
29. Farrand, *The Records of the Federal Convention of 1787*, 1:431–32.
30. Farrand, *The Records of the Federal Convention of 1787*, 1:426, 432–33.
31. Farrand, *The Records of the Federal Convention of 1787*, 1:408. The phrase in brackets is taken by Madison from Yates's notes.
32. Main, *The Upper House in Revolutionary America, 1763–1788*; Pauline Maier, *Ratification: The People Debate the Constitution, 1787–1788* (New York: Simon and Schuster, 2011).
33. Jonathan Elliot, *Elliot's Debates: The Debates in the Several State Conventions on the Adoption of the Federal Constitution*, vol. 2, n.d., 48, http://memory.loc.gov/ammem/amlaw/lwed.html.
34. Merrill Jensen, John P. Kaminski, and Gaspare J. Saladino, eds., *The Documentary History of the Ratification of the Constitution*, 31 vols. (Madison: Wisconsin Historical Society Press, 1976–), 5:66–67.

35. In addition to reading widely in the secondary literature and collections of primary sources on ratification, I did an electronic search of *Elliot's Debates* using several search terms. The eleven just noted include six veterans of the Constitutional Convention.
36. Elliot, *Elliot's Debates*, 2:246.
37. Bernard Bailyn, ed., *The Debate on the Constitution: Federalist and Antifederalist Speeches, Articles, and Letters during the Struggle Over Ratification*, 2 vols. (New York: Library of America, 1993), 1:367.
38. Bailyn, *The Debate on the Constitution*, 2:588–89.
39. Elliot, *Elliot's Debates*, 2:318–19.
40. See Wirls and Wirls, *The Invention of the United State Senate*, for much greater detail on the multiple and sometimes contradictory aspects of the Senate's construction.
41. William Blackstone, *Blackstone's Commentaries with Notes of Reference to the Constitution and Laws of the Federal Government of the United States and of the Commonwealth of Virginia by St. George Tucker* (Philadelphia: Young Birch and Abraham Small, 1803), book 1, 196; Joseph Story, *Commentaries on the Constitution of the United States* (Boston: Little, Brown, 1873), sections 709–12, 724.
42. *Congressional Globe*, Twenty-Seventh Congress, special session, 240.
43. For example, *Congressional Record*, March 7, 1917, 11. The 1841 debate furnished the earliest example cited in a congressional collection of extracts of Senate discussion of its status as a continuing body. See Legislative Reference Service, *The Senate as a Continuing Body: Extracts from the Congressional Globe Relating to Debates in the Congress of the United States on the Question of the Senate as a Continuing Body* (Washington, DC: US Government Printing Office, 1917).
44. Franklin L. Burdette, *Filibustering in the Senate* (New York: Russell and Russell, 1940), 22.
45. For example, according to the Senate Historical Office, in 1841 the Senate "conducted its first continuous filibuster on March 5, over the issue of dismissal of the printers of the Senate. The filibuster continued until March 11." Senate Historical Office, "Senate Chronology," https://www.senate.gov/history/chronology.htm. Koger finds that 1841 does not qualify as a filibuster by his definition, and that two earlier filibusters took place. Gregory Koger, *Filibustering: A Political History of Obstruction in the House and Senate* (Chicago: University of Chicago Press, 2010), 63. Lauren C. Bell, *Filibustering in the U.S. Senate* (Amherst, NY: Cambria Press, 2011), includes it in her comprehensive list as the fourth filibuster in Senate history.
46. *Congressional Globe*, March 5–11, 1841, 236–56. Burdette, *Filibustering in the Senate*, 22.

47. *Congressional Globe*, Twenty-Seventh Congress, special session, 236–57.
48. Legislative Reference Service, *The Senate as a Continuing Body*; Aaron-Andrew P. Bruhl, "Burying the 'Continuing Body' Theory of the Senate," *Iowa Law Review* 95, no. 5 (2010): 1401–65.
49. *Congressional Record*, March 8, 1917, 35.
50. My criticisms of the continuing body parallel and draw on Aaron-Andrew Bruhl's thorough and trenchant treatment: Bruhl, "Burying the 'Continuing Body' Theory of the Senate." At least one scholar (Gerhardt, "The Constitutionality of the Filibuster") has defended the continuing body idea as substantial enough to provide a constitutional foundation for both of these Senate rules, supermajority cloture and the stipulation that the rules continue from Senate to Senate. The arguments are based, however, almost exclusively on the mere fact of staggered elections, not on any sustainable claims that the framers either intended the Senate to be a continuing body or added staggered elections to create any such thing, or that the words of the Constitution itself imply it. As such, they are little more than assertions based mostly on the deadweight of largely unchallenged tradition.
51. *Congressional Record*, March 6, 1917, 8.
52. *Congressional Record*, March 7, 1917, 11.
53. Reuther testimony quoted in US Senate, Republican Policy Committee, *Senate Rules and the Senate as a Continuing Body* (Washington, DC: US Government Printing Office, 1953), 13.
54. For Walsh's entire speech, with colloquies, see *Congressional Record*, March 7, 1917, 9–19.
55. *Congressional Record*, January 17, 1975, 762.
56. "Nominations neither confirmed nor rejected during the session at which they are made shall not be acted upon at any succeeding session without being again made to the Senate by the President." Senate Rule XXXI.
57. Senate Rule XXV.
58. For an example from Senate debate, see the *Congressional Record*, January 9, 1959, 194. See also Gerhardt, "The Constitutionality of the Filibuster," 464.
59. *McGrain v. Daugherty*, 273 U.S. 135.
60. *McGrain v. Daugherty*, 181.
61. Bruhl, "Burying the 'Continuing Body' Theory of the Senate," 1456.
62. Reuther testimony quoted in US Senate, Republican Policy Committee, *Senate Rules and the Senate as a Continuing Body* (1953), 13.
63. *Senate Manual*, 112th Congress, 1st sess., Senate Document 112-1, p. 5, http://www.gpo.gov/fdsys/pkg/SMAN-112/pdf/SMAN-112.pdf.
64. On the 1959 reforms, see Martin B. Gold and Dimple Gupta, "The Constitutional Option to Change Senate Rules and Procedures: A Majoritarian

Means to Overcome the Filibuster," *Harvard Journal of Law & Public Policy* 28, no. 1 (2004): 231, 240–47.
65. The compromise prevailed on a 72–22 vote, with the nays coming mostly from a strange-bedfellows combination of the core reformers and die-hard southerners who could not stomach any diminution of the cloture rule's protection of minority power. *Congressional Record*, January 12, 1959, 494.
66. *Congressional Record*, January 12, 1959, 493.
67. In the mid- to late nineteenth century, the combined impact of state selection and staggered terms decreased, in some cases, the effect of a national swing in partisanship, with party control changing in the House but not the Senate. Overall, however, the Senate typically matched the House in terms of party control: Abramowitz and Segal, *Senate Elections*, 14–26. Moreover, the cause of bicameral divided government in this era is complicated by such things as the admission in the late nineteenth century of a large number of low-population western states, producing the "free coinage" of Republican senators: Charles Stewart and Barry R. Weingast, "Stacking the Senate, Changing the Nation: Republican Rotten Boroughs, Statehood Politics, and American Political Development," *Studies in American Political Development* 6, no. 2 (1992): 223–71.
68. The years 1954, 1968, 1976, 1978, 1980, 1986, 1988, 2000. The results of 2004 and 2014 were very close, with House and Senate continuity within 1 percent of each other. Brookings Institution, *Vital Statistics on Congress: Data on the U.S. Congress,* https://www.brookings.edu/multi-chapter-report/vital-statistics-on-congress/.
69. Alan Abramowitz and Jeffrey Allan Segal, *Senate Elections* (Ann Arbor: University of Michigan Press, 1992); Jonathan S. Krasno, *Challengers, Competition, and Reelection: Comparing Senate and House Elections.* (New Haven, CT: Yale University Press, 1997).
70. Martin Thomas, "Election Proximity and Senatorial Roll Call Voting," *American Journal of Political Science* 29, no. 1 (1985): 96–111; Sunil Ahuja, "Electoral Status and Representation in the United States Senate," *American Politics Quarterly* 22, no. 1 (January 1994): 104–18; Kenneth A. Shepsle et al., "The Senate Electoral Cycle and Bicameral Appropriations Politics," *American Journal of Political Science* 53, no. 2 (April 1, 2009): 343–59.
71. Dennis F. Thompson, "Democracy in Time: Popular Sovereignty and Temporal Representation," *Constellations* 12, no. 2 (2005): 253.
72. *Congressional Record*, March 7, 1917, 17. Quoting from Lord Byron's *Manfred.*
73. *Congressional Record*, September 23, 1893, 1703.

## 5. The Filibuster

1. *Congressional Record,* June 13, 2005, S6365. Sheryl Gay Stolberg, "Senate Issues Apology over Failure on Lynching Law," *New York Times,* June 14, 2005.
2. "Lynching in America: Confronting the Legacy of Racial Terror" (Montgomery, AL: Equal Justice Initiative, 2017).
3. *Congressional Record,* June 13, 2005, S6365. Her words parallel those of the resolution (S. Res. 39) itself: ". . . between 1890 and 1952, 7 Presidents petitioned Congress to end lynching" and that "between 1920 and 1940, the House of Representatives passed 3 strong anti-lynching measures." The Senate, however, "considered but failed to enact anti-lynching legislation" (S6364–5).
4. The following senators used some form of the word "filibuster" (with page references to the *Congressional Record,* June 13, 2005): Landrieu (6371), Allen (6372), Feingold (6385), Boxer (6386), Harkin (6386), Bennett (6388).
5. *Congressional Record,* June 13, 2005, S6388.
6. General Henry M. Robert, *Robert's Rules of Order* (New York: Pyramid Books, 1967).
7. It should be noted that Robert's Rules of Order specify that a successful previous question motion requires support of two-thirds of those voting.
8. Sarah A. Binder and Steven S. Smith, *Politics or Principle? Filibustering in the United States Senate* (Washington, DC: Brookings Institution Press, 1997), 35–39.
9. *Rules of the Senate,* https://www.rules.senate.gov/rules-of-the-senate.
10. See the website http://www.senate.gov/reference/glossary_term/filibuster.htm.
11. Franklin L. Burdette, *Filibustering in the Senate* (New York: Russell and Russell, 1940), 14.
12. Gregory Koger, *Filibustering: A Political History of Obstruction in the House and Senate* (Chicago: University of Chicago Press, 2010).
13. Daniel Wirls, "The 'Golden Age' Senate and Floor Debate in the Antebellum Congress," *Legislative Studies Quarterly* 32, no. 2 (2007): 193–222.
14. Frank W. Mondell, "Pro: Should Debate in the Senate Be Further Limited?" *Congressional Digest* 5, no. 11 (November 1926): 315.
15. *Annals of Congress,* April 7, 1789, 104.
16. "The First Parliamentary Procedure to Limit House Floor Debate, July 07, 1841," US House of Representatives, History, Art & Archives, http://history.house.gov/HistoricalHighlight/Detail/35501?ret=True.
17. *Rules of the U.S. House of Representatives,* https://rules.house.gov/sites/democrats.rules.house.gov/files/documents/116-House-Rules-Clerk.pdf.

18. *Rules of the U.S. House of Representatives,* https://rules.house.gov/sites/democrats.rules.house.gov/files/documents/116-House-Rules-Clerk.pdf.
19. Sarah A. Binder, *Minority Rights, Majority Rule: Partisanship and the Development of Congress* (New York: Cambridge University Press, 1997); Douglas Dion, *Turning the Legislative Thumbscrew: Minority Rights and Procedural Change in Legislative Politics* (Ann Arbor: University of Michigan Press, 1997); Koger, *Filibustering a Political History of Obstruction in the House and Senate.*
20. Burdette, *Filibustering in the Senate,* 80.
21. Including Arizona's Henry Ashurst, who held up a revenue measure in the waning days of a 1917 short session, exclaiming: "Now the iron hand: You will pass the Indian bill, or you will get nothing," Burdette, *Filibustering in the Senate,* 72 and 117.
22. *Congressional Record,* February 27, 1917, 4389; Burdette, *Filibustering in the Senate,* 116–17.
23. Lauren C. Bell, *Filibustering in the U.S. Senate* (Amherst, NY: Cambria Press, 2011), 151–53.
24. Burdette, *Filibustering in the Senate,* 123.
25. *Congressional Record,* March 5, 1917, 1, and March 8, 1917, 20.
26. For the original wording of the cloture amendment to Rule XXII, see *Congressional Record,* March 8, 1917, 40.
27. See, for example, *Congressional Record,* March 8, 1917, 20 and 31, for the remarks of Senators Pomerene and Stone, respectively.
28. Before 1917, the creative and aggressive use of procedural motions, particularly quorum calls, by the member or members conducting the filibuster could shift the burden onto the majority by forcing them to muster a quorum or deal with some other dilatory motion. Burdette, *Filibustering in the Senate,* puts some emphasis on this in his account of filibusters prior to the change in Rule XXII.
29. Bell, *Filibustering in the U.S. Senate,* provides direct evidence for this claim. Her analysis divides years after the creation of Rule XXII into four eras: 1917–36, 1937–1970, 1970–2004, and 2005–2010. In the 1937–70 period "civil rights, minority issues, and civil liberties" were the cause of 31 percent of all filibusters, by far the highest percentage for any issue area during any of the four eras. The same category fell to 6 percent in the following period from 1970–2004.
30. "Fatal Flood: James K. Vardaman," n.d., PBS.org, http://www.pbs.org/wgbh/americanexperience/features/biography/flood-vardaman/.
31. *Congressional Record,* March 8, 1917, 39.
32. Burdette, *Filibustering in the Senate,* 57.
33. Richard E. Welch, "The Federal Elections Bill of 1890: Postscripts and Prelude," *Journal of American History* 52, no. 3 (December 1965): 511–26.

The Senate could not defeat the filibuster even with the addition, by the time debate started on the bill, of twelve additional Republican senators from the six freshly minted western states of North Dakota, South Dakota, Montana, Washington, Idaho, and Wyoming.

34. Quoted in David Bateman, Ira Katznelson, and John S. Lapinski, *Southern Nation: Congress and White Supremacy after Reconstruction* (Princeton, NJ: Princeton University Press, 2020), 216. *Congressional Record,* May 20, 1897, 1199.
35. Eleanor Flexner and Ellen Fitzpatrick, *Century of Struggle: The Woman's Rights Movement in the United States, Enlarged Edition,* 3rd rev. ed. (Cambridge, MA: Belknap Press of Harvard University Press, 1996). Tennessee is famous for becoming the decisive thirty-sixth state to ratify, by the margin of one vote in the legislature. States of the former Confederacy made up eight of the eleven states that had not ratified by the end of 1920.
36. *Congressional Record,* January 26, 1922, p. 1795. The House of the Sixty-Seventh Congress had a membership of 302 Republicans and 131 Democrats (https://history.house.gov/Institution/Party-Divisions/Party-Divisions).
37. *Congressional Record,* December 4, 1922, p. 450. For a detailed account of the genesis and fate of this first attempt, see Claudine L. Ferrell, "Nightmare and Dream: Antilynching in Congress, 1917–1922," Ph.D. diss., Rice University, 1983.
38. US Congress, Senate Committee on Rules and Administration, *Senate Cloture Rule: Limitation of Debate in the Congress of the United States and Legislative History of Paragraph 2 of Rule XXII of the Standing Rules of the United States Senate (Cloture Rule),* prepared by the Congressional Research Service, 112th Cong., 1st sess. (Washington, DC: Government Printing Office, 2011), 47; Geoge C. Rable, "The South and the Politics of Antilynching Legislation, 1920–1940," *Journal of Southern History* 51, no. 2 (1985): 201–20; Robert L. Zangrando, "The NAACP and a Federal Antilynching Bill, 1934–1940," *Journal of Negro History* 50, no. 2 (1965): 106–17.
39. Lindsay Rogers, *The American Senate* (New York: Knopf, 1926), 169.
40. George Henry Haynes, *The Senate of the United States: Its History and Practice* (New York: Russell and Russell, 1938), 419.
41. *Congressional Record,* March 3, 1927, 5547–55. The incident likely had little to do with the woman supposedly involved. Heflin accosted the Black man, Louis Lundy, for drinking alcohol on the streetcar (Heflin was a teetotaler and had sponsored unsuccessful legislation to segregate the capital's streetcars). See also Burdette, *Filibustering in the Senate,* 152–62.
42. Donald Nieman, *Promises to Keep: African Americans and the Constitutional Order, 1776 to the Present* (New York: Oxford University Press, 1991), 106–7.

43. US Congress, Senate Committee on Rules and Administration, *Senate Cloture Rule*, 47–48; Bell, *Filibustering in the U.S. Senate*.
44. Janice E. Christensen, "The Constitutionality of National Anti-Poll Tax Bills," *Minnesota Law Review* 33, no. 3 (1949): 218–21.
45. Ira Katznelson, *Fear Itself: The New Deal and the Origins of Our Time* (New York: Liveright, 2013), 198–216.
46. Five southern states continued poll tax enforcement for *state* elections until stopped by the Supreme Court two years later in *Harper v. Virginia State Board of Elections*.
47. As one form of evidence, see the timeline of attempts to reform Rule XXII, in US Congress, Senate Committee on Rules and Administration, *Senate Cloture Rule*, 17–41.
48. *Congressional Record*, March 11, 1949, 2233.
49. Congressional Research Service, "Amending Senate Rules at the Start of a New Congress, 1953–1975: An Analysis with an Afterword to 2015," February 23, 2016, 35.
50. Alexander Keyssar, "How Has the Electoral College Survived for This Long?," *New York Times*, August 3, 2020; Congressional Research Service, "Senate Cloture Rule," 53–54.
51. *Congressional Record*, January 17, 1975, 756.
52. Barbara Sinclair, *The Transformation of the U.S. Senate* (Baltimore, MD: Johns Hopkins University Press, 1989).
53. Alan Abramowitz and Jeffrey Allan Segal, *Senate Elections* (Ann Arbor: University of Michigan Press, 1992).
54. Walter J. Oleszek, *Congressional Procedures and the Policy Process*, 9th ed. (Thousand Oaks, CA: CQ Press, 2014), 270–71.
55. Bell, *Filibustering in the U.S. Senate*, 65; Walter J. Oleszek et al., *Congressional Procedures and the Policy Process*, 10th ed. (Thousand Oaks, CA: CQ Press, 2016).
56. For a thorough recent overview of Senate holds, see Mark J. Oleszek, "'Holds' in the Senate" (Washington, DC: Congressional Research Service, January 24, 2017).
57. https://www.senate.gov/reference/glossary_term/hold.htm.
58. Walter J. Oleszek, *Congressional Procedures and the Policy Process*, 7th ed. (Washington, DC: CQ Press, 2007), 200–202.
59. Manu Raju and Meredith Shiner, "Shelby Puts Hold on Obama Noms," *Politico*, February 2, 2010, https://www.politico.com/story/2010/02/shelby-puts-hold-on-obama-noms-032584.
60. Oleszek, "'Holds' in the Senate."
61. Steven S. Smith, *Call to Order: Floor Politics in the House and Senate* (Washington, DC: Brookings Institution Press, 1989), 94–119.

62. James I. Wallner, *The Death of Deliberation: Partisanship and Polarization in the United States Senate* (Lanham, MD: Lexington Books, 2013).
63. Barbara Sinclair, "The '60-Vote Senate,'" in *U.S. Senate Exceptionalism*, ed. Bruce I. Oppenheimer (Columbus: Ohio State University Press, 2002), 241–61; David R. Mayhew, "Supermajority Rule in the U.S. Senate," *PS: Political Science and Politics* 36, no. 1 (January 2003): 31–36; Gregory J. Wawro, "The Supermajority Senate," in *The Oxford Handbook of the American Congress* (Oxford: Oxford University Press, 2011), 426–50.
64. Richard S. Beth, "Filibusters in the Senate, 1789–1993" (Washington, DC: Congressional Research Service, 1994); Bell, *Filibustering in the U.S. Senate*.
65. Frances E. Lee, *Beyond Ideology: Politics, Principles, and Partisanship in the U.S. Senate* (Chicago: University of Chicago Press, 2009), 3.
66. Lee, *Beyond Ideology:* 4.
67. Steven S. Smith, *The Senate Syndrome* (Norman: University of Oklahoma Press, 2014), 3.
68. Smith, *The Senate Syndrome*, 9.
69. Megan Lynch, "Unanimous Consent Agreements Establishing a 60-Vote Threshold for Passage of Legislation in the Senate" (Congressional Research Service, May 19, 2008), 1. As Lynch notes, "By incorporating a 60-vote threshold, such UC [unanimous consent] agreements avoid the multiple requirements associated with Senate Rule XXII, both for invoking cloture and for consideration under cloture."
70. Lynch, "Unanimous Consent Agreements Establishing a 60-Vote Threshold for Passage of Legislation in the Senate."
71. Senate roll call data compiled and provided to the author by Gregory Koger.
72. This excludes only the relatively few supermajority votes specified by the Constitution and requiring two-thirds of all senators voting, particularly veto overrides.
73. The Senate Defense Authorization Bill is another notable example. By tradition, that bill has come to the floor trailed by a long list of amendments, to be voted up or down.
74. Barbara Sinclair, "The New World of U.S. Senators," in *Congress Reconsidered*, ed. Lawrence C. Dodd and Bruce Ian Oppenheimer, 9th ed. (Washington, DC: CQ Press, 2009), 10–11.
75. Keith E. Whittington, *Constitutional Construction: Divided Powers and Constitutional Meaning* (Cambridge, MA: Harvard University Press, 1999).
76. Whittington, *Constitutional Construction*, 11–12.
77. Gregory Koger, "Filibusters and Majority Rule in the Modern Senate," in *Congress Reconsidered*, ed. Lawrence C. Dodd and Bruce I. Oppenheimer, 11th ed. (Washington, DC: CQ Press, 2017), 317.

78. Article I, section 7, by specifying that any bill not "returned by the President within ten Days (Sundays excepted) after it shall have been presented to him, the Same shall be a Law," ensures that the president cannot just refuse to act on measures that have received congressional approval.
79. *Congressional Record*, February 15, 2018, S1141. Emphasis added.
80. For contrasting discussions of the Court's possible role, see Catherine Fisk and Erwin Chemerinsky, "The Filibuster," *Stanford Law Review* 49, no. 2 (January 1997): 224–38; and Josh Chafetz, "The Unconstitutionality of the Filibuster," *Connecticut Law Review* 43, no. 4 (May 2011): 1036–37.
81. Assuming, that is, that none of the basic constitutional powers attached to the branches are, as worded, controversial. Any such changes would require a constitutional amendment.
82. The exceptions might be those signing statements—including George W. Bush's most famous, attached to the 2005 Detainee Treatment Act—that involve secret presidential action, such that Congress would not know whether the president had ignored something Congress had legislated; in this case, a prohibition against torture. Even so, the social construction behind Bush's extraordinary assertions—the unitary presidency—was openly contested and not widely accepted.

## 6. "Cooling the Coffee"

1. *Congressional Record*, January 27, 2011, S42.
2. At least one journalist covering this episode invoked the movie in the same way to refer to allegedly traditional filibusters. Paul Kane, "Senate in Long Recess as Leaders Seek to Rein in Democrats' Filibuster Rebellion," *Washington Post*, January 22, 2011.
3. Reid quoted by Senator Lamar Alexander, *Congressional Record*, January 5, 2011, S29.
4. *Congressional Record*, March 8, 1917.
5. Five senate debates on cloture—from 1917, 1949, 1959, 1975, and 2011—were examined in their entireties as recorded in the *Congressional Record*. Any comment, however long or short, that made an argument either in support of or opposition to filibusters or supermajority cloture was recorded and categorized. These debates are spread across the one hundred years from the creation of supermajority cloture to the present and are the longest debates on the filibuster and Rule XXII. As supermajority cloture became more controversial, there was a number of relatively brief debates from 1993 onward, with the one of some length in 2011. But as the one in 2011 was short, I have supplemented it with the hearings on congressional reform from 1993–1994 and from Senate action on judicial nominations in 2005, 2013, and 2017. I also draw on, in a less systematic fashion, the long

floor debate in 1959, as well as on opinion essays by politicians and pundits across the century from 1917 to 2017.
6. Richard A. Arenberg and Robert B. Dove, *Defending the Filibuster: The Soul of the Senate* (Bloomington: Indiana University Press, 2012), xiv–xv.
7. I would argue that this is the principal problem with Arenberg and Dove, *Defending the Filibuster*, but they are not alone in this regard.
8. *Congressional Record*, 1917, 22–23.
9. Robert C. Byrd, *The Senate, 1789–1989*, edited by Mary Sharon Hall, 2 vols. (Washington, DC: Government Printing Office, 1988), 2:162–63.
10. Arenberg and Dove, *Defending the Filibuster*, 77.
11. Senator Barack Obama, Remarks to the National Press Club, April 26, 2005, https://www.c-span.org/video/?186464-1/social-security.
12. Carl Hulse, "Senators Agree to Disagree on How to Fix a Split Senate," *New York Times*, December 6, 2020, 16.
13. *Congressional Record*, January 23, 1975, 1150.
14. Jennifer Steinhauer, "What if the Senate Goes Beyond the Filibuster 'Nuclear Option,'"? *New York Times*, April 5, 2017.
15. Joint Committee on the Organization of Congress, "Floor Deliberations and Scheduling," 103, 1st, pp. 98 and 225.
16. *Congressional Record*, March 11, 1949, 2227.
17. The quotation is from Moncure D. Conway, *Republican Superstitions as Illustrated in the Political History of America* (London: Henry S. King & Co., 1872), 47–48. See "Senatorial Saucer," https://www.monticello.org/site/research-and-collections/senatorial-saucer. This brief entry notes that there is no evidence that the conversation took place. "Senatorial Saucer" cites the 1872 book as the earliest publication of the anecdote.
18. Quoted in Sarah A. Binder and Steven S. Smith, *Politics or Principle? Filibustering in the United States Senate* (Washington, DC: Brookings Institution Press, 1997), 20. From *Congressional Record*, June 22, 1995, S8864.
19. Senator Royal S. Copeland, in *Congressional Digest*, vol. 5, no. 11 (November 1926), 302.
20. Chuck Hagel and Gary Hart, "Restoring Democracy to the U.S. Senate," *Time*, December 21, 2010. Reprinted in the *Congressional Record*, January 5, 2011, S22.
21. Section 359, "impertinent, superfluous, or tedious speaking," http://www.gpo.gov/fdsys/pkg/HMAN-111/html/HMAN-111-pg172.htm.
22. US Senate, Committee on Rules and Administration, *Examining the Filibuster*, 2010, 111th Cong., 2nd sess., Washington, DC: US Government Printing Office (italics added).
23. *Congressional Record*, January 5, 2011, S30.
24. To supplement the 2011 debate, I also drew on three more sources for the contemporary period: the congressional deliberations over congressional

reform in 1993 and 1994, the squabble over judicial nominations in 2005, and the brief cloture reform debates in 2011 and 2013. While precise comparison is unavailable, from the 1990s onward almost any skirmish over the filibuster featured arguments that tied it directly or indirectly to the founding. We can conclude confidently that they are a bigger percentage of the arguments made than in 1917, 1949, and probably 1959.

25. *Congressional Record,* January 27, 2011, S297.
26. Senator Mitch McConnell testimony before Senate Rules Committee, "Examining the Filibuster," 111th Congress, 2nd sess., April 22, 2010, https://www.govinfo.gov/content/pkg/CHRG-111shrg62210/html/CHRG-111shrg62210.htm.
27. US Senate, Committee on Rules and Administration, Legislative Reorganization Act of 1994.
28. *Congressional Record,* January 27, 2011, S315.
29. *Congressional Record,* 1949, 2083.
30. *Congressional Record,* 1949, 1916.
31. *Congressional Record,* March 7, 1975, 5634.
32. Senator Larry Craig, Hearings Before the Joint Committee on the Organization of Congress, Open Days for Members and Outside Groups, June 16 and 29, 1993, S Hrg. 103–128. US Government Printing Office, 114–15.
33. *Congressional Record,* 1975, 5636.
34. Senator Howard Smith, *Congressional Record,* March 11, 1949, 2237.
35. *Congressional Record,* 1949, 1921.
36. *Congressional Record,* March 10, 1975, 5532.
37. Roll Call, "Take Five," April 17, 2012, http://www.rollcall.com/news/take-five-daniel-inouye.
38. *Congressional Record,* October 21, 1996, S12421.
39. *Congressional Record,* November 30, 2010, S8278–79.
40. William Safire, "Not 'Ready to Go,'" *New York Times,* April 8, 1993, A15.
41. George Will, "The Filibuster Isn't What It Used to Be: It's Time to Bring the Old Way Back," *Washington Post,* March 29, 2017.
42. Neil MacNeil and Richard A. Baker, *The American Senate an Insider's History* (New York: Oxford University Press, 2013), 359. This is basically the thought that ends their book, aside from some brief and general discussion of tradition and reform. The authors take no stand whatsoever on the need for Senate reform, but they apparently are firmly convinced that equal representation is a constitutional warrant for supermajority cloture in service of minority rights.
43. Virginia A. Seitz and Joseph R. Guerra, "A Constitutional Defense of Entrenched Senate Rules Governing Debate," *Journal of Law & Politics* 20, no. 1 (2004): 1–32.

44. Lindsay Rogers, *The American Senate* (New York: Knopf, 1926), 163.
45. *Congressional Record,* March 9, 1949, 2066. See also the remarks of Senator Lyndon Johnson on the same day (p. 2043) and Senator Joseph Lister Hill on March 5, 1949 (p. 1916).
46. Arenberg and Dove, *Defending the Filibuster,* 156–57.
47. Emmet J. Bondurant, "The Senate Filibuster: The Politics of Obstruction," *Harvard Journal on Legislation* 48, no. 2 (Summer 2011): 467.
48. Stephen Ansolabehere, James M. Snyder, Jr., and Michael M. Ting, "Bargaining in Bicameral Legislatures: When and Why Does Malapportionment Matter," *American Political Science Review* 97, no. 3 (August 2003): 471–81; Frances E Lee, "Bicameral Representation," in *Oxford Handbook of the American Congress* (Oxford: Oxford University Press, 2011).
49. This combines the provisions of subsections 2 and 3 of Article I, section 7.
50. Bondurant, "Senate Filibuster," 481. Bondurant goes on to show how the Supreme Court in decisions from *Marbury v. Madison* to *Clinton v. New York* has applied *expressio unius* in major decisions about the powers of Congress.
51. Michael J. Gerhardt, "The Constitutionality of the Filibuster," *Constitutional Commentary* 21, no. 2 (2004): 456.
52. Gerhardt, "Constitutionality of the Filibuster," 456.
53. Richard S. Beth, "The Discharge Rule in the House: Recent Use in Historical Context" (Washington, DC: Congressional Research Service, April 17, 2003).
54. Bondurant, "Senate Filibuster," 494–95.
55. Jed Rubenfeld, "Rights of Passage: Majority Rule in Congress," *Duke Law Journal,* 1996, 79.
56. Bondurant, "Senate Filibuster," 481.
57. Bondurant, "Senate Filibuster," 480.
58. Julian N. Eule, "Temporal Limits on the Legislative Mandate: Entrenchment and Retroactivity," *American Bar Foundation Research Journal* 12, no. 2/3 (April 1, 1987): 379–459.
59. Seitz and Guerra, "A Constitutional Defense of Entrenched Senate Rules Governing Debate," 25.
60. John O. McGinnis and Michael B. Rappaport, "Symmetric Entrenchment: A Constitutional and Normative Theory," *Virginia Law Review* 89, no. 2 (April 1, 2003): 385–445. Blackstone is quoted in Seitz and Guerra, "A Constitutional Defense of Entrenched Senate Rules Governing Debate," 2.
61. Eric A. Posner and Adrian Vermeule, "Legislative Entrenchment: A Reappraisal," *Yale Law Journal* 111, no. 7 (May 1, 2002): 1665–705.
62. Ernest Young, "The Constitutive and Entrenchment Functions of Constitutions: A Research Agenda," *Journal of Constitutional Law* 10, no. 2 (2008): 399–411.

63. Catherine Fisk and Erwin Chemerinsky, "The Filibuster," *Stanford Law Review* 49, no. 2 (January 1997): 181–254; Josh Chafetz, "The Unconstitutionality of the Filibuster," *Connecticut Law Review* 43, no. 4 (May 2011): 1003–40; Bondurant, "The Senate Filibuster."
64. Tonja Jacobi and Jeff VanDam, "The Filibuster and Reconciliation: The Future of Majoritarian Lawmaking in the U.S. Senate," February 20, 2013, 64, http://papers.ssrn.com/sol3/papers.cfm?abstract_id=2221712.

## 7. The Supermajority Senate Curtailed

1. All quotations from *Congressional Record*, December 6, 2012, S7664.
2. Including *The Daily Show* (http://www.thedailyshow.com/watch/mon-december-10-2012/mitch-mcconnell-s-self-filibuster).
3. Floyd S. Riddick and Alan S. Frumin, "Riddick's Senate Procedure: Precedents and Practices," S. Doc. 101-28, 1992, https://www.gpo.gov/fdsys/pkg/GPO-RIDDICK-1992/content-detail.html.
4. Franklin L. Burdette, *Filibustering in the Senate* (New York: Russell and Russell, 1940), 55–57; Richard E. Welch, "The Federal Elections Bill of 1890: Postscripts and Prelude," *Journal of American History* 52, no. 3 (December 1965): 511–26; Gregory J. Wawro and Eric Schickler, *Filibuster: Obstruction and Lawmaking in the U.S. Senate* (Princeton, NJ: Princeton University Press, 2006), 76–87.
5. Wawro and Schickler, *Filibuster*.
6. For discussions of the "constitutional option," see Martin Gold, *Senate Procedure and Practice*, 3rd ed. (Lanham, MD: Rowman and Littlefield, 2013), 48–63; Martin B. Gold and Dimple Gupta, "The Constitutional Option to Change Senate Rules and Procedures: A Majoritarian Means to Overcome the Filibuster," *Harvard Journal of Law & Public Policy* 28, no. 1 (2004): 205–72.
7. *Congressional Record*, 85th Cong., 1st sess., Jan. 4, 1957, pp. 178–79. Quoted in Gold, *Senate Procedure and Practice*, 2013, 50.
8. Gregory Koger and Sergio J. Campos, "The Conventional Option," *Washington University Law Review* 91, no. 4 (2014): 867–909.
9. And that was not its only use to modify the application of Rule XXII. Roll Call, "Democrats' Memo on Senate Precedent Changes," July 15, 2013, https://www.rollcall.com/2013/07/15/democrats-memo-on-senate-precedent-changes/.
10. Koger and Campos, "The Conventional Option."
11. For a detailed history and discussion of these legislative exceptions, see Molly E. Reynolds, *Exceptions to the Rule: The Politics of Filibuster Limitations in the U.S. Senate* (Washington, DC: Brookings Institution Press, 2017).

12. US Senate, Committee on Rules and Administration, "Hearing on Senate Rule XXII and Proposals to Amend this Rule," June 5, 2003, https://www.rules.senate.gov/public/index.cfm?p=CommitteeHearings&ContentRecord_id=6CB1CE4E-45EC-4410-A512-6CAD59DCED9B&Statement_id=FB558D4F-3501-4D78-A0F2-B09AC153B032&ContentType_id=14F995B9-DFA5-407A-9D35-56CC7152A7ED&Group_id=1983a2a8-4fc3-4062-a50e-7997351c154b&MonthDisplay=6&YearDisplay=2003.
13. 295 US 495 (1935).
14. See sections 6(a)-6(d) and 7(a)-7(d) of The War Powers Act of 1973, Public Law 93–148, 93rd Congress, H. J. Res. 542, November 7, 1973.
15. National Emergencies Act (50 U.S.C. 1601, 1621, 1622).
16. For an excellent overview of the importance and use of the reconciliation process, see Barbara Sinclair, *Unorthodox Lawmaking: New Legislative Processes in the U.S. Congress,* 4th ed. (Washington, DC: CQ Press, 2012).
17. Trade Act of 1974, Public Law 93–618, as amended. See section 151.
18. For a history and analysis of how Congress did this, see Charlotte Twight, "Department of Defense Attempts to Close Military Bases: The Political Economy of Congressional Resistance," in *Arms, Politics, and the Economy: Historical and Contemporary Perspectives,* ed. Robert Higgs (New York: Holmes and Meier, 1990); and Kenneth R. Mayer, "Closing Military Bases (Finally): Solving Collective Action Problems through Delegation," *Legislative Studies Quarterly,* August 1995, 393–413.
19. Four rounds of BRAC—in 1988, 1991, 1993 and 1995—resulted in ninety-seven closures and fifty-five realignments of major installations, as well as over two hundred minor closures and realignments. US Government, General Accounting Office, "Military Bases: Analysis of the DoD's 2005 Selection Process for Base Closures and Realignments," GAO-05-785, July 2005, 18.
20. See, for example, E. Martin Enriquez, "Tyranny of the Minority: The Unconstitutional Filibuster and the Superimposed Supermajority on the Advice and Consent Clause of the Constitution," *T. M. Cooley Law Review* 21 (2004): 215–56.
21. Michael J. Gerhardt, "The Constitutionality of the Filibuster," *Constitutional Commentary* 21, no. 2 (2004): 459.
22. Data taken from Richard S. Beth, "Cloture Attempts on Nominations: Data and Historical Development" (Washington, DC: Congressional Research Service, June 26, 2013).
23. Beth, "Cloture Attempts on Nomination," 2.
24. For more detail and analysis of the Senate's increasing conflicts over judicial nominations, see Sarah A. Binder and Forrest Maltzman, "The Politics of Advice and Consent: Putting Judges on the Federal Bench," in *Congress Reconsidered,* ed. Lawrence C. Dodd and Bruce I. Oppenheimer, 9th ed. (Washington, DC: CQ Press, 2009), 241–61.

25. Miguel Estrada (7 votes), Charles Pickering, William Pryor (2), Priscilla Owen (4), Carolyn Kuhl (2), Janice Brown. See Beth, "Cloture Attempts on Nominations," 12.
26. The Senate website describes the Fortas nomination as having been filibustered. Some disagree that Fortas's Senate opponents were determined to prevent an up or down vote, but the historical record seems clear that they were determined, and motivated not just by disagreement with Fortas but also by the prospect of preventing LBJ from replacing the Chief Justice before the end of his presidency. See http://www.senate.gov/artandhistory/history/minute/Filibuster_Derails_Supreme_Court_Appointment.htm; John Dean, "The Facts About the Fortas Filibuster: Why Orrin Hatch Is Wrong," May 9, 2005, http://hnn.us/articles/11753.html; Charles Babington, "Filibuster Precedent? Democrats Point to '68 and Fortas; but GOP Senators Cite Differences in Current Effort to Bar Votes on Judges," *Washington Post*, March 18, 2005, A03.
27. US Senate, Committee on Rules and Administration, "Hearing on Senate Rule XXII and Proposals to Amend this Rule," June 5, 2003, https://www.rules.senate.gov/public/index.cfm?p=CommitteeHearings&ContentRecord_id=6CB1CE4E-45EC-4410-A512-6CAD59DCED9B&Statement_id=FB558D4F-3501-4D78-A0F2-B09AC153B032&ContentType_id=14F995B9-DFA5-407A-9D35-56CC7152A7ED&Group_id=1983a2a8-4fc3-4062-a50e-7997351c154b&MonthDisplay=6&YearDisplay=2003.
28. US Senate, Committee on Rules and Administration, "Hearing on Senate Rule XXII and Proposals to Amend this Rule," June 5, 2003.
29. William Safire, "Nuclear Options," *New York Times*, March 20, 2005; Jim VandeHei and Charles Babington, "From Senator's 2003 Outburst, GOP Hatched 'Nuclear Option,'" *Washington Post*, May 19, 2005.
30. Alexander Bolton, "Frist Finger on 'Nuclear' Button," *Hill*, May 13, 2004.
31. "Memorandum of Understanding on Judicial Nominations," 109th Congress, n.d.; Seth Stern, "Deconstructing the Judges Deal," *CQ Weekly*, May 30, 2005, 1443. http://library.cqpress.com/cqweekly/weeklyreport109-000001700755.
32. Sarah A. Binder, Anthony J. Madonna, and Steven S. Smith, "Going Nuclear, Senate Style," *Perspectives on Politics* 5, no. 4 (December 2007): 729–40.
33. With the help of such things as the use of budget reconciliation to evade any possible Senate filibuster of the Affordable Care Act.
34. Carl Hulse, "Senate Approves Reforms, but Leaves Filibuster Intact," *New York Times*, January 27, 2011.
35. President Barack Obama, "Address before a Joint Session of the Congress on the State of the Union," January 24, 2012, The American Presidency

Project, University of California, Santa Barbara, http://www.presidency.ucsb.edu/ws/index.php?pid=99000.

36. Other minor reforms, many of which were written to expire at the end of the 113th Congress, did little if anything to decrease the power of minority obstruction. Two resolutions containing the reforms were agreed to by large bipartisan margins on January 24, under an agreement that mandated a sixty-vote threshold for approval: *Congressional Record,* January 24, 2013, S270–74.
37. Republicans dutifully introduced a bill to reduce the size of the court, which had no chance of passing.
38. Jeremy W. Peters, "Reid Preparing to Move for Limits on Filibuster," *New York Times,* November 20, 2013, A16.
39. For the entire episode, see *Congressional Record,* November 21, 2013, S8414–8428.
40. All forty-five Republican senators voted to sustain supermajority cloture. They were joined by three Democrats—Carl Levin, Joe Manchin, and Mark Pryor.
41. Jeremy W. Peters, "Tempers Flare as New Rules Strain Senate," *New York Times,* December 13, 2013, 1,18; Christina L. Boyd, Michael S. Lynch, and Anthony J. Madonna, "Nuclear Fallout: Investigating the Effect of Senate Procedural Reform on Judicial Nominations," *Forum* 13, no. 4 (2016): 623, https://doi.org/10.1515/for-2015-0042; Ian Ostrander, "The Politics of Executive Nominations in the Post-Nuclear Senate," *Congress & the Presidency* 44, no. 3 (2017): 323–43.
42. Charles Krauthammer, "The Democrats' Outbreak of Lawlessness," *Washington Post,* November 28, 2013. Not even halfway through this column, Krauthammer, who by this point in time was using nearly every one of his op-eds to excoriate President Obama and everything the president said or did, switches abruptly to presidential "lawlessness" related almost exclusively to the Affordable Care Act's implementation.
43. Charles Krauthammer, "Nuclear? No, Restoration," *Washington Post,* May 13, 2005.
44. See, for example, the comments of Senator Charles Grassley, *Congressional Record,* April 4, 2017, S2408.
45. April 4 in the legislative calendar of the Senate.
46. Burgess Everett and Glenn Thrush, "McConnell Throws down the Gauntlet: No Scalia Replacement under Obama," *Politico,* February 13, 2016.
47. As this argument had no constitutional basis, Republican and Democratic senators also engaged in an unproductive debate about which side was being more hypocritical and whether there was any precedent for taking such an action. The Senate had never done anything like what McConnell was proposing. In July 1968 President Johnson, who had announced

in March that he would not be seeking reelection, nominated Abe Fortas to replace retiring Chief Justice Earl Warren. Senator Robert Griffin, a Michigan Republican, organized more than half of his fellow Republican senators to oppose any nomination because such should be left to the next president. The Senate, however, did consider Fortas's nomination, but it was blocked by a filibuster, and LBJ withdrew the nomination: Neil MacNeil and Richard A. Baker, *The American Senate an Insider's History* (Oxford: Oxford University Press, 2013), 127–28.

48. CBS News poll, February 12–16, 2016, https://www.scribd.com/doc/299653496/CBS-News-poll-The-next-Supreme-Court-justice-Obama-and-the-economy. The question was: "As you may know, U.S. Supreme Court Justice Antonin Scalia passed away. Would you like to see the next Supreme Court justice appointed by President Obama before the election in November or appointed by the President who will be elected in November?"

49. An early entry was a letter to Senate leaders, signed by more than 350 law professors, who deemed consideration a "constitutional duty" (https://law.stanford.edu/publications/350-legal-scholars-letter-to-united-states-senate-leaders-mitch-mcconnell-charles-grassley-harry-reid-patrick-leahy-urging-them-to-fulfill-their-constitutional-duty-to-give-president-barack/). Michael J. Gerhardt and Richard W. Painter, "Majority Rule and the Future of Judicial Selection," *Wisconsin Law Review*, 2017, 263–8; Josh Chafetz, "Unprecedented? Judicial Confirmation Battles and the Search for a Usable Past," *Harvard Law Review* 131 (2017): 96–132. See also Michael Gerhardt, "Getting the Senate's Responsibilities on Supreme Court Nominations Right," *SCOTUSblog*, March 9, 2016, http://www.scotusblog.com/2016/03/getting-the-senates-responsibilities-on-supreme-court-nominations-right/; David H. Gans, "Republicans Who Block Obama's Supreme Court Pick Are Violating the Constitution," *New Republic*, March 16, 2016; Michael D. Ramsey, "Why the Senate Doesn't Have to Act on Merrick Garland's Nomination," *Atlantic*, May 15, 2016; and Jonathan H. Adler, "The Erroneous Argument the Senate Has a 'Constitutional Duty' to Consider a Supreme Court Nominee," *Washington Post*, March 15, 2016.

50. This would leave a very large number of federal judgeships to be filled by President Donald Trump. Patrick Caldwell, "Senate Republicans Are Breaking Records for Judicial Obstruction," *Mother Jones*, May 6, 2016; Charlie Savage, "Courts Reshaped at Fastest Pace in Five Decades," *New York Times*, November 12, 2017, 1, 14.

51. Amber Phillips, "Senate Republicans Could Block Clinton Supreme Court Nominees Indefinitely. But It Wouldn't Be the Best Idea.," *Washington Post*, November 2, 2016; Sabrina Siddiqui, "Republican Senators Vow to Block Any Clinton Supreme Court Nominee Forever," *Guardian*, November 2, 2016, sec. Law.

52. Ashley Killough and Ted Barrett, "Here's How Senators Plan to Vote on Supreme Court Nominee Neil Gorsuch," *CNN,* April 4, 2017.
53. This means, in effect, that the option of filibustering the "motion to proceed" is not available as far as nominations, which are always considered in executive sessions.
54. Tessa Berenson, "Senator Jeff Merkley Protests Neil Gorsuch With 15-Hour Speech," *Time,* April 5, 2017.
55. As the new Congress was convening, at least one Democratic Senator, Charles Schumer, the newly-minted Minority Leader, expressed regret about the 2013 nuclear option, even though he was caucus leader of Senate majority at the time and voted for it. Mallory Shelbourne, "Schumer Regrets Dems Trigger of 'Nuclear Option,'" *Hill,* January 3, 2017.
56. For the entire episode, see *Congressional Record,* April 4, 2017, S2383–2417. Despite the events happening on April 6, the executive session on this nomination was on the legislative day of April 4.
57. Georgia's ailing Johnny Isakson was there for the crucial votes on April 6, but was back in Georgia recovering from back surgery on April 7.
58. *Congressional Record,* April 4, 2017, S2390–91. On restoration, see also McConnell, S2389.
59. *Congressional Record,* April 4, 2017, S2406.
60. *Congressional Record,* April 4, 2017, S2398.
61. *Congressional Record,* April 4, 2017, S2400.
62. *Congressional Record,* April 6, 2017, S2402.
63. *Congressional Record,* April 6, 2017, S2394.
64. James I. Wallner, *On Parliamentary War: Partisan Conflict and Procedural Change in the U.S. Senate* (Ann Arbor: University Of Michigan Press, 2017); Gregory J. Wawro and Eric Schickler, "Reid's Rules: Filibusters, the Nuclear Option, and Path Dependence in the US Senate," *Legislative Studies Quarterly* 43, no. 4 (2018): 619–47.
65. *Congressional Record,* April 6, 2017, S2388.
66. Elana Schor, "Bipartisan Pitch to Save Filibuster Gets 61 Senators' Endorsements," *Politico,* April 7, 2017.
67. Just after the Senate failed to advance what appeared to be its final attempt to repeal and replace the ACA, which as a reconciliation measure required only a simple majority vote, Trump tweeted: "The very outdated filibuster rule must go. Budget reconciliation is killing R's in Senate. Mitch M, go to 51 Votes NOW and WIN. IT'S TIME!" (https://twitter.com/realDonaldTrump, July 29, 2017). This was not a first for the president. On May 2 he had tweeted, "We either elect more Republican Senators in 2018 or change the rules now to 51%."
68. Carl Hulse, "Filibuster Fight Subsides, for Now, as Democrats Assume Full Senate Control," *New York Times,* January 26, 2021; Jordain Carney,

"Senate Passes Organizing Resolution after Schumer-McConnell Deal," *The Hill*, February 3, 2021; Annie Linskey, Sean Sullivan, and Maria Sacchetti, "Pressure Grows on Biden to End the Filibuster," *Washington Post*, March 5, 2021.

69. Burgess Everett, "Anti-filibuster Liberals Face a Senate Math Problem," *Politico*, March 9, 2021, https://www.politico.com/news/2021/03/09/anti-filibuster-liberals-senate-474729; Editors, "The Filibuster Has Changed Before. It's Time to Reform It Again," *Washington Post*, March 9, 2021; Editors, "For Democracy to Stay, the Filibuster Must Go," *New York Times*, March 11, 2021; Editors, "The Filibuster Is an Oddity That Harms American Democracy," *Economist*, March 13, 2021.

## Conclusion

1. Richard Hofstadter, *The Age of Reform: From Bryan to F.D.R.*, reprint (New York: Vintage Books, 1990).
2. Frances E. Lee, "Patronage, Logrolls, and 'Polarization': Congressional Parties of the Gilded Age, 1876–1896," *Studies in American Political Development* 30, no. 2 (2016): 116–27.
3. Jeffrey Jones, "Americans Split on Proposals for Popular Vote," Gallup, May 14, 2019, https://news.gallup.com/poll/257594/americans-split-proposals-popular-vote.aspx; "Gallup Polls: Consistent Super-Majority Support for a National Popular Vote," n.d., archive.fairvote.org/electoral_college/Gallup_Polls.pdf.
4. Pew Research Center, "Senate Legislative Process A Mystery to Many," January 28, 2010, https://www.pewresearch.org/politics/2010/01/28/senate-legislative-process-a-mystery-to-many/.
5. Steven S. Smith and Hong Min Park, "Americans' Attitudes about the Senate Filibuster," *American Politics Research*, 2013, 1–26.
6. Pew Research Center, "The Public, the Political System and American Democracy," April 26, 2018, http://www.people-press.org/2018/04/26/5-the-electoral-college-congress-and-representation/.
7. Ronald Brownstein, "Small States Are Getting a Much Bigger Say in Who Gets on the Court," *CNN Politics*, July 10, 2018, https://www.cnn.com/2018/07/10/politics/small-states-supreme-court/index.html; Paul Krugman, "Real America Versus Senate America," *New York Times*, November 8, 2018; Eric W. Orts, "The Path to Give California 12 Senators, and Vermont Just One," *Atlantic*, January 2, 2019; Hans Noel, "The Senate Represents States, Not People. That's the Problem.," *Vox*, October 13, 2018; David Leonhardt, "The Senate: Affirmative Action for White People," *New York Times*, October 19, 2018.

8. As we have seen, many senators have blamed their behavior rather than the rules of the Senate, for example. In the same way many prescriptions for how to fix American politics emphasize behavioral rather than institutional change. See, for example, Mickey Edwards, *Parties Versus the People: How to Turn Republicans and Democrats into Americans.* (New Haven, CT: Yale University Press, 2013).
9. For a closely related categorization and discussion of the differences, see Arend Lijphart, *Patterns of Democracy: Government Forms and Performance in Thirty-Six Countries,* 2nd ed, (New Haven, CT: Yale University Press, 2012). Lijphart distinguishes between what he calls the Westminster model of democracy and the consensus model of democracy. The Westminster model is the same as what I discuss above. The United States or Washington system is not a pure example of the consensus model, but it fits most of the characteristics in Lijphart's typology.
10. Woodrow Wilson, *Constitutional Government in the United States* (New York: Columbia University Press, 1908).
11. Robert A. Dahl, "On Removing Certain Impediments to Democracy in the United States," *Political Science Quarterly* 92, no. 1 (1977): 5.
12. Joseph S. Clark, *The Senate Establishment* (New York: Hill and Wang, 1963), 15–16.
13. Lindsay Rogers, *The American Senate* (New York: Knopf, 1926), 164. This is part of Rogers's argument that the American system in the early twentieth century was neither a true separation of powers system nor a parliamentary system with the clear responsibility of majority control. Senate deliberation was a way to check the dangers of this hybrid system. For a strong defense of the system as a logical form of majority rule tempered by legal mechanisms to protect fundamental rights, see Jonathan Riley, "American Democracy and Majority Rule," *Nomos* 32 (1990): 267–307. Riley does concede indirectly that the United States is at the outer edge of what might be practical or necessary (p. 287).
14. In making his argument that *The Federalist,* contra many interpretations, relies on public virtue, Garry Wills argues that Publius really sees the seemingly formidable system as only modestly antimajoritarian and that bicameralism is the only effective check. Gary Wills, *Explaining America: The Federalist* (Garden City, NY: Doubleday, 1981).
15. Sheryl Gay Stolberg, "The Decider," *New York Times,* December 24, 2006.
16. For one of the most comprehensive reviews of various proposals, see James L. Sundquist, *Constitutional Reform and Effective Government,* rev. ed (Washington, DC: Brookings Institution Press, 1992). Other critiques of the American system that tilt toward or advocate specific reforms (especially in the direction of Westminster) include Daniel Lazare,

*The Frozen Republic: How the Constitution Is Paralyzing Democracy* (New York: Harcourt Brace, 1996); Sanford Levinson, *Our Undemocratic Constitution: Where the Constitution Goes Wrong (and How We the People Can Correct It)* (Oxford: Oxford University Press, 2006); and Stephen M. Griffin, *Broken Trust: Dysfunctional Government and Constitutional Reform* (Lawrence: University Press of Kansas, 2015).

17. On the proposal from political scientists William Howell and Terry Moe to give the president universal "fast-track" authority see their book, *Relic: How Our Constitution Undermines Effective Government, and Why We Need a More Powerful Presidency* (New York: Basic Books, 2016). Arguably the biggest problem with the Supreme Court is its unlimited tenure and the politics of the appointment process. For a comprehensive argument for staggered and limited terms, see Steven G. Calabresi and James Lindgren, "Term Limits for the Supreme Court: Life Tenure Reconsidered," *Harvard Journal of Law and Public Policy* 29 (2006): 769–877.

18. Daniel Lazare, "Abolish the Senate," *Jacobin*, December 2, 2014; John D. Dingell, "I Served in Congress Longer Than Anyone. Here's How to Fix It," *Atlantic*, December 4, 2018.

19. Lynn A. Baker and Samuel H. Dinkin, "The Senate: An Institution Whose Time Has Gone?," *Journal of Law and Politics* 13 (1997): 21–103.

20. Orts, "The Path to Give California 12 Senators, and Vermont Just One."

21. In 2020, the House of Representatives passed a bill to make D.C. the fifty-first state, but that initiative had no chance of consideration, let alone passage, in the Republican Senate. On efforts to advance D.C. statehood early in the Biden administration, see Edward-Isaac Dovere, "The Window for D.C. Statehood Won't Be Open Forever," *Atlantic*, February 19, 2021, https://www.theatlantic.com/politics/archive/2021/02/will-dc-become-state-year/618065/. Note, among others, "Pack the Union: A Proposal to Admit New States for the Purpose of Amending the Constitution to Ensure Equal Representation," *Harvard Law Review*, January 10, 2020.

22. Raymond Winbush, ed., *Should America Pay? Slavery and the Raging Debate on Reparations*, reprint ed. (New York: Amistad, 2003); Alfred L. Brophy, *Reparations: Pro and Con* (New York: Oxford University Press, 2008); Ta-Nehisi Coates, "The Case for Reparations," *Atlantic*, June 2014.

23. Google Trends, for example, shows a small but consistent increase in reparations-related searches starting in 2015 followed by a large surge around the start of 2019 and another spike in June 2020 in the wake of the massive Black Lives Matter protests. On its history leading into the 2020 campaign, see Emma Goldberg, "How Reparations for Slavery became a 2020 Campaign Issue," *New York Times*, June 18, 2020.

24. Congressional efforts, such as HR 40, a bill promoted for many years by Representative John Conyers, have focused on the formation of a

commission to study the issue and make recommendations. For a directly monetary estimate and proposal, see William A. Darity and A. Kirsten Mullen, *From Here to Equality: Reparations for Black Americans in the Twenty-First Century* (Chapel Hill: University of North Carolina Press, 2020).

# INDEX

*The page references in italics represent figures and tables in the text.*

Adams, John, "Thoughts on Government," 89
Affordable Care Act (2010), 176, 246n33, 247n42
African Americans: disenfranchisement of, 40, 55, 67, 71–72; lynching of, 110; political and social equality for, 58; rights of, 8, 51, 105, 111, 120; as soldiers, 126; underrepresentation of, 73; urban population of, 62–63, 71; voting rights of, 122. *See also* minorities
Alabama, 45, 65
Alaska, 59–60, 69, 74, 223n2
Albright, Madeleine, 4, 212n7
Aldrich, Nelson, 122, 171
Alexander, Lamar, 147, 181–82
Allen, James, 129
American constitutionalism: equal representation in, 40; implicit understanding of, 145; problems of, 13. *See also* constitutionalism
American exceptionalism, 3–5, 201, 211n6, 212n7
Ames, Fisher, 94
antifederalists, 93
antilynching legislation, 110–13, 124–26, 142, 235n3. *See also* civil rights legislation; lynching
Apportionment Act (1842), 61
Arenberg, Richard A., *Defending the Filibuster*, 145, 147, 158
Arizona, 54, 58
Arkansas, 45
Articles of Confederation, 15–17, 30–33, 89, 93

Baker, Howard, 25
Baker, Lynn, 73

*Baker v. Carr,* 64, 66
balance of powers, 35, 162
Bennett, Bob, 111
bicameralism, 16–17, 20, 32–33, 78–79, 86, 206, 210, 215n2; advantages of, 147; consensus on, 21; creation of, 156; defense of, 79, 149; the essence of the Senate and, 146–47. *See also* Congress
Biden, Joseph, 191, 208
Bill of Rights, 152. *See also* Constitution
Binder, Sarah, 48
bipartisanship, 133
Birmingham, 62
Black Lives Matter movement, 209, 252n23
Blumenthal, Richard, 189
British House of Commons, 33–34, 113. *See also* Westminster
Brown, Scott, 181
*Brown v. Board of Education,* 58–59, 65–66, 104, 203
Bruhl, Aaron-Andrew, 103
Buchanan, James, 84, 96–98
Buffett, Warren, 81
Burdette, Franklin, 117
Burr, Aaron, 4
Bush, George W., 111, 140, 174, 176, 179, 188, 203, 211n6, 240n82
Byrd, Robert, 5, 85, 98, 147, 150, 173, 212n13

Calhoun, John C., 46–48, 115, 153; *A Disquisition on Government,* 47
California, 45, 60–63, 70–71, 74–78, 82, 152, 159, 209
Caro, Robert, 87
Carpenter, Jesse T., 47

255

census, 33, 43, 60–62, 223n4; percentage urban population in the, 62
checks and balances, 10, 47, 78, 112, 143–49, 194, 200–201, 206; the filibuster and the system of, 151, 166; revised system of, 139, 143, 210. *See also* Constitution
Cheney, Dick, 179
Chicago, 62
civil religion, 4, 211n6
Civil Rights Act (1957), 128, 142
Civil Rights Act (1964), 128
civil rights legislation: filibusters of, 85, 104–5, 122, 125–28, 142, 236n29; opposition to, 10, 105; triumph of, 129, 194. *See also* antilynching legislation; civil rights movement; voting rights legislation
civil rights movement, 38, 58–59, 103, 154. *See also* civil rights legislation
Civil War, 5, 8, 40, 48–50, 58; memory of the, 51, 60; prior to the, 193–94
Clark, Joseph, 201
Clay, Henry, 115
Clayton, Henry, 122
Cleveland, Grover, 122
Clinton, Hillary, 186, 211n6
Clinton, Bill, 1
cloture: changes to, 100, 105, 136; closure or, 115; legislative restrictions on supermajority, 173–77; majority, 119, 126, 145, 180, 207–8; reform of, 100, 105; rules on, 104, 113–17; senate debates on, 240n5; statistics on, *121*; supermajority, 10–11, 25, 39, 83, 86, 112, 118–22, 126–33, 138–66, 170–78, 187, 190, 194–96, 207–10, 240n5; and supermajority decision rule, 129–38; votes of, 138. *See also* filibuster; holds; rules of procedure; supermajority
Coby, Patrick, 27
Cold War, 5, 58, 130; the end of the, 177
Colorado, 49–50
common law, 160
Compromise of 1850, 46

concurrent majority, 46–48, 153
Confederacy, 55, 59, 122; states in the former, 126, 223n2; statues of leaders and generals of the, 209
Congress: activist, 130; bicameral, 13, 16; as a check on presidential power, 166; of the Confederation, 22, 24, 33–34, 43, 89; continuity in, 106; federal spending as dictated by, 74; "Fighting 112th," 136; "lame duck," 117; legislative committees in, 138, 176, 202; new western states in, 8; powers of, 243n50; role of committees in, 161–62; state sovereignty in, 157; struggles over civil rights measures in, 59; study of, 212n14. *See also* bicameralism; Congressional Budget Office; Congressional Research Service; House of Representatives; Senate
Congressional Budget and Impoundment Control Act (1974), 174–76
Congressional Budget Office, 202
*Congressional Record*, 111, 117, 126, 132, 240n5
Congressional Research Service, 202
Connecticut, 31, 71, 89, 156
Constitution: Article I of the, 60, 64, 139, 161, 172, 207; Article II of the, 180, 215n3; Article III of the, 215n3; Article IV of the, 48; Article V of the, 154, 184; critiques of the proposed, 93; drafting and approval of the, 3; the filibuster as a subversion of the, 160–65; inventions of the, 4, 35–36; the judiciary in the, 31–32; ratification of the, 210; republican theory of government in the, 112; sections of the, 14; substantive debate on the proposed, 37; three-fifths clause of the, 44; veto points specified in the, 139; as the will of the majority, 109. *See also* Bill of Rights; checks and balances; constitutional amendments; Constitutional Convention; ratification debates; separation of powers

constitutional amendments: Fourteenth, 65; Fifteenth, 51, 122, 171; Sixteenth, 124, 195; Seventeenth, 40, 52–58, 73, 79–83, 116, 119, 124, 157, 195, 198, 201, 214n19; Eighteenth, 124; Nineteenth, 58, 124, 195; Twentieth, 117; Twenty-third, 38; Twenty-fourth, 126. *See also* Constitution

constitutional construction, 138–40

Constitutional Convention (1787), 8, 13–37, 52, 149; apportionments at the, 219n10; compromises at the, 153, 156; debates at the, 86–87; map of the states at the time of the, 42; political philosophy of the, 199; politics of the, 13, 40–41; role of the vice president considered at the, 162; rotation at the, 90–93; secrecy of the, 204; small-state delegations to the, 216n17, 216n23. *See also* Constitution; Great Compromise; New Jersey Plan; three-fifths compromise; Virginia Plan

constitutionalism: evolution of political institutions and, 205, 213n15; loose, 146; modern, 9; partisanship and, 195; politics and, 195–200, 205; questions of, 6; of the Senate, 3, 8, 10, 83; of the Supreme Court, 203. *See also* American constitutionalism

constitutional option, 172–73, 180, 207

continuing body doctrine, 7–9, 19, 83–86, 96–108, 128, 207, 232n43; defense of the, 233n50. *See also* staggered terms

Conway, Moncure D., 141
Cornyn, John, 188
corruption, 4–5
Craig, Larry, 131, 155

Dahl, Robert, 201
Davie, William, 23
debate: alternative to public, 133; cloture as a threat to unlimited, 146; collective quality of, 10; floor, 204; rules of procedure and, 8, 141, 207; as superfluous, 202; unlimited, 10, 146, 155. *See also* deliberation; extended debate

Declaration of Independence, 3
Defense Department, 131
Delaware, 17, 60, 70, 72, 78, 90, 219n15, 220n19

deliberation: collective, 8, 203–5; and compromise, 11; in contemporary government, 202–5; diminishing of, 133, 205; distortion of, 194; and the filibuster, 112, 131; Madisonian ironies and, 133; mockery of, 136; quality of, 18, 20, 23–24, 35–36, 153, 159. *See also* debate

democracy: bedrock tenet of modern, 57; central standard of modern, 9; distortions of, 72; equal representation and, 194; evolution of the concept of, 205; institutions of, 58, 164, 199; Madisonian, 201; models of, 251n9; republican, 146; the Senate as a check on, 20, 23; simple, 80; theory of, 213n15; universe of contemporary, 200. *See also* "one person, one vote"; representation; republicanism

Democratic Party: apex of the power in Congress of the, 39; fragmentation of the, 46; as the liberal party, 75; return of a nationally competitive, 50; support for filibuster reform in the, 191. *See also* party politics

Detroit, 62
Dickinson, John, 17, 91
Dinkin, Samuel, 73
districting: highly engineered, 107; intervention by the judiciary in apportionment and, 63–64. *See also* elections

District of Columbia Voting Rights Amendment, 39. *See also* Washington, D.C.

Dodd, Christopher, 30, 156
Dove, Robert B., *Defending the Filibuster*, 145, 147, 158
Durbin, Richard, 168
Dyer, Leonidas, 124

elections: House, 105–8, *107*; midterm, 179, 181; in a parliamentary system, 200; presidential system of, 195; primary, 134; Senate, 75, 105–8, *107*, 134. *See also* districting; Electoral College
Electoral College, 53, 129, 195–98, 206. *See also* elections
Ellsworth, Oliver, 30, 156
England, 49
equality: contemporary notions of democratic, 193; electoral, 205; political, 58–83, 194, 206, 208; racial, 58–83, 165; social, 58, 165
Equal Protection Clause, 65
equal representation (two senators per state), 7–11, 17, 20–26, 37–83, 153–59, 165, 193–94, 208–9; the antebellum irony of, 42–44; elimination of, 209–10; in an era of democratic equality, 77–83; fairness of, 44; and minority interests, 46–48, 163; original relevance of, 9; policy consequences of, 74; politics of, 8, 58; positions on, 197; practicality or pragmatism and, 82; and principles of good government, 78; the "slave power" and, 44–46; and supermajority cloture, 158, 194, 213n14. *See also* minority rights; representation
executive branch: nominations to the, 131–32, 137; presidential appointments to the, 11. *See also* president/presidency
Executive Reorganization Act (1939), 174–75
extended debate, 46–48, 96, 113–17, 149, 153; and supermajority cloture, 83. *See also* cloture; debate; filibuster

fast-track (legislative procedures), 174–76, 206, 252n17
federal funding: of entitlement programs, 81; small-state bias in, 73, 81
federalism, 13, 47, 56, 79, 200; defense of, 80, 94; question of, 21; the Senate as the bastion of, 99; states and, 25, 204–5

*Federalist, The,* 20, 27–31, 41–42, 47, 148, 159, 204–5, 251n14. *See also* Hamilton, Alexander; Madison, James
Federal Reserve, 204
female suffrage. *See* women
filibuster, 9–10, 25, 46–48, 59, 110–66; avoidance of the, 133; bipartisan cooperation to end the, 207; classic, 115; and cloture motions, 130–34, 178–79; as a constitutional provision, 151; debate on the, 101, 104, 154, 240n5; defense of the, 145, 160, 180, 208; dysfunction of the, 144–46, 166; elections bill killed by a, 51; the evolution of the, *127*; as the founders' intent, 148–52, 160–65; history of the, 86, 96, 129, 232n45; limitation of the, 118–22, 129, 170–74; nineteenth-century use of the, 153–54, 171; protection of the, 104; protracted, 151–52; public knowledge of the, 197; reform of the, 127–29, 143–44, *151*, 181, 191, 196, 202, 207–8; silent, 130, 132, 134; by southern senators, *123*, 129, 221n31; as a subversion of the Constitution, 160–66; and supermajority cloture, 83, 129–38, 154, 196–97; unpopular, 100; use and abuse of the, 140; and the use of procedural motions, 236n28. *See also* cloture; extended debate; minority rights; nuclear option; Senate Rule XXII
Florida, 45, 72, 126
Fong, Hiram, 155
Ford, Gerald, 176
Fortas, Abe, 179, 246n26, 247n47
Franklin, Benjamin, 16, 28, 147, 150
free silver movement, 50
free states, 42–46. *See also* North; states
Frist, Bill, 174, 179–80, 184
fugitive slave laws, 80
Fulbright, William, 155

Garland, Merrick, 186–87, 189, 197
Georgia, 30, 64, 73, 220n16
gerrymandering, 76–77, 227n52

INDEX  259

Gilded Age, 5
Gingrich, Newt, 1
Gladstone, William, 5
Gorham, Nathaniel, 24, 91–92, 231n24
Gorsuch, Justice Neil, 185–88, 197
governance: crisis of, 1–3, 6; modern republican, 7
Government Accountability Office, 202
Graham, Lindsay, 189
Gramm, Phil, 149
Grant, Ulysses S., 50
Grassley, Charles, 139
*Gray v. Sanders*, 64
Great Britain, 184
Great Compromise, 17, 23, 26–30, 37, 40–48, 56, 63, 69, 95, 99, 153–56, 162–63, 218n50, 219n14. *See also* Constitutional Convention
Great Migration, 62
Great Recession, 74
Great Society, 130
Gregg, Gary L., II, 80
gridlock: at the Constitutional Convention, 91; governmental, 198, 208; legislative, 134; over nominations, 190; potential, 201
Guerra, Joseph, 157
gun control legislation, 163

Hagel, Chuck, 150
Halverson, Reverend Richard C., 1
Hamilton, Alexander, 18, 31, 41, 94, 204
Harding, Warren, 117–18, 124
Harkin, Tom, 179
Harkwick, Thomas, 98
Harris, Kamala, 191
Harrison, William Henry, 110, 122
Hart, Gary, 150
Hawaii, 59–60, 69, 223n2
Haynes, George, 84, 98, 125
Health Care and Education Reconciliation Act (2010), 176
Heflin, J. Thomas, 125, 237n41
Helms, Jesse, 147
higher law, 164
Hill, Joseph, 154

Hoffer, Peter Charles, 31
holds, 131–32, 178; reform of, 132. *See also* "hostage" holds
Hollis, Henry French, 142–43
Honest Leadership and Open Government Act (2007), 132
"hostage" holds, 131. *See also* holds
House of Representatives: adoption of rules in the, 172; African Americans in the, 73; antislavery measures of the, 46; apportionment for the, 44, 60, 223n4, 225n34; Democratic control of the, 50, 122, 181, 191; democratic nature of the, 33, 95, 153; elections for the, 105–8, *107;* innovation of the, 32; majority rule in the, 116; nonvoting delegates in the, 38; obstructive tactics in the, 115; potential domination by the South of the, 43; proportional representation in the, 22; representation in the, 60, 73; Republican control of the, 181; rules of the, 116; two-year terms in the, 85. *See also* Congress; proportional representation
Humphrey, Hubert, 173
hyperpartisanship, 107, 133, 167. *See also* partisan politics

Idaho, 50, 131
Illinois, 45, 72
immigration, 50–51; reform of the system of, 139
imperialism, 59
Indiana, 45
indigenous populations, 59
inequality, 5, 193; of separate educational facilities, 203. *See also* Jim Crow; underrepresentation
Inouye, Daniel, 155
Iowa, 45
Iredell, James, 94
Isakson, Johnny, 152, 189, 249n57

Jackson, Andrew, 47, 53, 204
Jacobi, Tonja, 164

Jefferson, Thomas, 141, 149–50, 204
Jim Crow, 5, 51, 55, 126; emergence of, 194; political disenfranchisement of, 129; segregation of, 129. *See also* inequality; poll taxes; racism
Johnson, Lyndon, 104–5, 128, 247n47
judiciary: as a deliberative institution, 202, 206; federal, 11, 63, 164, 179, 186, 248n50; imperial, 2; independent, 31–32; intervention in apportionment and districting by the, 63–64; nominations to the, 11, 137, 169, 174, 178–89, 193, 245n24, 246n26; power of the, 205; structure of the, 215n3. *See also* Supreme Court

Kansas-Nebraska Act (1854), 46
Kavanaugh, Brett, 197
Kennedy, John F., 38
Kennedy, Ted, 181
Kentucky, 43–44, 220n18
King, Rufus, 23–24, 36
Klobuchar, Amy, 142
Krauthammer, Charles, 184, 247n42

LaFollette, Robert, 118
Landrieu, Mary, 110
Lansing, John, 41
Latinx populations, 73
Leahy, Patrick, 183
Lee, Frances, 74, 134
Lieberman, Joe, 181
Lincoln, Abraham, 48–49, 204
Lincoln-Douglas debates, 53–54
Lindblom, Charles, *Politics and Markets*, 11
Los Angeles, 63
Lott, Trent, 179–80
Louisiana, 44
Louisiana Purchase, 46
lynching, 110–13, 124–26, 142. *See also* antilynching legislation

Macedo, Stephen, 80, 82
Madison, James, 15–21, 26–35, 41–42, 47, 52, 90, 143, 149, 159, 201, 230n21

Maine, 45, 73
majority tyranny, 8, 15, 27–29, 47; protection against, 35, 47, 156
malapportionment, 61–71, 70, 156
Mansfield, Mike, 130
Martin, Luther, 24
Maryland, 39, 89–90, 219n15, 230n18
Mason, George, 16, 24, 28, 33
Massachusetts, 30–31, 231n24
McCain, John, 147
McClellan, John, 154, 157
McClure, James, 155
McConnell, Mitch, 150, 152, 167–70, 185–90
*McGrain v. Daugherty*, 102–3
McKellar, Kenneth, 127–28
media: cities as the centers of the, 80; elections in the contemporary era of the, 107; news, 202. *See also* newspapers
Memphis, 62
Merkley, Jeff, 181, 187
Mexico, 46
Michigan, 45, 72
Millett, Patricia, 183
Minnesota, 45, 159
minorities: discrimination against, 83; government on behalf of, 165; rights of, 145–46. *See also* African Americans
minority power, 7, 10–11, 14, 25–29, 40, 48, 193–94, 201; accommodations of, 132; antebellum, 46–48; and the filibuster, 59; protection of, 156, 234n65; and rules of procedure, 193. *See also* minority rights; minority tyranny
minority rights, 8–9, 15, 25–29, 48, 126, 148, 153–59, 163, 217n40; abstract notions of, 51; mythology of, 112; the Senate as a bastion of, 84, 86, 109, 154. *See also* equal representation; filibuster; minority power
minority tyranny, 29. *See also* minority power
Mississippi, 45, 72
Missouri, 45–46

Missouri Compromise (1820), 45
Moffett, S. E., 38, 52, 54–56
Mondale, Walter, 101, 129
Mondell, Frank W., 115–16
Montana, 50
Morgan, Edmund, 33
Morris, Gouverneur, 24, 219n12
Moses, George, 125
*Mr. Smith Goes to Washington* (film, 1939), 141–43

National Emergencies Act (1976), 175
nationalism, 4
National Security Council, 204
Nebraska, 49
Nevada, 48–49, 59
New Deal, 58, 130, 174
New Jersey, 72–73
New Jersey Plan, 22, 33, 41. See also Constitutional Convention
New Mexico, 54, 58, 73
newspapers, 41; partisan, 96. See also media
New York, 30, 41, 43, 50, 60, 62, 72, 82
New York City, 81
Nixon, Richard, 38, 172–73, 175
nominations: crisis of, 179–81; for the executive branch, 131–32, 137, 169, 178, 182–83, 193; holds on, 131–32; for the judiciary, 11, 137, 169, 174, 178–89, 193, 245n24, 246n26; obstructions of, 177–78; and the sixty-vote Senate, 177–78
North, 51. See also free states
North American Free Trade Agreement (NAFTA), 176
North Dakota, 50
Northwest Ordinance, 34, 43
Northwest Territories, 43–44
nuclear option, 147, 167–91, 207, 249n55. See also filibuster
nullification crisis, 47

Obama, Barack, 132, 135, 140, 147, 163, 167–69, 177, 181–90, 197, 211n6
Ohio, 44, 162

Oklahoma, 54, 58
Omnibus Budget Reconciliation Act (1981), 176
"one person, one vote," 60–69, 82–83, 206, 209. See also democracy; equality
Oppenheimer, Bruce, 74
Oregon, 45, 49
Owen, Priscilla, 179–80
Owen, Robert, 100

partisan politics, 1–4, 9, 112, 135, 141, 163, 166, 178, 195, 206–8; antebellum, 54; equal representation in the era of, 75–77; era of, 137, 185; late nineteenth-century, 116; legislative, 134; national swing in, 234n67; of reform, 191, 196; senate representation in an era of, 76; steady rise in, 130. See also hyperpartisanship; polarization
party politics, 48–53; democratization and, 53. See also Democratic Party; Republican Party
Patterson, William, 22
Pell, Claiborne, 155–56
Pennsylvania, 16–17, 43, 50, 90, 219n14; constitution of, 30–31; unicameral, 147
Philadelphia, 13, 15–16, 62
Pinckney, Charles Cotesworth, 94, 216n22
*Plessy v. Ferguson*, 51
polarization: of America, 76, 186; battles between majority and minority that reflect, 112; of Congress, 132; and the crisis of governance, 194; extreme, 137; and obstruction, 183; partisan, 2–4, 9, 75–77, 76, 112, 130, 135, 163, 166, 178, 185, 206; rigid partisanship and, 141; of the Senate, 166, 183. See also partisan politics
poll taxes, 126, 238n46. See also Jim Crow
Powe, Lucas, 68

president/presidency: appointments and the, 193; as chief executive, 204; as a deliberative institution, 203–4, 206; direct election of the, 195–98, 206, 218n50; power of the, 2, 175, 201, 205–6; proposal of universal fast-track authority for the, 206; treaties and the, 193; veto power of the, 139. *See also* executive branch
progressive movement, 195
Prohibition, repeal of, 38
proportional representation, 14–15, 17, 21–23, 26, 41. *See also* House of Representatives
public law, 164
Puerto Rico, 40, 209, 223n1

race, 39; and civil rights, 66; and ethnicity, 72. *See also* racism
racism, 124–25; casual, 125; institutional, 209; systemic, 209. *See also* Jim Crow; race; slavery; white supremacy
Randolph, Edmund, 16, 92–93
Randolph Resolutions, 90
ratification debates, 93–95. *See also* Constitution
Read, George, 18, 91–92
Reagan, Ronald, 81, 176, 211n6
Reconstruction, 49–51, 226n38
Reed, Jack, 189
reform: cloture, 100–101, 104, 127–28, 143; constitutional, 206, 214n19; filibuster, 127–29, 143–44, 151, 181, 191, 196, 202; of holds, 132; institutional, 165, 199, 206; partisan politics of, 191, 196; of the rules of procedure, 104, 182–85, 247n36; of the Senate, 205, 247n36. *See also* reparations
Reid, Harry, 25, 142, 152, 167–68, 182–83, 188, 190
reparations: African American, 209–10, 252n23; constitutional repair and, 193–210. *See also* reform; slavery
representation: absurdity of, 39; distortion of, 83; inequities of Senate, 60, 67; injustices of, 71; multiple levels of, 205; regional, 42; of states, 155. *See also* democracy; equal representation; underrepresentation
republicanism, 205–6; modern, 206. *See also* democracy
Republican Party: bias of equal representation for the, 208–9; as the conservative party, 75; control of the presidency by the, 50–51; in the states in the North and West, 50–51. *See also* party politics
Reuther, Walter, 101, 103–4
*Reynolds v. Sims*, 65–69, 78, 203, 224n18
Rhode Island, 43, 78, 89, 208
Riker, William, 53–54, 56
Robert, Henry Martin, *Robert's Rules of Order*, 113–14, 235n7
Roberts, Pat, 150
Rogers, Lindsay, 87, 125, 157, 251n13
Roosevelt, Theodore, 116
rotation: at the Constitutional Convention, 90–93, 231n27; in the late eighteenth century, 88–90, 230n15; and staggered terms, 107–8, 228n5
rotten boroughs, 49–50
rules of procedure, 6–10, 14, 36, 59, 113–17, 161, 171, 201, 209; dysfunction of, 112; limits on filibusters in the, 118–22; majority vote on the, 103–4; minority power and, 193; reform of the, 104, 182–85, 247n36; supermajority protections to, 85, 102–3. *See also* cloture; Senate
Russell, Richard, 105

Safire, William, 156
Sanders, Bernie, 181
Sandy Hook mass shooting, 135
Scalia, Justice Antonin, 185–86, 248n48
school desegregation, 66
Schumer, Chuck, 187, 190, 249n55
segregation, 5
Seitz, Virginia, 157

Senate: absurdity of representation in the, 39, 70; and American democracy, 1–12; budget resolution of the, 137; citizenship and the, 19–20; compromised, 20–25, 34, 36; conservative purpose of the, 108; as a countermajoritarian body, 157; deliberative, 153; dysfunction of the, 6–7, 112, 129–38, 143, 168, 175, 193–95, 207; elections for the, 105–8, *107;* gerrymander of the, 77; history of the, 3–4, 8, 11, 84, 87, 104, 129, 142, 156, 167–68; independent and stable, 90; liberal government and the, 130; mythology of the, 3–6, 48, 141–66, 193; "obstruct and restrict" pattern in the, 135; overriding presidential vetoes in the, 28–29, 160, 162; power of smaller states in the, 158; and protection of property, 18; quorum in the, 28; racial bias of the, 165; refined selection of the, 22–23; reform of the, 52, 242n42; republican purpose of the, 15–21, 25, 35, 93; role in foreign affairs of the, 20; size of the, 7–8, 17–18, 20–23; as a supermajoritarian body, 129–38, 165–91. *See also* cloture; Congress; continuing body doctrine; equal representation; extended debate; filibuster; holds; nominations; rotation; rules of procedure; Senate exceptionalism; Senate Rule V; Senate Rule XIX; Senate Rule XX; Senate Rule XXII; Senate Rule XXX; Senate Rules Committee; senators; sixty-vote Senate; six-year terms; smaller membership; staggered terms; state equality; supermajority; tracking system; unanimous consent agreements

Senate exceptionalism, 3–6, 13–37, 84, 146, 193, 210, 211n1, 212n14. *See also* Senate

Senate Rule V, 104–5, 109, 128, 164, 207. *See also* Senate

Senate Rule XIX, 114. *See also* Senate

Senate Rule XX, 170. *See also* Senate

Senate Rule XXII, 86, 104–5, 109, 119–20, 126–29, 141–49, 158, 164, 168–72, 178, 183–84; change in the wording of, 179–82; reform of, 238n47; reinterpretation of, 188–90; rewriting of, 207. *See also* filibuster; Senate

Senate Rule XXX, 102. *See also* Senate

Senate Rules Committee, 101, 152, 174, 179. *See also* Senate

senators: African American, 73, 226n38; behavior of, 251n8; direct election of, 40, 52–58, 124, 195, 201; electoral and partisan interests of, 159; progressive, 55; Republican, 163; selection by state legislatures of, 23, 40, 52–56, 82, 106, 214n19, 221n38, 222n42, 226n38; slave state, 46; southern, 40, 55, 128. *See also* Senate

separation of powers, 47, 78, 112, 200–201; rethinking the, 205–6; revised system of, 210. *See also* Constitution

Shelby, Richard, 131–32

Sherman, Lawrence, 146–47

Sherman, Roger, 28–30, 37, 92, 156

sixty-vote Senate, 10–11, 112–13, 129–39, 144, 152, 166–70; as a fourth veto point in the legislative system, 138–40, 143, 193; nominations and the, 177–78; realities of the, 161; the rise of the, *137. See also* Senate; supermajority; unanimous consent agreements

six-year terms, 19, 193. *See also* Senate

slavery, 5, 37, 58; absence of, 42; defense of, 47–48; extension of, 80; presence of, 42; prohibition in territories of, 46; protection of, 194. *See also* racism; reparations; slave states

slave states, 8, 42–46, 219–20nn15–16, 220n19. *See also* slavery; states

smaller membership, 7–8, 18, 20, 193. *See also* Senate

small-state sovereignty, 80, 155. *See also* states

Smith, Steven S., 48, 134, 148, 217n40
South, 50–51, 62; disenfranchisement in the, 126; suffrage rights in the, 51, 122; white control in the, 67. *See also* slave states
South Carolina, 31, 89, 220n16
South Dakota, 50, 221n34
southern Democrats, 59, 85, 104–5, 122, 126, 129, 171–73
Specter, Arlen, 181
staggered terms, 7, 14, 19, 84–88, 93–100, 103–9, 193, 229n13, 233n50; consequences of, 101; origins of, 228n5; in the ratification debates, 93–95; rotation and, 107–8, 228n5; state selection and, 234n67. *See also* continuing body doctrine; rotation
state constitutions, 88–90. *See also* states
state equality, 13–15, 21–27, 43, 60, 68, 72, 159; consequences of, 44; unicameral legislature based on, 33, 41. *See also* Senate
state legislatures, 8, 13, 22, 113, 221n38; malapportionment of, 71; reapportionment of, 61–62; selection of senators by the, 23, 40, 52–56, 82, 106, 214n19, 221n38, 222n42; and state policy, 56; and state senates, 63. *See also* states
states: admissions of, 44–45, 50–52, 58–59, 194, 220n18, 234n67; border, 43; diverse, 72; and federalism, 25, 204–5; heavily urban, 72, 75–77; and the House of Representatives, 33–34; least urban, 75–77; moderately urban, 75–77; northern, 43–44, 59, 62; size of, 42–43, 51, 80, 155–58; southern, 43–44, 45, 60, 62, 73; as specific political entities, 27; western, 52. *See also* free states; slave states; small-state sovereignty; state constitutions; state legislatures
Stennis, John, 154
Story, Joseph, 95
supermajority, 10–11, 102–4, 109, 112–13, 119–22, 126–40, 164; politics of the, 177; rationale for the, 85, 152; as required in the Constitution in some instances, 160, 162; substantial, 105. *See also* cloture; sixty-vote Senate; unanimous consent agreements
Supreme Court: apportionment cases before the, 82; composition of the, 13; constitutionalism of the, 203; control of the, 2, 51; deliberation of the, 202–3; interpretation of the Constitution of the, 9; intervention by the, 140; major decisions about the powers of Congress by the, 243n50; nominations to the, 185–89; ruling from the, 174; size of the, 138; tenure and selection of the, 206; vacancy in the, 185. *See also* judiciary; Warren Court

tariffs, 47
Tennessee, 43–44, 60–61, 64, 126
Texas, 45–46, 74, 82
three-fifths compromise, 43. *See also* Constitutional Convention
Thune, John, 189
Thurmond, Strom, 128, 142
Tillman, "Pitchfork Ben," 117
Tocqueville, Alexis de, 3–4
tracking system, 130–34. *See also* Senate
Trade Act (1975), 176
trade agreements, 176
Trans-Pacific Partnership (TPP), 177
treaties, 102, 178, 193; approval of, 160
Truman, Harry, 59, 110, 127, 223n1
Trump, Donald, 81, 162–63, 177, 185–86, 190–91, 248n50, 249n67
Tseytlin, Misha, 79–80
Tucker, St. George, 95
Turpie, David, 4, 109

unanimous consent agreements, 132–36, 161, 207, 239n69. *See also* sixty-vote Senate; supermajority
underrepresentation, 69–74, 193; of urban and minority voters, 83, 165, 209. *See also* inequality; representation

UN General Assembly, 113
unicameralism, 206, 215n2
United States: crisis of governance in the, 194, 205; deliberative policy-making institutions of the, 205–6; history of race in the, 6, 111, 193–94; as the indispensable nation, 212n7; and other democracies, 211n2; as a predominantly urban nation, 116; as a republic instead of a democracy, 205
Utah, 54, 58, 73

Van Dam, Jeff, 164
Vandenberg, Arthur, 149
Vardaman, James K., 120, 122
Vermont, 44, 74, 220n18
veto points, 138–40, 143, 161, 165, 193, 201, 205
Virginia, 41, 43, 70, 73, 90, 230n21
Virginia Plan, 17–19, 22, 26, 34, 52, 90, 156, 230n21. *See also* Constitutional Convention
Voting Rights Act (1965), 128–29, 227n52
voting rights legislation, 126–29. *See also* civil rights legislation

Wallop, Malcolm, 152
Walsh, Thomas, 100–101, 108–9
War Powers Act (1973), 175
Warren, Chief Justice Earl, 60, 66–69, 224n22, 247n47
Warren Court, 60–69, 78–79, 224n22. *See also* Supreme Court
Washington, 50, 221n34

Washington, D.C., 38–40, 81, 200; enfranchisement for, 223n1; statehood movement for, 39, 208, 252n21
Washington, George, 141, 143, 149–50, 204
Wawro, Gregory, 46
Webster, Daniel, 4, 115
*Wesberry v. Sanders,* 64
Westminster, 200. *See also* British House of Commons
West Virginia, 48–49
White, William, 5, 85, 98
white supremacy, 7, 9, 58, 124, 193–94, 209; in the apportionment cases, 67; the continuing body doctrine and, 103–5, 128; defense of, 10–11, 51, 112, 120–29, 153; direct legislative threat to, 124; equal representation and, 40; filibusters in support of, 86, 122–29, 142–44. *See also* Jim Crow; racism
Will, George, 156, 251n14
Williamson, Hugh, 29, 91
Wilmot Proviso, 46
Wilson, James, 16, 29, 92, 218n50
Wilson, Woodrow, 116, 118, 124
Wisconsin, 45
women: government on behalf of, 165; oppressed groups such as, 165; suffrage of, 58, 124, 195, 237n35
Wooddy, Carroll, 56
World War I, 100
World War II, 58–59, 61, 130
Wyoming, 50, 70–71, 74, 76, 82, 159, 162, 208

Yates, Robert, 41, 231n24

RECENT BOOKS IN THE SERIES
## Constitutionalism and Democracy

*High Courts in Global Perspective: Evidence, Methodologies, and Findings*
Edited by Nuno Garoupa, Rebecca D. Gill, and Lydia Tiede

*Of Courtiers and Princes: Stories of Lower Court Clerks and Their Judges*
Todd C. Peppers, editor

*Lighting the Way: Federal Courts, Civil Rights, and Public Policy*
Douglas Rice

*The Battle for the Court: Interest Groups, Judicial Elections, and Public Policy*
Lawrence Baum, David Klein, and Matthew J. Streb

*Of Courtiers and Kings: More Stories of Supreme Court Law Clerks and Their Justices*
Todd C. Peppers and Clare Cushman, editors

*Voters' Verdicts: Citizens, Campaigns, and Institutions in State Supreme Court Elections*
Chris W. Bonneau and Damon M. Cann

*Diversity Matters: Judicial Policy Making in the U.S. Courts of Appeals*
Susan B. Haire and Laura P. Moyer

*The View from the Bench and Chambers: Examining Judicial Process and Decision Making on the U.S. Courts of Appeals*
Jennifer Barnes Bowie, Donald R. Songer, and John Szmer

*A Storm over This Court: Law, Politics, and Supreme Court Decision Making in Brown v. Board of Education*
Jeffrey D. Hockett

*In Chambers: Stories of Supreme Court Law Clerks and Their Justices*
Todd C. Peppers and Artemus Ward, editors

*Merely Judgment: Ignoring, Evading, and Trumping the Supreme Court*
Martin J. Sweet

*Battle over the Bench: Senators, Interest Groups, and Lower Court Confirmations*
Amy Steigerwalt

*Law, Politics, and Perception: How Policy Preferences Influence Legal Reasoning*
Eileen Braman

www.ingramcontent.com/pod-product-compliance
Lightning Source LLC
Chambersburg PA
CBHW021821300426
44114CB00009BA/275